VOLUME 3

WOMEN'S HISTORY IN GLOBAL PERSPECTIVE

VOLUME 3

PUBLISHED WITH THE
AMERICAN HISTORICAL ASSOCIATION

WOMEN'S HISTORY

IN GLOBAL PERSPECTIVE

Edited by Bonnie G. Smith

UNIVERSITY OF ILLINOIS PRESS

URBANA AND CHICAGO

∞ This book is printed on acid-free paper.

Library of Congress Cataloging-in-Publication Data
Women's history in global perspective, volume 3 /
edited by Bonnie G. Smith.
p.   cm.
"Published with the American Historical Association."
Includes bibliographical references and index.
ISBN 0-252-02990-9 (cl. : alk. paper)
ISBN 0-252-07234-0 (pbk. : alk. paper)
1. Women—History. I. Smith, Bonnie G., 1940–
HQ1121w88585   2005
305.4'09—dc22   2003024938

Contents

Introduction

BONNE G. SMITH

This volume and the two that precede and follow it testify to an exciting new stage in teaching women's and gender history: development of a global perspective on the past. For several centuries scholars in the West have produced world history textbooks, including those of Johann-Christophe Gatterer (1761) and Johann Gottfried von Herder (1784–91). These usually began with the appearance of the human species as an advance over animal life and followed what can be called a Christian trajectory that saw other "civilizational" groups in relationship to the unfolding of Judeo-Christianity. There were also parallel efforts by earlier historians of women—Lydia Maria Child's *History of the Condition of Women* (1835) is just one among many possible examples—to investigate the experience of the world's women.

As imperialism, debates over the slave trade, more rapid communication and transport, and global trade itself brought people into greater contact, histories of women in the Mideast, China, Africa, and elsewhere poured from the pens of amateur scholars during the nineteenth and early twentieth centuries. The professionalization of history and the cataclysmic wars from 1914 on curtailed some of those efforts. More recently, the vast new evidence of global connectedness has revived the imperative to better understand the world, especially the worldwide history of women. The volumes are devoted to surveying the most recent findings on women and gender in the hope of bringing teachers at all levels a practical introduction to the new data, historical issues, and historiographical debates from all regions of the world.

The volumes are part of the evolution of women's history since the 1960s, and many authors of these chapters were pioneers in that development. The 1970s revived and professionalized the study of women's past, particularly in the form of social history in which the experience of women as workers, mothers, outcasts, prostitutes, and homemakers took center-stage. Historians of women during these and subsequent years quantified many aspects of women's past, often looking at such new issues as the female lifecycle. Investigations of the workplace and the household were primary, but there were also forays into issues of reform and women's participation in great national events such as war. In addition to concern for class as a determinant of women's experience, the women's history written during the 1970s and 1980s brought the study of race to the fore. Work in this field focused on difference and incommensurability, especially as it traced African American women's unique past as slaves, reformers, and free workers. One culminating moment in the development was the appearance of a groundbreaking biographical dictionary, *Black Women in America: An Historical Encyclopedia* (1994).

During the mid-1980s, gender theory emerged to reorient and even contest the path that women's history was taking. In brief, this theory proposed looking at masculinity and femininity as sets of mutually created characteristics shaping and even producing the lives of men and women. Gender theory replaced—or at the very least challenged—ideas of masculinity and femininity and of men and women as operating in history according to fixed biological determinants. Many established historians who observed the emergence of the history of women had thought it belonged more appropriately to natural history. Women's history, some believed, had to be told in conjunction with the history of the family and women's biology. Gender history changed all that. By removing these categories of men and women from the realm of biology, it made a history possible.

For some, the idea of gender history was but another term for women's history, but serious students of gender theory transformed the ways in which they approached writing and teaching about both men and women. To some extent it may be hypothesized that the major change gender theory offered was to problematize the study of men, making them as well as women gendered historical subjects who operated in a culturally constructed universe of symbols developed around the issue of gender. The leading proponent of gender theory, Joan Wallach Scott, pointed to the ways in which the operation of gender produced hierarchies of meaning and value that were part of the operation of power in the world. The subsequent investigation of gender in history placed an enhanced variety of subjects under the expanded mandate of gender theory.

As these developments continue to play themselves out in the form of important new scholarship the last decade of the millennium vividly highlighted the need for more global and comparative perspectives in teaching and scholarship. World and global history appeared more insistently in the curriculum of schools and universities owing to the rapid unfolding of world events such as migration, communication technology, wars, and increased global trade. Because of the expanded subject matter teachers had to convey, attention to women and gender dropped by the wayside. This material was seen as secondary to the more important subject matter of global politics directed by men or of global economic systems such as the Silk Road or routes on the Indian Ocean. In the first forays of a new world history, as in the earlier textbooks in German universities or Arnold Toynbee's extension of their paradigm, women were rarely discussed. Even when making an appearance it would be to extend an earlier paradigm. Books introduced unique topics—footbinding, for example—to point to the barbaric treatment of women outside the (Christian) West. This situation had to be changed, many educators felt.

In the midst of the development of a modern version of world history in the academy, activists from around the world were also at the forefront of highlighting the importance of a fresh, global perspective in women's and gender history, and their insights contributed to developing new scholarship on women and gender in global perspective. Almost two centuries ago Lydia Maria Child's work on women in various parts of the world was born of her commitment to abolitionism, and it allowed her to see slavery as part of a world system—a perspective reborn in the decades since World War II. More recently, the international meetings of women connected with second-wave feminism inspired participants, especially those from Central and South America, Africa, and Asia, to insist on a more encompassing and diverse global perspective. Issues taken as normative by U.S. and West European feminists had little relevance from the vantage point of activists in Africa, South Asia, and Latin America. Outside the prosperous northern tier of countries, family, work, politics, and nation had different meanings and entailed different political strategies. Gender was multiply constructed, non-Westerners maintained. Western ignorance and U.S. dominance were called into question during these meetings, and an entire system of scholarly priorities and values was thrown into question as well. No where was that more evident than in the study of history.

The dissolution of the Soviet Union and the collapse of state socialism in Eastern Europe and Central Asia have also challenged the orientation of traditional historical research in the United States. The scholarship on women and gender that emerged from that region raised an alternative array of historical questions, particularly concerning democratization, the free market, and citizenship. In what was euphemistically called the "transition," women suddenly found themselves both without jobs and without the social services that had provided health care from them and their children. Following free-market values meant unemployment for women, and belief in women's equality was equated with a failed and often brutal socialist system. Women's inequality became prized in these countries because of its association with American and Western European success, inspiring bursts of feminist activism from women in the post-Soviet world. As nongovermental organizations sponsored women's and gender history programs in Budapest and Moscow, scholars and activists used the insights of Western scholars and devised many new questions of their own, often contesting the would-be hegemony of U.S. feminists and their scholarly concerns. Historians in eastern and east central Europe helped shift attention to issues of citizenship and democratization as global processes. Eastern European scholars have helped their counterparts elsewhere address issues of historical evidence and feminism from a fresh point of view.

These events alone have shown that a global perspective calls for examining the past from more than one point of view. Beyond that, however, questions of what constitutes world history and global studies still remain open to zestful debate. As Margaret Strobel and Marjorie Bingham describe so well in volume 1, world history has had many metamorphoses and will probably have many more. Orthodoxies have come and gone while the field of knowledge about women and gender in world history has expanded exponentially. For some, a global perspective has meant examining and integrating the history of all countries except the United States. According to this view, global history is best taught by specialists in the Chinese, African, or similarly non-U.S. fields. Others have seen global history as best when it additionally excludes Europe, which is perceived as so hegemonic in historical narrative that studying it irremediably distorts attempts at understanding the global past. In these two versions of global history, such a history means "the rest" and has led to a much-criticized pedagogy. While Americanists and Europeanists have focused on relatively specialized scholarship and teaching, specialists from outside those fields have been charged with teaching the world in its entirety.

In contrast, this book and the two others try to integrate both North America and Europe into a global perspective in the belief that such inclusion is necessary for a holistic history that encompasses the world. Similarly, the most innovative textbooks in the field have increasingly rejected this strategy. The initiator of the three volumes, the Committee on Women Historians of the American Historical Association, envisioned a wide-ranging series that would make available the insights and information from recent scholarship from *all* geographic regions. Moreover, it aimed for inclusive topical chapters that would bring into play women's experience of such large-scale institutions and movements as nation-state, feminism, and religion from around the world and would be written by specialists in a variety of geographic fields. We see the virtues of inclusiveness, for example, in the chapter on work, which establishes discernible patterns, topics, and analytical themes that can unify the study of work in many parts of the world over the centuries. Material on women in the United States and Europe helps establish those themes and patterns but does not dominate the analysis. More important, the global sweep of this analysis of work prevents the omission of the United States and Europe from distorting our understanding. Instead, the centrality of gender to the organization, remuneration, and conditions of work globally comes into true focus.

Because of the vast amounts of potential historical coverage in both topical and geographical volumes, the distinguished authors of the essays in the three volumes have been ruthlessly selective, providing a usable model to teachers who also must prune their classroom presentations. Understanding that there are many world religions, the chapter on religion, written by a specialist in North Africa, has focused on Islam, Christianity, and Judaism while omitting other systems of belief that are treated in other chapters and volumes. Regional and national presentations of women's and gender history are also pared to the most central and useful topics and themes. These are not necessarily uniform across the volumes because each region's history and central concerns differs. The chapter on China, for example, provides a detailed overview of the family system as a prelude to the more general treatment of women and gender in Chinese history. The early history of Latin America, in contrast, brings into play the impact of contact on indigenous women and on the evolution of gender. The author of the early history of North America emphasizes the interaction and diverse lives of the multiple ethnicities there, offering excellent material for teachers wishing to establish a background to the complex gendering of North American history.

Several classroom uses are intended for this volume, the one preceding it, and the one that follows—and we stress again the practical intent of these overviews. First, the books allow more material on gender to be introduced into the study of any particular area of the world. The volumes are designed to help teachers and students of Chinese history or Latin American history, for example, learn more about the gendered aspects of that history and add the history of women to their understanding. Women were present in the evolution of classical Chinese thought and the nation-building processes of modern Latin America. The regional histories provide an overview of women's history from around the world and can enrich the gendered component in national and regional courses. A second step, one that has shaped the world history course, is to encourage comparisons among the historical experiences of women from various continents, regions, nations, and religious traditions. The topical chapters on family, religion, race, and ethnicity and other basic subjects allow nearly any course to have a comparative gendered component. Critical insights develop when the study of such phenomena as nationalism or work contains material on women and gender. Material from the regional volumes, however, also allows for comparative study and teaching.

Because women's activism has led to seeing history in a more inclusive, comparative manner, activism brings to light still another perspective on globalism that involves thinking about the very nationalist bias of women historians in the United States in writing and conceptualizing history. A substitute way of thinking considers the histories that crossed borders. Transnational women's movements parallel contemporary phenomenon such as global migration, multinational corporations, global communications, and transnational ruling structures like the World Bank. These developments, however, have been accompanied by new findings in world history that suggest the enduring nature not of nations but of global contact.

The surprising constancy going back tens of thousands of years of global migration, cultural exchange, and the spread of disease and epidemics opens new vistas for the history of women and gender. Among these phenomena are women's relationship to overland and overseas trade, their variegated participation in migration and diasporas, and their contributions to culture both nationally and internationally. Women throughout time have been part of regional and transregional slave systems and international prostitution; they have also participated in international movements against slavery and forced prostitution. The transregional spread of religion has involved women, and it has simultaneously often been a highly gendered process.

The chapters in this book and the two others include material that allows teachers to focus on the place of women and the role of gender in the transnational aspects of world history. Various components of women's work have implications beyond national and regional borders, and information on their labor appears in the chapters on race and work, among others. Women's relationship to world religions and philosophical systems appears in multiple chapters, including most of the regional chapters and topical ones. Women's transnational activism is also prominent, especially in the investigation of feminism and nationalism. The three books are intended to encourage gendered study in the exciting evolution of world history as it comes to examine processes that operate across current national and regional boundaries.

A "global perspective" allows for several different approaches to women's and gender history in the classroom. First, it can mean simply bringing to the fore historical material from most of the discrete areas of the globe—what might be called a "civilizational approach" that many teachers find important. Reading this volume and the next, which contain regional chapters, will provide an overview of women's history from around the world and permit teachers to enrich the gender component in national and regional courses. It also permits cultural literacy in women's history that is worldwide. A second step in developing a global perspective would be to encourage comparisons among the historical experiences of women from various continents, regions, and nations. The seven topical chapters on family, religion, race and ethnicity, and other subjects that appear in volume 1, for example, allow courses based on a topical approach to have a gender component.

Many teachers find that organizing a course by topic allows for clear organization that students can follow. Insights develop when a study of such phenomena as nationalism or work contains material on women and gender. If the study of women and gender has helped to transform historical study, there is still more to be done—opening for students a still wider window on the historical world using multiple strategies.

As historians of women struggle to meet the need to inform students and themselves more broadly about global processes and pressing international issues, the sheer mass of information in the ever-expanding historical field seems overwhelming. The chapters that follow provide economical coverage of basic themes and facts. In the face of the current information overload, however, the greater danger is to continue to claim only marginal importance for issues of women and gender and omit any coverage at all. In the face of great world events and the need to understand major cultural influences, women's importance can appear to shrink. The chapters that follow also demonstrate a distinctly opposite historical world in which issues of gender and the presence of women have been pivotal to political, economic, and cultural development.

From the opening salvos of this volume, where women appear as critical players in Islam, to the final chapters on women in the twentieth-century Americas, there are perils to accurate understanding if women's experience and the construction of gender are omitted from the historical account. Both have been central to the development of nationalism, the economy, and religious life, and individual regions and nations have mobilized both women and gender to advance political and economic agendas.

Responsible and accurate historical understanding depends on considerations of women and gender, and this volume and its two companions seek to provide usable overviews of the latest issues, central facts, analytical tools, and current scholarship. The Committee on Women Historians of the American Historical Association seeks to enrich the connection of all teachers and students to the vital world of women's and gender history.

1

Women and Gender in the History of Sub-Saharan Africa

CHERYL JOHNSON-ODIM

It is a daunting task to think of discussing the history of women in sub-Saharan Africa in a short essay. I have relied heavily on the work of many scholars, in particular the synthetic essays by Iris Berger (on Eastern and Southern Africa) and E. Frances White (on Western and West Central Africa) in *Women in Sub-Saharan Africa: Restoring Women to History*, part of the series "Restoring Women to History," which I coedited along with Margaret Strobel and to which we provided a lengthy introduction. The research of others kept me from reinventing the wheel, but I take full responsibility for all interpretations and conclusions in this essay, as well as errors of fact.

What this essay and other recent work on African women make clear is that although the category "woman" does have salience, we often best understand women's experiences by deconstructing that category. That is, women have several identities, each of which has meaning for their lives. Some of those identities change over time—age, marriage, motherhood—and effectively change women's experiences. Women can also have multiple identities simultaneously, such as being a daughter, a wife, and a mother. I will discuss how multiple simultaneous identities had great importance in the lives of women in Africa.

Where women *meet* historical circumstances could also have as great an impact as gender. If a woman were a subsistence farmer, or a marketwoman trading on a small scale, or a member of a royal household, for example, her experience of the same historical circumstance, colonialism, would differ due to her particular status. There is no denying gender as an important element in the experiences of women, but even with that factor held steady the addition of others could profoundly differentiate women's status and experience.

Even though there are tremendous gaps in the record, the physical area and time period to be covered in this essay are so vast that selectivity is a necessity. This is all complicated by not being able to assume any knowledge of the history of the continent and its people. African history has not generally been taught in K-12 curricula until recently and then only in selective locations.

Even now African history is often unavailable not only at the K-12 level but also at many institutions of higher education. No reputable history department could fail to offer U.S., Latin American, European, and probably even Asian history. African history, however, is another matter. Although courses have proliferated, few look aghast at schools where there is no specialist on Africa. That is changing (even this essay is aimed at K-12 teachers), but courses on African women's history are in even shorter supply. It is for all these reasons that I have written such a lengthy introduction.

Beginning in the 1970s the historical literature on women in sub-Saharan Africa exploded. Analyses of women's agency, gender construction, and gender relations over time begin to be undertaken in a systematic and historical mode. I do not see Africa as unique in this regard but rather as part of the general recovery of women's history and the history of gender that increased around the globe.

Observations about sub-Saharan African women were written long before the twentieth century, although we are able to recover them unevenly across historical periods. Both the Greeks and the Romans left some commentary on women in Nubia and the Nubian centers at Kush, Meroe, and Aksum— all ancient African civilizations. Nubia, Kush, and Meroe (all civilizations of the Upper Nile Valley, south of Ancient Egypt and well down into the present-day country of Sudan) had trade and other relationships with Egypt. Notably, they do not figure in contemporary controversies (centered on Egypt) over whether their people were part of "black" Africa, and, clearly, they were so identified by ancient sources. Stanley Burstein notes that the Greeks and Romans referred to them as "burnt-faced people."[1]

At various times Egypt expanded into Nubian territories, and reverse expansion also occurred. Nubians, for instance, ruled Egypt for sixty years, beginning around 730 B.C.E. when they invaded Egypt and controlled the kingdom from Thebes. Nubian control of Egypt was the twenty-fifth dynasty, also known as the Ethiopian dynasty. Kingship emerged in Nubia around the same time or perhaps earlier than in Egypt. Some scholars believe that the idea of pharoah traveled from south to north, originating in Nubian civilization and traveling north to Egypt.

Meroe, the last and most famous capital of Kush, was located near the center of the present-day country of Sudan and developed its own written script. Modern inability to decipher Meroitic script, however, retards efforts to chronicle Meroitic civilization. Aksumite civilization (in the area of present-day Ethiopia) also developed a written script, Ge'ez, although little information can be gleaned about women.

Some African languages such as Hausa were written in Arabic script before they were in Roman script. Some writing by Africans, for instance, was in Arabic and in Hausa and Swahili using Arabic script. Moreover, the writing of Arabic travelers and explorers began as early as the eighth century, and those of Europeans as early as the fifteenth. Although traveler and explorer accounts (primarily in Arabic and European languages) sometimes remarked on women's statuses and conditions, they did so most frequently from the biases of the worldviews of their particular authors and rarely provide anything more than commentary representing the "ethnographic present." Still, they are useful in helping reconstruct jobs performed by non-elite women, for example, or activities of women (such as the famed women warriors, the so-called Amazons of the West African kingdom of Dahomey, now Benin) that most differed from those of the foreigner's own geographical area.

In many sub-Saharan African cultures, commentary by indigenes on the statuses and conditions of women before the nineteenth century is found in nonwritten sources—proverbs, folktales, and myths of origin. Although the nature of those sources as living literature exemplifies their protean nature, they nonetheless provide some insight into the cosmology of gender as well as actual gender roles. Even when not preserved in written sources, pre-nineteenth-century indigenous oral commentaries on women and prescriptions of gender yield information on gender construction and relations.

Closer to the present day, and as might be expected, more sources are available that treat women and gender relations over time and systematically. Increasingly, contemporary historical literature also treats women and gender relations comparatively; a growing body of work examines women within Africa (for instance, those in urban and rural areas) or by region (West Africa compared to East Africa). In addition, the scholarship that compares sub-Saharan Africa with places outside the continent is expanding, being the most prevalent where the largest African diaspora populations are found—South America (especially Brazil), the United States (particularly during the era of slavery), and the Caribbean.

There is also a growing body of literature produced by African scholars, work that one African scholar who investigates African women has referred to as *nzagwalu* ("answering back" in the Igbo language) literature.[2] This literature, not all of it by historians, critiques much Western feminist theory regarding African women. In its most radical analyses it posits that African societies were originally matriarchal, never became as patriarchal as Western societies before the onslaught of colonialism, and that even as matriarchy ebbed they became complementary in gender roles. That complementarity, they suggest, privileged men in some ways and women in others, although most agree that men at some point became, overall, more privileged than women.

• Ifi Amadiume theorizes an original African matriarchy based on three factors: women's control of the subsistence economy and the marketplace, women's self-government, and women's control of their own religion or culture. Arguing that much of women's economic and political power is not immediately visible because it is not symbolically reflected in ritual, Amadiume suggests that the reality of women's power juxtaposed to the image of men's power embedded in ritual symbolizes what she refers to as the "perennial contest" between matriarchy and patriarchy. For instance, masking, a ritual attendant to a wide variety of religions, was often used as a way of excluding women, for example, in *oro* or *egungun* (secret society) ceremonies among the Yoruba. *Eku* (a male masking tradition among the Ebira people of middle Nigeria, the area of the Niger-Benue confluence) excluded women but did so as a means of men counteracting women's power. Because counteracting women's power lay at the heart of the ritual (and thus was implied acknowledgment of that power) some women were inducted into eku as the surrogate mothers of masked male performers so their "female" power could help the men achieve various objectives. The ritual, which seems rooted in the mid-nineteenth century, was practiced as late as 1966 to minimize damage from a smallpox epidemic, as Christians, for example, might pray for the end to an epidemic. Others have argued that gender neutrality in language and naming is symbolic of a lesser patriarchal structure in much of sub-Saharan Africa.[3] Not all scholars agree. •

Feminist theories about matriarchy as the first form of human hierarchical organization, and about what caused women to become generally subordinated to men over much of the globe, have differed. It appears, in sub-Saharan Africa at least, that there is increasing evidence that the development of centralized political systems was accompanied by increasing gender differentiation and women's greater subordination to men. As long as women remained central to the economy, however, they continued to have important, culturally sanctioned political roles.

In Ancient Egypt, for example, the earliest African civilization with a centralized political system and one in which women played important economic roles, there were at least five women pharaohs. Moreover, upper-class (particularly royal) women exercised considerable power within the state and enjoyed a number of freedoms.

The importance of royal women, the existence of women rulers, and women's critically important roles in the economy all would be equally characteristic of later African civilizations south of the Sahara. Sub-Saharan African people would also share with Egypt the veneration of motherhood and motherhood as a primary expectation of all women. That belief seems likely related to a high infant and maternal mortality rate, although some scholars have argued that it is a remnant of earlier, matriarchal societies, interpretations that are not mutually exclusive. Yet powerful women (for example Hathshepsut, one of the best-known female pharohs) were sometimes gendered male; they took, that is, male titles or dressed as males. The opposite could be true as well, men could be gendered female in important religious rituals honoring female deities (e.g., certain Yoruba ceremonies).

In some areas of the world, land as private property emerged fairly early. This is not generally true for sub-Saharan Africa, where for the vast majority of people kinship-based communal ownership of land pertained, with individual usufruct rights, until well into the twentieth century. This fact helped shape gender and class relations, particularly before the era of high colonialism (approximately 1920 to 1960) that signaled greater capitalist penetration and greater Western cultural imperialism. Women's roles as members of their natal families (the families into which they were born) remained as important—more important in some ways—as their roles in families by marriage (their affinal families) because land, the primary source of wealth, was inalienable from the natal family. The labor of people, however, was another major source of wealth, and though women often continued as important economic actors in their natal families, their children's natal family was considered to be that of their fathers, except among matrilineal people.

As economic actors African women were always an important part of the labor force. As well, they gained political "space" from the economic interdependence of women and men in precapitalist African economies. That space resulted from acknowledgment of women's critical economic contributions, especially in agriculture, and in trade and craft production as well. Thus public, political space was not gendered as only male although it was often organized in parallel male/female sectors. Direct and acknowledged involvement in the economy did not guarantee women's total equality with men, yet being seen (or construed) to have little economic involvement seemed to guarantee women's subordination.

A major pillar of African cultures from ancient times until well into the twentieth century was religion. Some would argue that is still the case, although perhaps differently configured in postcolonial states that are multiethnic and in other ways very diverse. Religion for many African people was synonymous with culture. If one were Wolof, Yoruba, Igbo, Kikuyu, or Shona, for instance, that ethnic identity defined one's religion as well as one's culture. Most religions, complexly and intricately bound to specific cultures, did not spread beyond an ethnic group, and ethnic groups varied in membership from thousands to tens of millions. States, initially based on ethnicity, were sometimes ruled by queens or kings who were simultaneously political and spiritual heads.

Early empires such as those of the western Sudan (from the fourth to the sixteenth centuries C.E.) did not force conquered people to accept their religions or cultures. Although later, as their rulers converted to Islam, conversion and adherence to Islam could provide a more privileged relationship to the bureaucracy of the state.

Belief in a supreme deity was common throughout sub-Saharan Africa before the spread of Christianity or Islam and helped both be accepted as monotheistic religions. Most African religions also included a belief in lesser deities, some thought to have power over particular places or things. Most people embraced a cycle of life that included the unborn, the living, and the dead (or ancestors) and considered those planes to interact. Women were important in all indigenous religions as deities, diviners, healers, priestesses, and prophetesses. They were barred from some religious rituals, but there were all-female rituals as well.

Any perusal of religious art in sub-Saharan Africa will reveal many female symbols. The "spirit possession" characteristic of many indigenous religions could be freeing and empowering to women. Certain behaviors that would have been unacceptable in daily life could be engaged in while possessed. One woman in Southern Africa during the early twentieth century, said to be spirit-possessed, insulted her father-in-law with impunity: "My father-in-law slanders me. I shall do the same! He is a mad fool! My father-in-law insults me. I shall insult him also!"[4] It is not likely that she would have been allowed such freedom of expression under other circumstances.

Africa also exported religions via the Atlantic slave trade. Bahía in Brazil, Santería in Cuba, and Vodún in Haiti are syncretic (combining elements of Roman Catholicism with principally Yoruba religious beliefs) religions that are easily recognizable as African in origin and among the major African religious influences outside the continent itself. These have all spread to North America, although slowly. There are, for instance, Yoruba temples in U.S. cities such as New York and Chicago where both descendants of Africans and descendants of Europeans practice Yoruba religion as converts. In addition, a number of African American Christian practices in the United States and the Caribbean carry African religious influences.

Christianity and Islam spread in sub-Saharan Africa soon after each was founded in the Near East, beginning in the fourth and seventh centuries c.e., respectively, and throughout the twentieth century their practice continued to be influenced by the indigenous religions still being practiced among many rural people as well as in urban centers. Some people "hedged their bets" by combining indigenous religions with Christianity and Islam, praying to various powerful gods. Many in contemporary sub-Saharan Africa practice Christianity (in various denominations) and Islam (both Shi'ite and Sunni, although mostly Sunni). Indigenous African religion does continue to be practiced.

Likely as a result of the gendered division of labor, what I have called elsewhere the "community of women" had as much importance in a woman's life, particularly in the long era still most often known as the precolonial period (referring to European colonialism), as the overall heterosexual community. The community of women socialized young girls and had great influence over many day-to-day aspects of their lives. Women-to-women relationships were central to females. Girls were likely to learn a trade from women and practice it with them, or farm with women, or be a co-wife, sister-in-law, or daughter-in-law to a woman. Their children would be delivered by women, and they would depend on women to help with child care. Memberships in all-female organizations would facilitate everything from rites of passage to business loans.

There were as many rules connected to woman-to-woman relationships as to those between women and men, and they were based on age, kin relations, and other factors. Because women as a collective, a community, wielded the power to punish men (discussed later in this essay), the community of women could also provide protection from physical harm and male—sometimes female—exploitation. Thus women's power with respect to other women needs to be understood as a social dynamic similar to men's power over women. Women's associations, whether economic, political, or sociocultural in nature and scope, were also a mode of responding to patriarchy. Through the use of collective domestic strikes, ridicule, outright physical attack, and control of certain rituals women negotiated power as a group within kinship units, the community, and, if applicable, the state.

Many scholars of African women argue convincingly that the lifecycle was as much a determinant of gender as biological sex was, especially for women. That is, women's power and autonomy ebbed and flowed according to such lifecycle events as childhood, daughter-in-law status, motherhood, mother-in-law status, and being postmenopausal. These various stages could have profound impact on what was considered appropriate behavior and therefore on ascribed status and its attendant rights, freedoms, and obligations. Moreover, a woman might simultaneously hold a variety of statuses that operated on profoundly different levels. She could, for instance, be a grown daughter in her natal lineage (and therefore exercise the status of a "husband" over sisters-in-law and have the right to inherit land-use rights and other property) as well as a new and/or childless wife in her affinal family, subject to sisters-in-law and mother-in-law and without the ability to inherit, even from her husband. The historical complexity of women's multiple and sometimes simultaneous statuses will be explored later.

The historical lack of teaching about Africa in general in the K-12 curricula means that most North Americans have been little exposed to the geography of the African continent. Students frequently think (and speak) of Africa as a country rather than a continent of fifty-four independent countries. That lack of geographical knowledge obscures the tremendous size of the continent (the United States can fit into it about three and a half times) as well as its diversity and commonalities. Due to a lack of attention to the continent, Africa is not as familiar to students as other world areas such as Europe and Latin America, where students might not know the exact location of particular countries but are still aware of the diversity of languages and people. It is important, therefore, to use a map of Africa during classroom discussion.

Often, the five countries of North Africa—Morocco, Algeria, Tunisia, Libya, and Egypt—are not seen as being "truly" Africa. The attention in this essay to sub-Saharan Africa, unfortunately, lends credence to that perception. Africa has experienced a continental history, however, and now African history is generally taught that way. It is equally true that geographical location (being situated on the Mediterranean Sea, for example) or ecological formation (e.g., a thick, rain forest terrain) combined with the size of the continent influenced the degree and length of contact between its various areas and between the continent and areas external to it.

North Africa was very early drawn into the Near Eastern, and subsequently the Mediterranean, world through trade and the migration of people. However obvious it may be that there was contact between sub-Saharan Africa and North Africa from the earliest human development through to the present, the greater incorporation of countries bordering the Mediterranean into the intercommunicating zones of Mediterranean and Near Eastern history means that those histories often overlapped. Particularly after the spread of Islam, beginning in the seventh century, areas closer to the Middle East became not only Islamized but also Arabized through migration. For certain things, therefore, it has become more convenient to study North Africa as part of Middle Eastern culture, especially given the shared language of Arabic.

Islam, however, did not stop north of the Sahara desert, even though the cultures it encountered as it spread south had as much impact on Islam as Islam did on them. At no time in African history did North or Northeast Africa float off into the Mediterranean or the Red Sea or completely cease contact with the sub-Saharan portion of the continent. The Sahara desert was a bridge as much as a barrier from the time it was the "green" Sahara (until about 3000 B.C.E.) through the desiccation that still continues. Even the language of the trans-Saharan trade is that of "bridge." The word *sahel* (area at the edge of the desert), for example, comes from the Arabic *sahil* ("shore" or "coast"). Trading caravans navigated the desert as they would have an ocean, with safe "harbors" between "shores" and at each end. Thus a steady stream of the gold, with which North Africa kept Europe amply supplied from at least the ninth to the sixteenth centuries, was ensured. By the fourteenth century, two-thirds of the gold that circulated in Europe was from sub-Saharan Africa.[5] Like "Moroccan" leather, most of which was crafted in northern Nigeria, gold was traded from North Africa to Europe but did not originate in North Africa. It is important to note that ancient African civilizations (including Egypt) looked south as well as north, west as well as east, and that they were of Africa as well as in it.

From Human Origins through Antiquity

The earliest Homo sapiens evolved in Africa between two hundred thousand and one hundred thousand years ago. It is believed that farming developed independently in the Nile Valley (including Nubia) as early as 10000 B.C.E., maybe as early as 16000 B.C.E. Other possibly independent sites of agricultural development are China (ca. 5000 B.C.E.) and Mexico (ca. 3000 B.C.E.).[6]

Sorghum and millet of indigenous African origin were being harvested in the region of the Upper Nile (near Khartoum in present-day Sudan) by 6000 B.C.E. Scholars speculate that farming likely had its origins in the gathering of wild grains, work done mostly by women. In the savannah areas of West Africa there would have been abundant wheat and barley to be gathered at least as early as the peak of the Sahara's most recent wet phase, around 7000 B.C.E. It is believed that farming spread as far west as present-day Senegal and Gambia sometime between 4000 and 1000 B.C.E.

Farming and the attendant production of food surpluses would have led to diversification in the economy and society. Women bore more children in settled, permanent communities, tying them ever more to the domestic sphere. Women, as primary gatherers, would likely have had greater responsibility for farming (just as they still do in most of the continent) and developing early agricultural techniques and food storage. The founding of farming communities, and the resulting development of strict kinship ties and their linkage to communal land ownership and rights, provided one framework for constructing gender relations.

Humans in early farming communities also hunted, gathered, and fished. By ten thousand years ago Later Stone Age people were experienced hunter-gatherers. By 8000 B.C.E., particularly in the savannahs of East, Central, and South Africa, it is likely that three-quarters of the daily diets of Later Stone Age people consisted of fruits, nuts, and roots in addition to protein-rich food such as termites, caterpillars, and locusts—all of which women gathered.[7]

They also had communal and kinship-based economies that appear to have been very egalitarian. There was a gendered division of labor, but hunter-gatherers were economically interdependent for survival. There also seem to have been few significant status distinctions between women and men. The Mbuti (pejoratively called "Pygmies") and the San (pejoratively called "Bushmen") of the twentieth century retained much of that egalitarian behavior between the sexes. At least one scholar suggests, however, that although gender roles were fluid and decision-making across the sexes was collective, making hunting and gathering societies remarkably egalitarian compared with sedentary people of a later time—women were a little "less equal" than men.[8]

Fishing communities were also common among Later Stone Age people and produced some of the earliest baked clay storage pots. Evidence of the pots' existence appeared in the savannah areas of the Upper Niger River area in West Africa and the Great Lakes region of East Africa between 8000 and 4000 B.C.E., indicating settled communities even before the large-scale development of farming or the domestication of animals.

Women in ancient Africa were important to the economy in areas other than agriculture. They worked in the gold mines of Nubia.[9] They were also involved in the economy of Kush, a politically independent Nubian state as early as 1000 B.C.E., probably in craft production as well as agriculture, although little is known of the division of labor along gender lines. Animal husbandry, an important barometer of wealth in Kush, appears to have been male-dominated.[10] Female deities appear to have existed in Kush, and women were priestesses. The women rulers of Kush were referred to in the Greco-Roman world by the title "Candace" and sometimes co-ruled with their sons. Queen Amanitore, for instance, ruled jointly with King Notakamani in the first century C.E.[11] The role of queen mother existed in Kush, and queen mothers often played significant political roles, particularly in Meroe, where Kushitic civilization was centered from about 300 B.C.E.[12] The occasional passage of power from aunts to nieces and the occasional succession by the son of a queen's sister have sometimes been interpreted as evidence of matrilineal succession.[13] There does not appear to be, however, a tradition of royal women wielding as much power as men (or as often) or controlling as much wealth. There is also evidence of women soldiers among the Kushites.[14]

Aksum began its rise during about the fourth century B.C.E. as a syncretic civilization of migrants from southwestern Arabia and indigenous people in the area of present-day Ethiopia. After several generations of intermarriage people evolved a spoken and written language, Ge'ez, from which the modern Ethiopian language of Amharic developed. By the first century C.E. Aksum was a powerful state, siphoning both sea and land trade from Meroe and also trading with Romans. By the fourth century C.E. the Aksumite King Ezana (320–50 C.E.) had adopted Christianity, introduced by Christian scholars from Alexandria in Egypt, and was involved in lucrative trade with the Greeks.

Little is known about women in Aksum. The earliest Ethiopian queen, Makeda, identified in the Aksumite origin myth with Sheba, is supposed to have decreed that only men rather than women would rule.[15] The fact, however, that a woman, as legend goes, had the power to make this transformation, coupled with the existence of the title *negeshta nagashtat* (queen of queens) and a term for God that suggests a religion centered on female agricultural cults, gives one pause to wonder whether women wielded more power than indisputable evidence can indicate. There is some speculation that women co-ruled with their sons and brothers. It also appears that they accompanied troops on campaigns, a custom that survived to later Ethiopian kingdoms.[16] New archeological evidence indicates that between 700 and 400 B.C.E. complexly organized communities settled in the area of present-day Eritrea. Gold earrings, bracelets, and rings have been found, although it is unclear whether they were obtained through trading or through mining. Archaeologists at the University of Asmara speculate that these were settlements of indigenous people; the gold jewelry could have been worn by women or men or both. Not enough is known to shed light on gender constructions, but— were resources available for further archaeological exploration—there are various such places on the African continent where the past could be given greater shape and form.[17]

The spread of people often known as the Bantu is at the base of many commonalities among those in sub-Saharan Africa. Bantu is not actually the name of a particular people or language but rather a linguistic designation for a family of African languages (belonging to the Niger-Congo group) that stretches across much of sub-Saharan Africa. Some posit the spread of Bantu speakers to have begun as early as 1600 B.C.E.[18] By 1000 B.C.E., it is evident that Bantu-speakers occupied most of the continent below the Sahara. Kin-

ship-based, the heads (usually male) of individual families constituted a ruling council, and when networked over large territories, councils could control the affairs of several hundred thousand people. They were primarily agriculturalists, although some hunting and gathering probably continued
during the early stages of expansion. In many places (particularly Eastern and
Southern Africa) Bantu-speakers kept livestock.

There is little other information on women's roles in these early stages,
although it would seem fair to suggest that they were important providers of
food and that intermarriage cemented relations between the Bantu and the
hunters and gatherers they eventually absorbed. It is likely that women also
effected ties among the various council heads through marriage and childbearing. Berger reports that early Bantu speakers followed bilateral forms of
descent.[19] We can also speculate that as people became more sedentary, control over land and the crops it produced became more important, as did control over livestock. That resulted in more control being exercised over labor—
or people. The control of women as agricultural laborers and reproducers of
labor began to become more important.

One of the earliest settled societies in West Africa is that at Nok, a settlement named after the area in central Nigeria where it was first unearthed. The
Nok site is most famous for the discovery of beautiful terra-cotta figurines
dating to between 500 and 400 B.C.E. People at Nok appear to have had a
gendered division of labor that assigned child care and other domestic tasks
such as cooking to women (a speculation based on women's roles in early Iron
Age societies of which Nok was one) but very little is actually known about
women's roles at Nok.

Ironworking was established in Meroe by at least the fifth century B.C.E.
and at Nok by the fourth century B.C.E. Over time, knowledge of how to smelt
iron had tremendous implications for increasing the agricultural development
that came to be the basis of the economy of most early Iron Age communities, although people also continued to hunt and gather; to fish, depending
on location; and to keep livestock. Sometime between the fifth century B.C.E.
and the fifth century C.E. ironworking was spread by (or independently invented by) people in Eastern, Central, and Southeastern Africa.

Early Iron Age communities appear to have already developed a clear
division of labor between women and men and to have practiced polygyny
(taking more than one wife). Women cared for children, tended crops, and
prepared food while men hunted and tended livestock.[20] Still, Berger suggests
that very early Iron Age societies in some places were likely to be matrilocal
and matrilineal.[21] Perhaps that was due to women's central role in stabilizing
those societies by providing the most consistent source of food, being seen as

the "source" of others, and caring for the young until they could become productive members of a group. As Kevin Shillington reports, "In general in Later Iron Age societies [ca. 1000 C.E. to 1500 C.E.] there was a growing division between rich and poor and a greater domination by men over women."[22]

The Early Spread of Christianity and Islam

During the first century C.E., Christianity began to spread into Northeastern Africa, and Alexandria in Egypt became an important early center of activity. From Egypt, Christianity also spread south into Nubia sometime during the sixth century C.E. By that time, Egyptian Christianity had formed the Coptic Christian church, an act that resulted in expulsion by the church centered at Rome. Christianity thrived in Nubia, however, and church construction and monastery development withstood the spread of Islam in the seventh century—for a while. Christian Nubian men even participated in European-sponsored crusades to the Holy Land.

Although Nubians were matrilineal, the arrival of Christianity sparked a transition to some form of patrilineality as monarchies began to assume strict successions from fathers to sons. Although sometime during the eleventh century C.E. there was a temporary return to the tradition of sisters' sons succeeding their maternal uncles, patrilineal descent reappeared later.[23] Between the twelfth and sixteenth centuries, Islam continued to penetrate the Christian Nubian kingdoms centered in the Nubian states of Makurra and 'Alwa; by the sixteenth century, Islam had spread to the area and Islamic law was implemented.

By the middle of the fourth century, Christianity had spread to Aksum from Alexandria, and by at least 350 C.E. the Aksumite King Ezana had converted to the new religion. Surrounded by an expanding Islam in the seventh century, Christian developments were isolated in the northern Ethiopian highlands until about the twelfth century C.E., when a new dynasty encouraged the spread of Christianity. Although Aksumite Christianity developed its own trajectory, which was different in some ways from that centered at Rome, there does not appear to have been great divergence from the subordination of women as promulgated by the Roman church, although Roman influence certainly lessened after the expulsion of Coptic Christians from the Roman church and after the rise of Islam. In the tenth century a queen of Agao named Gudit (Yodit) rejected Christianity and rebelled against the Aksumite state.[24] Although it may be somewhat speculative to suggest that part of her rebellion was fueled by a desire to resist the greater subordination of women that accompanied Christianity and the accompanying turn from matrilineality to patrilineality, that would be a logical interpretation. During the sixteenth century Portuguese explorers arrived in Ethiopia and met African Christians, and Christianity continues to be strong in Ethiopia.

By the mid-fifteenth century the Portuguese had introduced Christianity into the kingdom of Kongo in Central Africa and won some converts among the ruling classes. They also made attempts to introduce Roman Catholicism to Benin on the west coast and Zimbabwe in Central Africa in the early sixteenth century, but such efforts met with little success. It is not at all clear that those developments had repercussions for women's status in this early phase.

Although Christianity spread to Africa before Islam was born, Islam preceded the spread of Christianity in most of the continent below the Sahara (with the exceptions that have been noted). Islam, founded in the seventh century, spread to Africa almost immediately; North Africa became gradually Islamized and Arabized due to intermarriage, particularly between Arabs and matrilineal Berber communities. There is evidence that in the fourth century C.E. there were female authority figures and holy women among the Berbers. The unearthed tomb of Ahaggar, for example, revealed a woman of considerable wealth and involvement in trans-Saharan trade.[25]

By 642 C.E. Arab invaders had conquered Egypt. During the early period Islam spread to sub-Saharan Africa, primarily through two routes: the trans-Saharan trade and the sea lanes of the Indian Ocean. It spread patrilineality where it did not already encounter it. Still, there were often great variations in Islamic practice over much of the sub-Saharan continent, depending on the resilience of local cultures and customs. Islam often championed certain rights for women in inheritance and divorce, for example, but it also projected women as the wards of men.

The expansion of Islam into sub-Saharan Africa between the seventh and sixteenth centuries (by which time it had also spread, although unevenly, throughout the continent, with the least direct contact in Central and Southern Africa) had far more profound implications than the extension of Christianity during this period. Islamic control of the trade routes of the Mediterranean and the Indian Ocean made conversion very attractive, particularly in the western savannah, where the rise of the Sudanic empires of Ghana, Mali, and Songhay (between the fourth and sixteenth centuries C.E.) was partially predicated on control of trans-Saharan trade routes.

From about the tenth century C.E., ruling families of the Sudanic empires embraced Islam, and the religion took strong hold throughout West Africa. In the East, Islam figured prominently in the rise of Swahili culture and the wealthy Swahili trading centers along the Indian Ocean coast. Women in this area were central to the religion's spread as marriage partners of resettled Arab traders.

Women in Early Societies, Communities, and States (ca. 1000 C.E.–ca. 1880 C.E., with Some Attention to Earlier Periods)

GOVERNANCE

This was a period of intensified state-building and expansion as well as major political, economic, and cultural developments. Women's roles in these developments, and the attendant constructions of gender, are easier to recover, especially from the seventeenth century on, although tremendous lacunae remain. The era as a whole is often referred to as the "precolonial period," although European contact was well established in coastal areas by the early sixteenth century, colonialism did not begin in earnest before the seventeenth century, and only that early in a few places. There are growing attempts by scholars of Africa to differentiate among periods within this long era and develop a periodization centered in African historical developments.

East Africa was drawn very early into the trade of ancient times. Indian and Persian sailors as early as 500 B.C.E. brought trade with China. Roman and Hellenistic mariners reached East Africa via the Red Sea. By the second century C.E., Bantu-speakers had begun to form small states in the interior of East Africa, states that traded overland with the East African coast. Central Africans also traded with the East Coast as early as the fifth or sixth centuries C.E. In West Africa, trade across the Sahara was ongoing in the early centuries of the Christian era, but the introduction of the camel sometime between the third and fourth centuries increased the trans-Saharan trade exponentially.

As trade grew along the East African Coast and across the Sahara, people of the interior of Eastern and Central Africa and those of the forest areas of Western Africa were drawn into trading in increasing numbers. By the middle of the fifteenth century, Portuguese explorers began their journey around the Atlantic Coast of the continent, partially in search of an alternate route to the East. Although early trade consisted of other commodities, by the early sixteenth century (subsequent to Columbus's return from the Americas) trade in people, the Atlantic slave trade, began to replace that in other commodities.

A number of states developed between the fourth and seventeenth centuries C.E. The listing in the following table, a selective example of approximately when some began, is provided as a chronology for the discussion that follows.

Women were important to state-building in a number of ways. They sealed alliances by marrying across family and clan lines, creating interwoven kinship groups and allegiances and thus cementing larger territories. A common method of securing allegiance to the state in sub-Saharan Africa was the mar-

Polity	Approximate Date of Origin
Western Sudanic States (Ghana, Mali, Songhay) situated in present-day Senegambia, Mali, Burkina Faso, and Niger	Ghana, fourth century C.E., Mali, twelfth century C.E., Songhay, fifteenth century C.E.
Hausa City States (present-day northern Nigeria)	Eleventh century C.E.– twelfth century C.E.
Ife/Benin (present-day midwest to southern Nigeria)	Twelfth century C.E.– thirteenth century C.E.
Swahili City States (East African Coast from Kenya to Mozambique)	Thirteenth century C.E.– fifteenth century C.E.
Zimbabwe (Zimbabwe)	Thirteenth century C.E.
Oyo Yoruba (southwestern Nigeria)	Fourteenth century C.E.
Luba/Lunda Kingdom (N. Democratic Republic of The Congo, DRC)	Fourteenth century C.E.
Kongo (Congo/DRC)	Fifteenth century C.E.
Ndongo (Angola)	Fifteenth century C.E.
Buganda (Uganda)	Seventeenth century C.E.
Asante (Ghana)	Seventeenth century C.E.
Dahomey (Benin)	Seventeenth century C.E.

riage of kings to women of important kin groups. Both Buganda (present-day Uganda) and Dahomey (present-day Benin) initially expanded in this way.

Between 1000 and 1599 C.E., the Swahili city-states arose. Located on the Indian Ocean coast of East Africa (from present-day Somalia south to present-day Zimbabwe), they were hybrid coastal societies that were primarily Islamic in religion and Bantu (indigenous African) in language and culture. The population was a mixture of indigenous Bantu speakers (the majority) inter-married with the Arab migrants who came to trade. One of the first rulers of one of the most important and largest of these towns, Mombasa (present-day Kenya), was a woman, Mwana Mkisi.[26]

Women not only created kinship and allegiance through intermarriage, but they also helped create states by integrating and stabilizing cultures through childbearing and childrearing. Even the role of concubine, which would seem to be a vulnerable one because concubines were protected nei-ther by blood relationship nor legal ties, could be used to exercise influence, and concubines could, potentially, be incorporated into the structure of state power. All the *askias* (kings) of the kingdom of Songhay, for instance, were the children of concubines.[27]

After an initial phase of kinship as a tool of expansion, many states began to develop complex military organizations and turned to expansion through conquest. Militaristic states tended to favor male symbols and a male hierarchy. Women, however, not only accompanied many state troops in their campaigns but were also sometimes combatants. In Dahomey, an elite corps of female troops that later European observers would dub "Amazons" were feared combatants. These female troops were nominally viewed as "wives" of the king and could have been the result of an earlier, kinship-based state expansion tool turned to a new use. Women were also important to the development of the economies of states. As agricultural laborers, reproducers of laborers, producers of crafts, and traders in the distributive sector they were always involved in African economies in very direct and public ways.

As states became more centralized and a bureaucracy developed that was less dependent on kinship, one clear avenue of women's influence and power in state formation eroded, but the role of marriage in cementing state loyalty, although dissipated, did not disappear. Royal women in particular (the ruler's mother, sisters, and wives) retained power based on kinship. Even where most formal political roles became dominated by men, women exerted profound political influence through collective associations such as age grades (a group created of children born around the same time), market associations, and secret societies. Women rulers also existed in several places, but in general the greater centralization attendant to state formation tended to underprivilege women compared to men as it attached greater importance to kinship and control of wealth based on kinship—therefore, control of women's reproduction.

Menstruation was something men seemed to fear, perhaps because they thought it to be connected to women's power of life-giving and, dialectically, to death, its opposite. Postmenopausal women, however, were invested with the power of being elders, making them equal to (or nearly equal to in some places) the men in their age cohort and superior to younger men. Being postmenopausal freed women from all kinds of restrictions imposed on their menstruating sisters because most women were isolated during menstruation.

Classification as an elder was an almost nongendered status for many African people. Being able to have children gave women one kind of positive status and being unable to have them any longer conferred another, equally positive, status. Not ever being able to have children, however, created a crisis for women in a society in which kinship was wealth in both the psychic and material senses. So-called barrenness was grounds for divorce or abandonment. Many people allowed women to circumvent the pariah status of not having biological children by giving the same maternal status to those who adopted children as to those who actually gave birth.

Many people lived in "stateless" societies. The idea of centralized political systems as more sophisticated/complex is problematic for much of sub-
Saharan Africa. One assumption to drop is that people who did not form
centralized states somehow lacked the know-how to do so. Amadiume has
called these societies "anti-state" decentralized political systems to emphasize
the element of choice in remaining decentralized.[28] Stateless societies frequently existed near highly centralized states and had various relations with
them. They were also often densely populated and controlled important resources. One could not argue, for instance, that the stateless Igbo of West
Africa were small in number, lacking in resources, or uninvolved with the large
centralized systems, such as Oyo or Benin, near them.

Although power was dispersed in stateless societies, it devolved to kinship
groups, usually as controlled by men as were large state systems. Because kinship was so important, control of women's reproduction was important. Dis-
persal of power from the center does not seem to have enhanced the autonomy of women with respect to men. The creation of sedentary society, and the
generation of surplus and differentiation in status that ensued, seems to have
been one of the main factors in the erosion of women's equal or complementary status with men.

Whether in large state systems or stateless societies, however, women
played important roles in social, economic, and political development and
challenged patriarchal authority. They could also exercise considerable power when they organized collectively, which is a distinct feature of women's
history in sub-Saharan Africa.

A number of states as well as stateless societies, such as Dahomey and the
Igbo people, respectively, had dual-sex political systems in which female offices
mirrored those of males. Among people who developed states or city-states,
queen mothers were important figures across a broad swathe of the continent.
The office did not necessarily redound to the status of women in general, but
queen mothers often exercised considerable power. They helped enthrone
and depose rulers, could control access to rulers, sometimes collected taxes
and controlled treasuries, presided over court systems, and exercised state
power in other ways. The actual power that queen mothers wielded differed
in degree and kind from place to place, but the role of queen mother represented one avenue through which elite women could exercise power over elite
and commoner men. The office of queen mother also made women visible
in state government.

Ridicule was one way in which women challenged patriarchy collectively.
It was ubiquitous, a weapon that was only effective if used publicly and collectively. Standardized rituals of ridicule such as flashing one's genitalia or dispar-
aging men in oral commentary were employed below the Sahara by women who

sought to adjudicate disputes with men and influence decision making on the part of the state. Whether in seventeenth-century Southern Africa or eighteenth-, nineteenth-, and twentieth-century Western and Eastern Africa (and likely for a long time before) women excoriated male and/or state actions that they felt harmed women's interests. Occasions that invited ridicule included wife beatings, appropriation of women's economic resources such as crops, and attempts to control women's trade or collect taxes from them. Women employed ridicule against European colonizers as well. Collective public protest by women that employed ridicule and disparagement of men is referred to variously as "sitting on a man" by scholars of Africa and by indigenous names such as *adjanu* by the Baulé of Côte d'Ivoire or *anlu* among the Kom of Cameroon. One scholarly study reports, "When the women of a village wished to resort to disciplinary action against a man . . . they assembled as *anlu.*"[29]

A main avenue through which individual women exercised state power was by ruling, although most rulers of the period were men. Among the Mossi people of West Africa there was a legendary warrior queen, Iyennegi, who is still glorified in song and celebration. She is reported to have led a strong army in defense of Mossi lands (the present-day Burkina Faso) sometime during the late first millennium C.E., and her tomb is still a site of visitation.[30]

During the early seventeenth century, a royal woman, Njinga, seized state control from her half-brother. Known to history as Njinga of Ndongo, she initially consolidated her power in the 1620s in the area of present-day Angola but was forced, due to Portuguese incursions, to move further eastward to Matamba. There she created woman-based rituals of state power and was able, in the middle of the seventeenth century, to bequeath power to her sister. Njinga is heralded as strong woman ruler and a heroine of the struggle against early Portuguese colonization.

Several Hausa city-states have legends about original female rulers. Although scholars have debated whether the legends describe actual historical events, at least one scholar argues convincingly that they do.[31] By the late sixteenth century there was a female ruler of Zazzau, one of the Hausa states, Queen Amina (or Aminatu), who succeeded her father. She, too, was a warrior queen who led her people in conquest, thus extending the boundaries and expanding the economy of Zazzau. At least two other women are said to have ruled among the Edo people of Benin (present-day Nigeria), Ogiso Emose and Ogiso Orhorho.[32]

The Mende people of Sierra Leone have a long history of female chiefs that dates at least to the sixteenth century. Madame Yoko of the Mende, who ruled from 1885 to 1905, is said to have used her role in arranging marriages for young girls as a way of cementing power. Moreover, she is said to have manipulated British colonizers to secure her power.[33]

Women also exercised power through various roles in the state and community. Among both centralized and noncentralized people they often held political offices that corresponded with those of men in a dual-sex political system. Such was the case, for instance, among both the Fon (highly centralized) and the Igbo (highly decentralized or "stateless"). In addition, among both centralized and decentralized people, women (particularly those who were postmenopausal) were appointed to committees that provided checks and balances on the rulers' power in centralized states or adjudicated important societal disputes among decentralized groups. Among the Yoruba (West Africa), for instance, women were appointed to the Ilu Committee at least as early as the nineteenth century. This committee advised the *oba* (king) and could call for his resignation and in earlier periods even for his suicide. Women were also appointed to such committees as early as the sixteenth century in the kingdom of Kongo (Central Africa).

The Igbo of present-day southeastern Nigeria remained decentralized, which is not to say unorganized, before the twentieth century. Beautiful bronze art dated to at least 900 C.E. is part of the Igbo cultural legacy. Among decentralized people such as the Igbo, postmenopausal women were often impaneled, with elder men, to adjudicate societal disputes. Because being an elder in sub-Saharan Africa was nearly a genderless status, elder women were generally venerated for being close to the ancestors and for the wisdom of their years, much as were men.

Another potential way for Igbo women to exercise greater autonomy, power, and influence was to take on a male role through an institution known as "woman marriage." This allowed women of wealth to take wives and become the heads of lineages, because children the wives bore were, legally, those of the female "husband." Women could also be treated as "male daughters." That is, if a man had no male heirs or favored a daughter who showed business acumen or some other valued quality, he could declare the daughter his heir. A daughter so-declared would exercise the same power a son would have, including having the power of a "husband" over lineage wives.[34] In both these instances, to exercise such power women had to be gendered (or socially constructed) male although they were biologically female. Neither "female husbands" nor "male daughters" much affected women's generally subordinate role to men among the Igbo, although both roles provided ways for individual women to resist the restrictions attendant to being a woman.

There were other roles for women in centralized states as well that allowed them to exercise considerable power as individuals. The *Iyalode* (literally, "mother of the town") among the Yoruba was a member of the ruler's council of chiefs and a spokesperson for the women of her city and often had her own court and council of subordinate female chiefs.

The Yoruba began forming city-states during the eleventh century. The first, Ife, well known for its beautiful wood, ivory, brass, copper, and iron work dating from the twelfth through the fifteenth centuries, was located in present-day southwestern Nigeria. By the fourteenth century, however, the role of Ife was usurped by that of a newly rising and powerful city-state, Oyo.

Although it is not clear exactly when the title of Iyalode originated, by the eighteenth century several major Yoruba towns had such an office.[35] An Iyalode was usually chosen by other women for her wisdom and achievements. She was considered to be a leader of women and represented the collective interests of nonroyal women to government. According to Awe, the role of the Iyalode would be transformed by greater state centralization in some places. During the successive internecine Yoruba wars of the nineteenth century the state usurped more control from citizens outside its direct bureaucracy and influence. Thus nonroyal individual powerholders such as the Iyalode were diminished in their ability to exercise that power in, for instance, New Oyo. "Upstart" Yoruba cities such as Ibadan and Abeokuta, however, became important during the instability of the nineteenth century, and in both cities there remained powerful roles for the Iyalode, at least until the end of the nineteenth century when colonization commenced in earnest.[36]

The role of queen mother was often a very powerful one. She was usually the birth mother of the king, but if the king's biological mother were dead or otherwise incapacitated the king or his counselors could choose another royal woman to exercise this function. Sometimes a woman could insinuate herself into the role of queen mother by successfully engineering the succession of her son to power. The queen mother among the matrilineal Asante, known as the *aasantehemaa,* is an example of the most powerful queen mothers. The Asante nation dates from the last quarter of the seventeenth century, when Osei Tutu unified various Akan states under one centralized ruler. His successor Opoku Ware (1717–50) expanded the state until it took up most of the territory of present-day Ghana and exercised control over most gold-fields of the West African forest. As one scholar has written of the role of the asantehemaa:

> As a full member and co-chairman of the governing council or assembly of state, the queen mother's presence was required whenever important matters of state were to be decided. She also had to hear all judicial cases involving the sacred oaths of state. She was entitled to, and did have, her own separate court where she was assisted by female counselors and functionaries. Her independent jurisdiction covered all domestic matters affecting women and members of the royal family. In certain cases, however, Male litigants could apply to have their civil cases transferred from the chief's court to the queen mother's where fees and fines were generally lower.[37]

The asantehemaa nominated candidates for the position of *asantehene* (king) and could wield considerable influence in his selection.

Particularly for the nineteenth century there is considerable detail about the activities of powerful women who occupied the office of asantehemaa. The asantehemaa Yaa Kyaa (also known as Akyaawa) went on military campaigns with asantehene Osei Yaw during the 1820s and negotiated at least one peace treaty with the British, with whom the Asante went to war many times in the nineteenth century in an effort to maintain the independence of the Asante state. Another well-chronicled asantehemaa, Yaa Akyaa, maneuvered her son Prempe I onto the throne. She is remembered for her role in fiercely resisting British efforts to colonize Asante. When the British finally took the Asante capital, Kumase, in 1896, Yaa Akyaa and her son were exiled to the Seychelle Islands.[38]

In centralized states women also exercised some power as the keepers of state secrets. The state of Dahomey (in present-day Benin), founded in the seventeenth century by Wegbaja (the first king) from a group of "stateless" rural villages, became highly centralized. Women occupied a number of high-status positions in Dahomey and controlled powerful areas of state bureaucracy. The famous female warriors of Dahomey, referred to as Amazons by Europeans, whose organization dates from the early eighteenth century, were housed within the palace walls and considered to be the king's bodyguards.

The so-called Amazons undertook police and military campaigns on behalf of the state. The royal women of Dahomey also played important roles and were very powerful. They had complete access to the king and a role in choosing his successor. The queen mother in Dahomey sometimes had a portion of the royal treasury allocated to her, and some queen mothers undertook pubic works on behalf of the state. In its early years the Dahomean state required every territory to send a wife to the king and thus cemented alliances with its citizenry.

The roles of powerful women in the state and women's offices to which power was attendant in both centralized and decentralized societies did not always affect the status of other women. Moreover, sometimes powerful women had to be gendered male in order to exercise power. Yet among some hunting and gathering people, women seem to have been the equals of men in general. The San of Southern Africa had a fairly egalitarian ethos despite their gendered division of labor—at least until the latter part of the twentieth century. As Berger observes, motherhood among the San, often posited as a major reason for women's subordination to men, did not automatically make women social inferiors. Of the Mbuti and the !Kung she notes, "These examples of highly egalitarian societies not only provide important insights into the African past but also challenge any notion that childbirth automatically relegates women to an inferior position in society. Clearly, it is the material and social conditions under which birth and mothering occur that determine their significance."[39]

It was in groups that most "ordinary" women, and therefore women in general, exercised power. One example is the ubiquitous existence of women's secret societies, which empowered women collectively among centralized and decentralized people. Men belonged to secret societies as well but rarely had control over the formation or operation of women's secret societies. The societies were secret not because people did not know about them but because they employed often elaborate secret rituals of initiation and called for detailed reciprocal rights and duties among members.

Secret societies were functional in a variety of ways. They initiated girls into womanhood and taught women medical and other skills that they might practice for remuneration and to increase their status. Secret societies served as incubator groups for future women leaders and as self-help groups from which women could borrow money and/or find help for entrepreneurial endeavors. In most secret societies, achievement, leadership, and an affable personality composed the democratic foundation that could allow individual women to succeed. Older women held more power in societies such as Bundu (present-day Sierra Leone), although all women joined.[40] Secret societies also often taught women the rules of gender and the history and philosophy of their people. Moreover, because they often served such important sociocultural functions, the societies were religious in nature as well.

RELIGION

There is a long history of female deities throughout sub-Saharan Africa. Among the Nnobi Igbo, Idemili is worshipped as the basis of all civilization and culture.[41] Amadiume posits that the worship of Idemili binds all Nnobi Igbo women in a "spirit of common motherhood" that reflects a past matriarchy. In addition to female deities, women often played important roles in religious rituals. Berger notes that Mang'anja women (in the area of present-day Malawi) were more prominent than men in rituals that honored the area's "guardian spirit," Mbona.[42] Among some Yoruba groups (primarily in present-day western Nigeria), *oriki* (praise poems) are performed mostly by women, who, consequently, are seen to exercise a great deal of control over communication with the *orisa* (gods).

Female deities were centralized in nearly all sub-Saharan religious traditions, even in those few from which women were barred or marginalized from centers of power, such as the *gelede* (masking ceremonies) among the Yoruba that allow participation of men only but have at their center a revered female deity, Inyanla. In part because religion was concerned with survival and therefore with the fertility of the land or the people, the transparent role of women in reproduction was seen as intrinsically powerful. Some people viewed menstruation as "polluting" and thus having the potential to defile anything

31

menstruating women touched, a concept that resulted in women being isolated during menstruation. At the base of such notions was often fear of the
potential power women had over reproduction and thus over life and group
survival.

In addition to the pervasive existence of female deities there were also
numerous women diviners and healers. Both divining (searching for the hidden truth and representation behind things) and healing had religion at their
centers. Religion and material life were often connected such that diviners
could probe for the problems that lay behind infertility, for example, or other illness or personal calamity. They could also predict the future. The concept of healing is fairly self-explanatory, although what was thought to make
a person ill most often had some social component, such as a failure to fulfill
some obligation or being the target of witchcraft. Thus the religious power
attendant to being a healer or diviner meant that such women also wielded
power in the physical world. Diviners and healers not only held status and
power but also usually expected economic remuneration.

A woman could also be a prophetess and thus wield important political
power. In one such example in 1856, a Xhosa prophetess, Nongquase, advised
her people to kill their cows and destroy their fields and stored food as a desperate measure to rid themselves of European colonizers and reclaim their
land and sovereignty. The ancestors, she reported, had advised that white
colonizers would be cast into the sea and would not disturb the Xhosa for at
least a thousand years if these things were done.[43]

Women were also spirit mediums, and such possession could be not only
an empowering experience but also a freeing one. Women could say and do
many things when possessed by a spirit that would otherwise be completely
unacceptable (and for which they might even be punished were the spirit not
speaking through them). Political power could also accrue to women spirit
mediums. In one example, Charwe, a medium of the spirit Nehanda of the
Shona people (of present-day Zimbabwe), led a rebellion in 1896 against
British rule. In so doing she mobilized other spirit mediums of Nehanda as
well as those of other spirits.

Depending on time and place, Christianity and Islam spread to sub-Saharan Africa both through conquest and peacefully. During the early periods of
their formation as religions they both expanded into Africa from their places
of origin in the present-day Near and Middle East. Conversion to Islam was
sometimes attractive because Islam provided greater entree to trading networks
and/or a lower rate of taxation, particularly before the period of European
colonization. Conversion to Christianity was sometimes attractive because
Christianity gave greater access to Western education, often a prerequisite for
greater economic and political rewards, especially during the colonial period

(and even after). Local people sometimes modified the religions to reconcile them with indigenous beliefs, rituals, and social organizations.

Small pockets of people (particularly among the ruling classes) who were in direct contact with Europeans due to trade relationships converted to Christianity even before the colonial era. King Affonso of Kongo (in the area of the Democratic Republic of the Congo in Central Africa), for instance, wrote in the early sixteenth century to the king of Portugal to ask that the burgeoning slave trade be stopped due to its ill effects on the economy and society of his people. A woman called Kimpa Vita (known to the Portuguese at Doña Beatriz or Beatrice), also of the Kingdom of Kongo, in 1702 claimed that St. Anthony had entered her body while she was dying and returned her to life. She formed a syncretic religious movement that combined elements of Catholicism and indigenous beliefs and challenged the Roman Catholic hierarchy and Portuguese influence in Kongo. Although a member of the Kongolese nobility, Kimpa Vita seems to have lost its support when, pointing to St. Anthony as the source of her power, she claimed the right to choose a new ruler for Kongo. Having challenged both the Portuguese and the Kongo rulers, she was castigated by both and burned at the stake in 1706.[44]

In places as diverse as the East African coast (particularly the Swahili city-states) and northern Nigeria (particularly the Hausa city-states), the seclusion of upper-class women occasioned by the spread of Islam was a very gradual process due to local customs. It often took several centuries. Even though by the sixteenth century the general seclusion of women prevailed in these areas, women of royal birth still sometimes ruled. During the sixteenth, seventeenth, and eighteenth centuries there were occasional women rulers on the island of Zanzibar (off the East Coast) and in the Swahili city-state of Pate (on the East Coast) as well as in the Hausa city-state of Zaria (the present-day northern Nigeria).

Even though orthodox Islam and the imposition of Shari'a (Muslim law) proscribed women from active participation in public life, the syncretic adoption of such laws, particularly among rural and/or nonelite populations, meant that women in many places still engaged publicly in pre-Islamic ceremonies. Among the Hausa, for instance, the *bori* religious tradition (in which both men and women could be possessed by the bori spirits) continued to thrive, even in heavily Islamic areas, into the nineteenth century despite the arrival of Islam as early as the eighth century. Islamic scholars did not condone continuation of the bori tradition, and over time the status and power of its practitioners waned as Islam gained prestige and influence. Still, there were places in which bori continued into the twentieth century, although diminished in social and religious importance.[45]

In early-nineteenth-century northern Nigeria, a jihad led by Uthman Dan

Fodio had many implications for women. The instability created while the jihad raged made some women more vulnerable to capture and even enslavement. Female seclusion, where it could be afforded, gained popularity and was advocated by Dan Fodio himself. Still, he held some relatively progressive views toward women. He believed that they should be educated and had a right to fair and just treatment from husbands, especially regarding inheritance. Although he argued that women were subordinate to their husbands, he also maintained that they had a right to disobey husbands who refused to educate them or who themselves disobeyed religious laws.

Dan Fodio educated the women of his own family and began a tradition that produced generations of women intellectuals in the Fodio family. His daughter Nana Asma'u is well known for her inspirational religious verse, which is considered to have made a major contribution to the development of Islam in northern Nigeria.[46] Khadija, also a daughter of Dan Fodio, translated an important Islamic law book, the *Mukhtasar* of Khalil, into the West African language Fulfulde.[47] Later generations of Fodio women, writing in Arabic, Fula, and Hausa (the latter two being West African languages that were written in Arabic script before Roman script) left a number of writings that commented on good character, religious piety, and current events. As one scholar has written of these women, "They wrote deliberately, purposefully, often burning with zeal. They taught and lectured, scolded, warned, exhorted, ridiculed; they marshaled recorded events and set them down."[48]

The Fodio women were not the only ones known to have been educated as a result of the jihad and to have written important religious works in nineteenth-century northern Nigeria. During the period of the jihad and afterward, other women organized themselves into teams called *yan taru*, which traveled around the nation, taking Islamic knowledge to women in rural areas.[49]

The jihad also strengthened the rights of concubines because orthodox Islam mandated that a concubine who gave birth to her owner's child had to be manumitted. Enforcement, however, was generally left up to the good conscience of the owner. The jihad also stated that women must inherit from husbands and girls from fathers (even if a lesser amount than sons and brothers) and awarded women the right to divorce (even if it was harder for them to initiate a divorce than for men to do so).

On the negative side of the equation of the jihad, at least insofar as women's autonomy is concerned, seclusion and women's exclusion from publicly sanctioned roles in government and trade operated to lessen women's power in the state, both as individuals and as a group. It also placed them at an economic disadvantage with respect to men. Although women in seclusion continued to trade by using young female relatives or slave women and/or men to represent them in public, seclusion made it more difficult to secure credit, expand trading networks, and increase their volume of trade, thus curtailing the scale of their businesses. Sometimes, if they were veiled, secluded women could go in public after dark and conduct business, but only with other women and never with non-kin men. Scholars have pointed out that some were able to use seclusion to their advantage by developing businesses built on marketing crafts or selling cooked food (both of which could be produced in seclusion) and thus accrue individual wealth.[50]

Seclusion was the ideal for orthodox Muslim women, but in practice even those of the upper classes did not always obey it, nor did men always enforce it. Moreover, poorer women and those from rural areas (especially poor, rural women) could not withdraw from agricultural labor and trade because their own survival (and often that of their families) relied on them. Overall, however, it is clear that dilution of women's economic access and direct political clout were among the jihad's effects. Diminution in women's public roles in governance, in fact, may be at least partially responsible for the fact that women in northern Nigeria, where the jihad took greatest hold, were kept from gaining the franchise until the central government gave it to them in 1976, more than a quarter of a century after it was awarded to their southern sisters.

In other places Islam took different turns. In Senegal (in West Africa) it was organized through powerful brotherhoods, particularly the major four: Tidjaniya, Muridiyya, Qadiriyya, and Layenne. Although, technically, women cannot be *talibes* (disciples) in brotherhoods, the state considers them to be members of the group to which their male household head belongs. Brotherhoods differ in attitude toward and treatment of women; the Layenne, for instance, permit women to worship in a mosque (albeit separate from male worshippers). In the mid-twentieth century, through the foundation of socioreligious organizations called *dahira,* women became even more involved in Islamic practice by serving in prominent positions in both mixed sex and all-female dahira. Moreover, in Senegal, in contrast to northern Nigeria, some women are highly placed in brotherhoods and publicly acknowledged as politco-religious leaders. A few, such as Sokna Mulimatou in the 1960s, had their own disciples. Callaway maintains that pre-Islamic traditions of women's pubic leadership among the Wolof and Serer people of the Senegambia area are continued indirectly in roles women play in brotherhoods.[51]

In other places, particularly coastal West Africa in the areas of present-day Sierra Leone and Nigeria, conversion to Islam did not include the seclusion or veiling of women. Muslim women interacted in public with non-kin women and men, were absent from home on long trading ventures, founded schools for girls, and were active in public life. Among the Yoruba, for instance, Madam Pelewura, a Muslim, was a politically powerful leader of Lagosian (the former capital of Nigeria) marketwomen, the majority of whom were also Muslim, from the 1920s to the 1950s. She led them in major battles with the British colonial government over women's taxation, right to vote, and right to control the location of markets and the prices of good sold in them.[52] She also was active in anticolonial politics, working with Herbert Macaulay and Nnamdi Azikiwe, two of the best known and most influential male anticolonial politicians of the twentieth century.[53] Pelewura served on the Ilu Committee that advised the traditional ruler of Lagos. Another Muslim woman, Humani Alaga, became a very wealthy trader in Ibadan, a major urban center in western Nigeria. She built a mosque and founded a school for Muslim girls, where religion was taught along with secular subjects.

On the East African coast, Muslim women in Kenya found novel ways of bypassing Islam's traditional strictures on dress and women's leadership by forming dance associations known as *lelemama*. These groups had many purposes, including enabling members to navigate the strict racial and class hierarchies of large urban centers such as Mombasa and the mutual provision of economic aid. At events such as weddings where members danced as group entertainment, women who would otherwise have been secluded or forbidden from dancing in front of men and not wearing the customary *buibui* (long black robes) did so, often in fierce competitions among dance associations. Although this activity was unaccompanied by political demands, women were putting their own perceived social needs first, and the associations operated as incubators for developing women's leadership. This activity, however, never seems to have directly translated into overt demands for larger roles for women in governance or even in religious observance—such as attendance at mosque. In fact, Strobel contends that lelemama associations were primarily organizations "of rather than specifically for [i.e., operating in the interests of] women."[54]

As seen from the few preceding examples, the influence of Islam and its role in constructing gender were quite varied throughout the sub-Saharan continent. Christianity had considerable influence during the colonial period but was less formative of gender construction than Islam during the precolonial era. Still, it was employed by women (and men as well) to attempt to exercise agency with Europeans. Despite the growing populations who embraced (fully or partly) Christianity or Islam, indigenous religions did not lose currency. They remained major forces in society and therefore in women's lives.

THE ECONOMY AND THE FAMILY

During this period women were the mainstay of the agricultural sector of African economies. As well, by the eighteenth and nineteenth centuries in some areas (such as among the Yoruba of present-day Nigeria) where polities were urban to provide protection from numerous internecine wars, men often went outside city walls to farm. Women, then, were in control of much of the distributive sector of the economy in marketing the goods that men farmed.

The interdependence of men's and women's roles in the economy of precolonial and precapitalist Africa affected family structure and relationships. Although a gendered division of labor existed in a vast majority of places, women's work was as integral to the survival of their families as was men's. Men's work was still considered more important in some cases, for instance in cattle herding in some areas of the northeastern part of the continent, and hunting, almost singularly engaged in by men, was also of high importance. There were a few areas in which women did hunt, though, such as among the Shona of present-day Zimbabwe.[55]

Still, the basis of most economies was agriculture, and for most of the continent women provided the main agricultural labor force. Men often cleared the land, but it was most often women who planted and tended the vast majority of crops. Although most land was owned communally by family, women often had usufruct rights to land in their natal families. In a few places where individual ownership of land obtained, such as among the Igbo in West Africa or the Amhara in Northeast Africa, women sometimes owned land as well.

Women had a variety of other roles in the economies of African societies and states. They were traders, both local and long-distance, and wove and dyed cloth and made clothing, although some textile products were reserved for men. Women braided hair, produced household goods such as bowls and crockery, and traded cloth and other items. Although the tradition of powerful female traders so well known in West Africa does not seem replicated in East and Southern Africa, women in those areas did do some trading and certainly provided the staple labor for their agricultural economies.

In most places women exercised some control over the fruits of their labor, particularly if they were free and often even if they were slaves. One route to political power, in fact, was election as head of a group of trading women such as the *Iyalode* of the Yoruba or the *Omu* of the Igbo (both people of present-day Nigeria). Because election to these positions was based on skill, trading success, and personality they were among the powerful positions that women could earn rather than inherit.

Royal or religiously powerful women, sometimes even elderly women, could control the labor of others and thus achieve a certain amount of wealth and power. Mothers-in-law, for example, sometimes controlled the labor of daughters-in-law or other younger women of the extended family. A woman might also own the slaves, both male and female, who worked for her or the products of whose labor redounded to her because of her place in the family.

Women's importance in the economy gave them public visibility and vested common interests as a group due to the gendered division of labor. Sometimes they were able to parlay that into recognition of their political salience. Groups of women traders could exercise considerable political influence, even securing appointments to ruling bodies. Even where women did not exercise strong trading roles that allowed access to political power they could strike or rebel, collectively, in order to protect their interests as women and as an economic class.

Most women who traded were "petty traders," they traded in small quantities and had very slim profit margins. As a result, they could only protect their interests through collective bargaining power. In West Africa, women were often organized into powerful trading organizations. That was much less true of Eastern and Southern Africa, where women were much more likely to be embedded on small family farms and have less access to urban centers and non-kin women. As were women in West Africa, those in coastal areas of East Africa, however, were more likely to belong to larger trading or economic collectives of non-kin women with whom they could work to control the supply and price of commodities, loans, and political influence.

Slavery had economic salience in Africa, both before and during the Atlantic slave trade. Given the tremendous variety of African forms of unfree labor, all often carelessly lumped together into the category *slavery* as it developed in New World capitalist economies, the ultimate objective of most African societies to absorb unfree labor into their populations as both clients and family has often been lost. Not all unfree labor was in perpetuity in Africa. Pawning, for instance, could be employed for a set period to repay a debt or even to secure credit. Usually, pawns were members of a group and had kin nearby to look out for their interests. People could also be enslaved (for set periods) due to capture during war, for debt, or as criminals.

In societies in which kinship meant everything and formed the basic organizational model and root of the economy and polity, to be without kin was a major crisis. Being without kin was, essentially, the first element of slavery in sub-Saharan Africa. Most indigenous African slavery had at its core the assimilation and productive use of captives of war who had no kin. Female slaves in particular were more easily assimilated as wives and could also expand a kin group by having children. In some places having children for an owner meant that those children were automatically free members of the lineage and gave special rights to their mother as well. All of indigenous African slavery was not benign, but it was different in particular and important ways from slavery in the New World and even from the impact of the Atlantic trade on slavery within Africa.

The rise of the Atlantic trade in slaves created a new, and for a while seemingly insatiable, market. For most of the period of the trade (roughly the early sixteenth century to the third quartile of the nineteenth century) males made up the bulk of those captured and sold across the Atlantic Ocean. Some scholars maintain that the reason for that appears to have been that Africans preferred to keep women who were captured and destined for slavery rather than because Europeans preferred men as slaves.[56] One scholar argues against that interpretation, reporting that the same-sex skewed ratio was not present in the contemporaneous trans-Saharan and Indian Ocean slave trades in which the numbers of women traded were often close to or in excess of men.[57] During the early days of slavery in the Americas, especially in the Caribbean and South America, where nearly 95 percent of enslaved Africans landed, enslaved women were worked as hard as men and in many of the same occupations. In fact, the treatment of men and women in the Atlantic system of slavery appears to have been conditioned more by the labor needs of the enslavers than by gender.[58]

Whoever is correct, women's labor was prized in Africa, particularly in agriculture. Women captives could be more easily assimilated than men, and the slave population in Africa became increasingly female. In West Central Africa during the nineteenth century men began to take slave wives rather than freeborn women so they did not have to meet economic obligations to the families of freeborn women. Slave wives would have been unprotected by kin and far more subject to the authority of husbands.[59]

The violent nature of slave procurement for the Atlantic trade contributed to increased violence in the internal trade and profoundly affected it. Women were especially disadvantaged, being more vulnerable to the rapes and beatings that became characteristic of the Atlantic trade and had some effect on internal African trade as well. During this time the numbers of slaves being shipped in the Indian Ocean and trans-Saharan trades increased, and from the eleventh century C.E. Africans began to replace the supply of slaves from Eastern Europe in these trades.

Some women, although very small in number, either became involved in the trade as intermediaries between European slave purchasers and African slave vendors or became slave dealers themselves. Along the West African coast, women known as *signares* or *senhoras* (depending on whether they dealt with the French or the Portuguese) established relationships (sometimes even households) with European traders. They interpreted for them, looked out for their interests, often had children with them or sometimes married them, and in other ways facilitated the traders' economic and political relationships with Africans. Some of these women were able to enrich themselves and their children considerably. Senhora Phillippa controlled an important trading center at Rufisque (Senegal) in the first half of the seventeenth century. The trading network between Gambia and Sierra Leone that Bibiana Vaz maintained during the late seventeenth century was so extensive that for awhile she established political power in the form of a coastal Afro-European Republic.[60] Madam Tinubu, heroine of the 1864 Dahomey-Egba war from which the famous Egba (Yoruba) city of Abeokuta was born, was also for a time a slave trader. Due to her extensive political and economic power, when the British annexed Lagos (Nigeria) in their first colonialist power grab in the area in 1861 Tinubu was expelled from the city as punishment for backing a local ruler with whom the British did not wish to negotiate.[61]

Africans did not see themselves as Africans collectively against Europeans collectively during much of this period. They warred among themselves for control of trade and territory, much as Europeans did. The Asante, for instance, were as concerned about the African states around them as they were about the British or the French. To understand how the slave trade was successful we must recognize three kinds of relationships: those between Africans and Africans (often in competition with one another); those between Europeans and Europeans (who were often in competition with one another within Africa as well as outside it); and those between Africans and Europeans. All of such relationships were protean.

The Atlantic slave trade skewed society in some ways, particularly in West and West Central Africa (areas from which most slaves hailed) for this period, but continued economic interdependence of men and women resulted in "space" for women in most sub-Saharan African societies' affairs. That space resulted from women's critical roles in the economy. There was not, strictly speaking, male/female equality, but women did have important negotiating power with respect to men in terms of economic and political influence and decision making. Among the Nupe of northern Nigeria, for instance, women's important roles in the economy and their ability to manage much of their own wealth meant they helped their sons with bridewealth. Sometimes even their husbands were indebted to them. To facilitate long-distance trading, women practiced both contraception and abortion and controlled provision of domestic services such as sex and cooking as a way of negotiating with men.

Women operated in two families and could have differing statuses in each. One family was that into which they were born, their natal family; the other was the one into which they married, their affinal family. Women were fullfledged members of natal families and thus, depending on particular circumstances, were sometimes able to inherit land outright or at least the use of land (usufruct rights) or other inheritable property. Women often had both material and ritual obligations to natal families. They were most often senior in rights and privileges to women who married into natal families, such as sisters-in-law (and would often even refer to these women as "our wife," meaning the wife of the lineage). Women often started out at the bottom rung of their affinal families, however. They could rarely inherit from them and derived status primarily from their roles as mothers and mothers-in-law. Motherhood was a major constituent element of women's status, and being unable to have children was a calamity. There were ways around that problem, however, because raising an adopted child from birth did not appreciably differentiate one's status as a mother from that of a woman who had a biological child.

Marriage was an institution between two families and not between two individuals. Because it was a major means of increasing the lineage in both human and material wealth, marriage was expected of all adults. Where male heirs were unavailable or unacceptable, women could operate as "husbands" for their natal lineage, taking other women as "wives" in a woman-to-woman marriage. Powerful and wealthy women could even begin a lineage in such a way. At least one scholar posits that this type of marriage links the evolution of gender relations from a matriarchy to a matrifocal patriarchy.[62]

Matrifocality centers society and family on a relationship to affinal women. This is not the same as matrilineality, tracing patterns of kinship and inheritance through the female line. In a matrilineal system women were not necessarily powerful; most power was in the hands of their brothers and sons. Women, however, generally held high status in matrilineal societies because status in the group was determined by relationship to the women of the group. Historically, a number of African people were members of matrilineal groups. In fourteenth-century Mali the early traveler and historian Ibn Battuta commented on the matrilineal organization of its people, and the Asante of Ghana are also well-known as being matrilineal.

In a matrifocal system, a woman and her kin children were seen as a unit of production and consumption, related to a larger unit through a husband. Due to the matricentric nature of the unit of a woman and her children, women gained a certain power of influence as well as a good deal of economic control. Amadiume sees the matricentric unit as a site of ideological construction of matrifocality (woman-centeredness) in the most basic social unit, that of the family.[63] Due to polygyny, a husband/father entered the unit at specific times and for specific purposes, but he was not omnipresent nor a completely overarching authority figure.

Most evidence indicates that over a broad swathe of sub-Saharan Africa, at least by the seventeenth century and probably much earlier, the matricentric unit, at least until late childhood or early puberty, was the primary one in which children were socialized. Some scholars posit that the widespread tradition of matrifocality made its way, along with enslaved Africans, across the Atlantic and influenced the organization of enslaved families and subsequently the structure of black families in the Americas.[64]

The effects of gender as a determinant of status, however, were fluid. The lifecycle of a woman was extremely important in affixing status. Whether she was a child, mother, mother-in-law, postmenopausal, married, or unmarried, for instance, could have as much to do with her freedoms, privileges, and power as being a woman. Moreover, her status in the nexus of one set of social relations (her natal family) might be totally different from that in another (her affinal family), even at the same stage of life. As well, elite women could hold power over men who were poor and older women over younger men.

Women as a collective wielded power in many parts of the continent through their associations, which were modes of responding to patriarchal authority. Through the use of domestic strikes, public ridicule, outright physical attack, or control of rituals, women negotiated power within kinship units and the state.

Another important mode of social organization for women (as well as men) was the age-grade, which crossed kinship lines. All individuals born within a few years of one another in societies that had age-grades (and most did) belonged to the same age-grade. Age-grades were same-sex and were also one way of organizing people to work for the state or larger group across kinship lines. They included the rendering of public service in the construction of roadways, maintenance of markets, and even military service. Age-grades also supported members in a variety of ways, including support and resources for ceremonies.

Bridewealth (bride-price, bride-service) was attendant to most marriages during this period and well into the twentieth century. Bridewealth was the exchange of goods and services between a groom and a bride's family to compensate them for her loss, particularly that of her labor and any children who might be born to the couple. The exchange of these gifts or services was also seen as a sign of respect to the bride and her family and helped legitimize a marriage, serving as a sort of contract or license. In the event of divorce, the gifts and services were often required to be returned to the groom and his family (unless he was considered culpable for the divorce). With the onslaught of colonialism, especially in places where the colonial power required wage labor because it was forced as service to the state or to pay newly imposed taxes, money began to sometimes substitute for bridal gifts or service to the bride's family. That often caused distortions in the custom.[65]

Divorce was quite commonly available to, and instigated by, women over much of the sub-Saharan continent, even among Muslims, until well into the colonial period. For a time in the colonial period the "management" of women became a challenge for both colonizers and indigenous men in an era of great space and upheaval created by the clash of cultures and interests. Divorce became harder for women in some circumstances, especially when collusion occurred between colonizers and indigenous men over the control of women's movements and roles in the economy. Postcolonial states, on the whole, seem to have returned to an easier pattern of divorce for women. In some areas, however, growing fundamentalist movements, whether Muslim or Christian, have risen to challenge this.

One cannot leave a discussion of family or economic organization without discussing polygyny (taking more than one wife). With land and people as the primary bases of wealth in most areas, and women (and sometimes their dependent children) providing the majority of farm labor, the material basis for polygyny is transparent. Although women often had the right to the use of land, and even its ownership where it was individually owned, by this period men exercised effective control over most land use. Multiple wives increased the wealth of men by making land produce and by producing people who enlarged kin networks. Women were not merely economic pawns or exploited labor, however. In many places they were entitled to trade a percentage of the crops they produced, even if the land "belonged" to their husbands, and they exercised autonomy over the financial gain from that percentage. Women also negotiated with husbands for start-up funds to set up a trade or other business venture or to have them pay for an internship that would provide a woman with a wage-earning skill, such as work as a hairdresser or seamstress. It was expected that women would engage in economic activity other than what they produced for their families and exercise control over some surplus they produced, even in strongly patrilineal families; women also often counted on help from and land use in their natal families. Colonialism, along with the attendant spread of Christianity, eroded many premises of women's economic activity, in particular the ability to control resources.

Where wives got along, polygyny could advantage women in some ways. They had the help of co-wives for childcare, particularly if a woman was a long-distance trader. Although they shared a husband, they also shared the chores associated with marriage, such as cooking for a husband or providing him with clean clothes. Wives, however, could also compete with one another or otherwise not get along, which could make life harder as well. A senior wife could exercise arbitrary authority over junior wives (seniority being based on marriage date, not age). The degree to which polygyny obtained was dependent on the ratio of women to men and also on the wealth of a society. Only men of certain means could afford more than one wife. That sometimes meant that older men, more likely to have wealth, practiced polygyny and often with younger wives.

The spread of European ideas and Christian ideals during the colonial period (beginning as early as the seventeenth century in some areas) posed challenges to the institution of polygyny, particularly among the small and emerging elite. The institution was also challenged, particularly in the early twentieth century, by an increasing number of urban women who sought to lessen both consanguinal (blood-related) and affinial kin male power over their lives.

Colonialism (ca. 1650s-1960, Later in Several Areas)

African women did not experience colonialism the same through space and time, nor were they merely the victims of colonialism. They exercised agency that at various times and in various places negotiated with the colonial encounter and modified it. Through accommodation, syncretism, and resistance African societies transformed colonialism and were transformed by it. Just as colonialism sought to remake Africa, Africans remade themselves and reshaped colonialism.

Still, colonialism did not have as its main mission the development of Africa nor the improvement of the lives of Africans. It was meant to develop Europe and improve the lives of Europeans. It was intended as a system of sociopolitical and economic control. Colonial ideology did not accept Africans as equals but attempted to "elevate" them to the level of European society. As such it had negative impacts on the lives of all Africans, female and male. There were individual Europeans who sought to improve society in ways that were beneficial to Africans. There were also institutions such as Christian religious denominations, for example, that believed they were "doing good" by converting Africans, saving souls, and, in the process, enacting certain concrete programs for Africans to avail themselves of and use. Religious denominations in particular often sought to save souls through Western education, which became a tool many Africans used to challenge the colonial enterprise. To the extent that colonialism benefited African populations, it did so through the efforts of individual Europeans, the aegis of private organizations such as churches, or colonial government responses to the insistent demands and/ or resistance of Africans.

Any social upheaval such as colonialism creates "revolutionary space." Upheaval challenges institutions and changes them, whether directly or indirectly. Thus the elements of an indigenous population that may be disadvantaged by certain aspects of existing institutions are sometimes able to parlay the "revolutionary space" created by social upheaval to their own advantage. When cultures meet, ideas and practices confront one another; they harmonize or clash, merge or subordinate, and fertilize each other and bring people into each other's worlds. In general, no meeting of cultures is all bad or all good. In forced encounters, however, one side or the other usually pays a higher price for the introduction. Africa paid a higher price than Europe.

Women were both disadvantaged by colonialism and sometimes able to have it work to their advantage. They were always active in the African movements resistant to colonialism as well as those that tried to negotiate for a "best terms" coexistent solution. Because it created crisis, colonialism both opened and closed opportunities for women. Most scholars agree, though, that its greatest effect on gender relations was to marginalize women as a group from political centers of power and from economic resources and to attempt to reinvent in Africa the seventeenth- through nineteenth-century European ideal of the apolitical, dependent woman whose highest calling was to motherly and wifely duties.

The earliest stages of African-European contact were shaped by a trade that initially included other items but soon became overwhelmingly a slave trade. By the middle of the fifteenth century the Portuguese were trading with Africans in the area of the Senegambia, and as the century progressed their contacts stretched along the Atlantic coastal areas of the continent, around the tip of Southern Africa, and up along the East African coast. By the seventeenth century, trade in slaves was the most important trade between Africa and Europe.

Other aspects of Afro-European contact in these early centuries affected women's status. Crops such as cassava, introduced from the New World, demanded more labor by women.[66] Women slaves who could be controlled by men sometimes displaced the labor of free women, particularly as men began to take slave women as wives. The large number of women available as slaves affected the formerly greater equality of gender relations. The instability created by the slave trade made centralized power, supported by military organization, even more important for security and trade, thus disadvantaging women in the public sector because they were much less likely to be involved in providing security. By the mid-seventeenth century there was European settlement in a few areas, such as Southern Africa. Khoikhoi women in the area were taken into Dutch homes and trained as servants in this early period, although soon they would be displaced by domestic labor recruited from the East Indies.[67]

In general, colonialism proceded in three stages (with notable exceptions, particularly in the Portuguese colonies and white settler colonies of Southern Africa): so-called pacification or conquest, when Europeans (sometimes with African allies or Africans pressed into service) were attempting to combat the military and political resistance of Africans (ca. 1860 to 1900, although most of this occurred after the Berlin Conference of 1885); early colonialism (ca. 1900 to 1920), when Europeans were "consolidating" colonialism by setting up colonial bureaucracies and legal, economic, and military systems were more flexible and there was often space for Africans to maneuver; and high colonialism (ca. 1920 to 1960), when European-controlled state bureaucracies were in place and African economies were controlled by them.

The greatest dislocation occurred in local African communities in colonies that had large numbers of white settlers (particularly in Southern Africa but also in East Africa). Family life was disrupted because the settlers appropriated land and expropriated labor for work in urban centers, mining areas, and on large, commercialized farms and plantations. African men in large numbers became migrant laborers, leaving women and children behind in rural areas to scrounge for food and other necessities. The men's wages could be kept depressed because, ostensibly, they had no families to support, given that the families were left in rural areas and were, according to European propaganda, "self-supporting." The twentieth-century government of apartheid South Africa gave voice to this long-standing policy when Prime Minister Hendrik Verwoerd declared the wives and children of South African male migrant laborers "superfluous appendages."

Although African women did increasingly, over the course of the twentieth century at least, become migrant laborers in factories and private homes, the state constantly attempted to limit their numbers. The women and children who migrated to urban areas to follow husbands and fathers made implicit demands on the state for a family wage for the men and for housing, medical care, and education, none of which the state or private capital wished to provide.

Just as some groups of women were disadvantaged by male migration to urban centers, small numbers of others attempted to turn this situation to their advantage. Women in the Zambian copperbelt, for instance, provided services such as cooking and laundry for African migrant miners and therefore were able to attain a certain degree of economic independence.[68]

In examining the ideological premises of colonialism it is necessary to consider the particular stage at which Europe developed into an occupying colonial power in Africa. Certainly by the late nineteenth century, when colonial occupation began in earnest over much of the continent, Western Europe at least embraced growing notions of individual rights and growing capitalist states. It promoted a cult of domesticity that (ideally) confined women to their homes as helpmates of men and gendered the public-sphere male. Educational systems were not only largely stratified by class but also informed more and more by science (although sometimes pseudo-science) and logic, as by Western classical ideas. The presence of Christianity and women's domestication was a barometer of "civilization." Capitalist states also competed among themselves as imperial powers for economic and nationalistic reasons. All of this would profoundly affect the ethos of the colonial enterprise in sub-Saharan Africa.

Commercial capitalism began to encroach on sub-Saharan African economies during the period of the slave trade, particularly from the seventeenth century through to the early nineteenth. It would, however, take a full-blown colonial presence to establish conditions for its real growth. The effects of that growth on the majority of women were more adverse than positive. Berger points out that in East Central and Southern Africa especially, commercial capitalism aggregated power in the hands of men and devalued women's economic activities such as their roles in the distributive sector of the economy.[69] She posits that the growing of cash crops, farm mechanization through the use of plows and ox-drawn sledges, and the use of men as migrant workers all contributed to enhancing men's economic position in an increasingly cash-oriented economy.

The growing of cash crops disrupted the complementary nature of male/female labor in several places. In West Africa, for instance, men often provided protein through hunting or fishing and cleared the land for women to plant subsistence crops. Women's roles in the productive sector of the economy became obscured because European colonizers looked to deal with men as the "owners" of land, even where women were the primary producers of crops, and because African men commandeered the labor of women to produce cash crops.

White traces the example of Baulé women in twentieth-century Côte d'Ivoire, who, before colonial penetration, enjoyed a fairly equal, economically beneficial relationship with men when it came to producing cotton and trading in finished cloth.[70] The women had grown cotton on land men cleared for them, cleaned the cotton, spun it into thread, and produced indigo with which to dye it. Men then wove it into strips to be sold, and both men and women shared in the profits. Women were, in this process, viewed as the real "owners" of the cloth because they produced the raw material. They began to be marginalized, however, when cotton became a major cash crop in the growing capitalist economy and the French dealt with the men who traded the finished product. The women lost out all around in the "development" of the textile market in Côte d'Ivoire once the cotton began to be shipped to Europe and then re-imported and sold in Africa.

Capitalism in general disadvantaged women for three reasons. First, they derived much of their economic power as sellers in the marketplace or producers of craft goods, organized collectively into cartels. That collective organization obstructed capitalist penetration and thus was attacked by colonizers. In the early twentieth century one colonial official pointedly criticized the degree of power that Yoruba women's market associations wielded in Lagos, saying that it should be "nipped in the bud."[71]

Second, women were disadvantaged in obtaining access to the credit necessary to capitalist development because Europeans viewed them as being "out of their place" as entrepreneurs. Where women were afforded small amounts of credit they were often forced to accept slow-moving goods (those harder to sell) along with faster-moving, more attractive goods, which affected their abilities to turn around merchandise and garner a profit.[72] As African men became more empowered in controlling land use and women's labor, women's traditional institutions lost power in representing women's interests in the economy. In the early twentieth century among the Igbo of Ossomari in eastern Nigeria, for instance, colonial authorities reassigned waterside market control, formerly the purview of the Council of Women, to the town council.[73]

Third, women competed with not only African men and European companies but also an increasing presence of East Indian and Middle Eastern male entrepreneurs. That left the vast majority of African women in the role of "petty traders"—those for whom the volume of goods was relatively small and the margin of profit both small and constantly precarious. There were women, however, who, although small in number, were able to marshal the resources and business acumen sufficient to become, relatively speaking, wealthy from the vastly increased volume of trade in the colonial economy. Humani Alaga, a Yoruba Muslim, for example, became a major philanthropist and founded a school for Muslim girls in the Nigerian city of Ibadan during the early period of independence. Although she earned most of her money after independence in 1960, she built on a textile empire she had begun during the colonial period.[74]

Many women formed credit cartels from which they could borrow to expand businesses and commodity associations that helped them to fix the prices, choose the sites, and control the maintenance of markets as well as the flow of goods. Particularly in West Africa, women's trade associations became powerful political allies of men during labor strikes and in the independence struggles of various African states.[75]

Land registration plans promulgated by colonial authorities often registered property to a male head of household or male head of an extended family, reinforcing African patriarchal traditions that gave men control over land. Registering land to individuals alienated it from the control of kin groups and distorted traditional land tenure systems in which women had access to the land in their natal families. In the process, women were disenfranchised from land ownership and sometimes even from usufruct rights. Colonial states attempted to assign male "owners" of land because the states promoted men as the "normal" heads of households and, moreover, as providers for women and children. In a severe famine in Malawi in 1949, colonial administrators who distributed food discriminated against women by giving the food to men with the expectation that it would "trickle down" to women and children.[76] As cash-cropping progressed (and this actually continued into the period of independence), men were trained in the new technologies and asked to make decisions about issues such as the growing of crops and use of pesticides even where women were the primary agricultural producers.

Originally, colonialism created even greater stratification among women than among men, in part because the economic and cultural markers that accompanied class formation bore more heavily on women in that they supported confining them to the domestic sphere as individual wives and mothers. The group gender-consciousness of women was challenged. In sub-Saharan African societies women had not, as a rule, been confined to the domestic sphere, and the domestic or familial sphere was defined very differently than that in nineteenth-century Europe, which was being forcibly imported to Africa. The domestic unit in nineteenth-century Africa was an extended family with a division of labor in which women were involved in some form of production for the family and the marketplace. Even the relatively small number of women secluded due to Islam continued, for the most part, to exercise a degree of economic autonomy. Women derived civic and cultural importance and influence as a result of direct labor force participation, their transparent roles in the productive and distributive sectors of the economy, and their group-consciousness as women. Due to a gendered division of labor that threw them together in these roles, they recognized common interests and often operated to protect one another from the abusive power of husbands, the larger ethnic group, and even the state. They also operated through their associations to oversee their economic interests. As colonial authorities and Christian missionaries began to promulgate the "cult of domesticity" with increasing efficiency, and as it began to be mirrored in the governance and economic structures of colonies, women became more invisible as citizens and economic producers.

Particularly during the consolidation period of colonialism, conservative African male elders sometimes found common ground with colonizers in their desire to control women. In many colonies, for example, Europeans wished African women to stay in rural areas as agricultural workers in order to stabilize colonial economic networks and more easily develop systems of taxation. As women attempted to use the upheavals of the period to move to urban areas or in other ways challenge traditional strictures such as arranged marriages and carve out space for themselves in newly emerging economic markets, the social fabric resisted change, seeking to keep the women where they were.

"Traditional" or "customary" African law began to be codified during the colonial period. Colonial authorities worked primarily with male elders and chiefs in this task. As a result, many rights of women became distorted to men's benefit as traditional law became codified. The presumption of men as heads of households for census data and tax purposes also distorted women's roles in the family and the economy. As bridewealth began to be paid more frequently in cash (especially in Eastern and Southern Africa), subtle changes began to be enacted that signified the payment as ceding to men rights over wives unavailable to them under customary law. It also made divorce more difficult for women because bridewealth had to be repaid in kind, and women were less likely to have access to cash.[77]

Women resisted control by colonizing and indigenous males. Especially because women had few opportunities in the formal wage-labor sector created by capitalism they became entrepreneurs in areas they could control and that required fewer resources to initiate. Single women and girls from rural areas migrated to urban spaces created by colonialism and set themselves up independently as brewers of beer, sellers of cooked food, laundresses, mistresses, and sometimes even prostitutes. Both colonial authorities (who rounded up women or blocked their arrival as they disembarked from trains) and indigenous male elders (who forbade women to leave rural areas) tried to stem the tide of urban migration among single women. The women might have had more autonomy in urban spaces, but they lacked the protection of their families and the familial safety net. Still, the encounter of European and indigenous social organizations created a negotiable space for redefining gender relations that women tested all over the sub-Saharan continent.

Colonialism had other gender-specific ways of impacting African women, particularly in the areas of sexual exploitation and education. On various plantations (coffee, tea, and cotton) organized by Western businesses in East Africa in particular but also in areas of West Africa, foreign men raped women or in other ways sexually harassed them.[78] The education provided by colonial governments was primarily aimed at men and sought to educate a class of African men who could staff the lower echelons of the colonial civil service.

Although elements of the African population sometimes resisted education for women and girls—seeing it as not arming females with the tools to earn a living, removing them too much from the control of parents, and proselytizing Christianity—it was African women who were the most insistent in demanding education for girls and themselves. In 1927 Queen's College was founded in Lagos (Nigeria) as a result of African women's agitation for the secondary education of African girls. Its curriculum consisted of needlework, domestic science, singing, and, only if specifically requested, mathematics and a foreign language. Despite the fact that parents of many students complained that the curriculum should be more academic, the European principal wrote in 1929, "The character of girls' education should be of a particular kind. It is almost universally agreed that it should not be a copy of that which is given to boys."[79] Still, a small Christianized African elite was produced in Nigeria as the result of Western education, and it was this elite that produced many leaders of the anticolonial struggle.

Although patriarchy was known to African societies before the arrival of Europeans, kinship-based cultural organization, extended family structure, and sexual division of labor all combined to blur the boundaries of patriarchy and create spaces that empowered women, particularly as a group. In Western European cultures of the colonial period, ideally, at least, women's protection and provision for by men was synonymous with a "civilized" and "progressive" society. Where it did not interfere with profit or political control, colonials sought to refashion African gender relations to mirror those in Europe. Christianity was a major factor in this activity. The Christianized African elite created during the colonial period both accommodated and resisted refashioning African gender relations to a European model.

Christianity promoted monogamy, even to the extent of sometimes asking men to give up other wives to whom they were wedded and with whom they had children. Some women welcomed monogamy and their attendant rights to be primary inheritors of their husband's estates under Christian marriage laws, but they also felt keenly isolation as well as dependency as Christian norms sought to withdraw them from the public sector, both economically and politically.[80]

Christian sects, particularly until the 1940s, were the primary providers of Western education for women. Although they concentrated primarily on providing training for women to be good wives, mothers, or household help for Europeans, they also taught them to read and write, providing a powerful new set of tools that some Christianized women used to represent women in literacy and suffrage struggles. Where Christian ideas about health care, cooking, and sewing seemed to lighten women's burdens or otherwise improve their lives and those of their children, women not only accepted parts of the new ideologies but also actively joined in promoting aspects of them. As one historian has stated, however, Christianity was "as much about new family forms as faith in Christ," and as such it frequently clashed with African cultures.[81]

The small, Christianized African elite began to form "breakaway" churches that allowed Africans access to roles in the church hierarchy and that harmonized more with African cultural practices by, for instance, labeling monogamy not a law of God but of Europeans, and forming the basis for resistance to colonialism. Kimpa Vita (a.k.a. Doña Beatriz) used Christianity in this way in the movement she led against the Portuguese in eighteenth-century Kongo. In Central and Southern Africa, women played important roles in the Watchtower movement that resisted colonialism.[82]

There were large numbers of European women in settler colonies, although their presence seems not to have affected the gender-specific oppression of African women. In some settler colonies where African women provided domestic labor for European families (often men did rather than women), they were sometimes maltreated by European wives who were concerned about the potential for sexual liaisons with husbands. There was also a small presence of European women in nonsettler colonies. Strobel posits that they did not challenge colonialism overtly but that their presence as travelers, chroniclers, and workers did challenge patriarchal notions of imperialism and adventure as being gendered male and of women's roles in the societies from which they hailed.[83] That may be true. It certainly is true that some colonial women studied women's roles in African societies and published their findings.

With the exception of missionary women who sometimes sheltered young girls whom they felt to be abused by their families, there is no evidence that European colonial women had any real effect on the nature of colonialism in Africa, particularly in the ways it affected women. In 1930s' Lagos, in fact, the opposite was true. Led by Charlotte Olujamoke Obasa and her Lagos Women's League, Western-educated women protested the fact that they were not hired in civil service jobs and in the nursing profession because such work was (unofficially) reserved for the European wives of colonial officials. Even as women began to be hired in some positions they were paid salaries much lower than those of comparably employed men. In fact, the confinement of women to certain grades of the civil service and lower pay scales for them was consistent with British practice toward women in Britain.[84] Although a relatively short period in African history, the colonial era was a profound one for the changes it wrought in the internal affairs of the continent as well as the relationships between the continent and the rest of the world.

RESISTANCE TO COLONIALISM

Women were very active in the anticolonial struggle from the earliest days in the seventeenth, eighteenth, and nineteenth centuries when Kimpa Vita, Njinga, and Tinubu resisted European imperialism through to the independence struggles and national liberation wars of the twentieth century. Women's resistance, widespread and varied, was engaged in by women who followed traditional religions or were Christian or Muslim, elite or non-elite, Western-educated or unlettered, and rural or urban.

In the earliest years of the "pacification" stage of colonialism, a number of women led resistance movements. Berger discusses the resistance movements of the 1890s against Europeans led by Charwe in present-day Zimbabwe, Muhumusa in present-day Rwanda, Empress T'aitu Bitoul in present-day Ethiopia, and Mekatililli in present-day Kenya.[85] During World War I, Aline

Sitoe Diatta, a Muslim of Senegal, led her village in uprisings against French policies that sought to conscript rice from the Casamance region. Eventually, French troops were sent to put down the uprising, and Diatta was exiled to the neighboring country of Mali, where eventually she was executed under mysterious circumstances.[86]

In 1929 in southeastern Nigeria one of most-studied uprisings of women, termed variously the "Aba Riots," the "Women's War of 1929," or by its Igbo name, "Ogu Umunwaayi," occurred.[87] In this uprising, women responded en masse to the spread of ideas about being taxed by colonial authorities, and tens of thousands attacked colonial symbols, both material and human, foreign and indigenous. The leadership was self-effacing, and later when the British convened a major inquiry into the affair they were unable to identify any individual leader.

In Nigeria, several groups of women were involved in protest from the 1920s to the 1950s. Led by a well-respected marketwoman, Madam Pelewura, women of the Lagos Marketwomen's Association protested taxation, especially because they were not enfranchised, and demanded both an end to female taxation and the right to vote.[88] They also demanded the right to keep their traditional roles in deciding the location of markets, the pricing of commodities sold by their market associations, and control of the fees charged for maintenance of the markets. During World War II the colonial government attempted to enact price controls for such indigenous staple foods as *gari,* including a proposal that it be sold at government-run centers, without consulting members of the Marketwomen's Association. Pelewura, who led the association in protesting the price controls, told the colonial Governor Bernard Bourdillon that she had lived through World War I, when "no white man sold gari." She also refused government attempts to bribe her to rein in the women's protests, accusing officials of trying "to break and starve the country where I live."[89] Addressing a rally during the 1940s, Pelewura is quoted as saying, "I am she who is called Pelewura." Noticing an overwhelmingly male audience, she continued, "We wonder why your womenfolk did not show up here today. Tell me of that thing which men can undertake alone without the help of the womenfolk?"[90]

One of the most famous Nigerian activists of the 1940s, Funmilayo Ransome-Kuti (later known as Funmilayo Anikulapo-Kuti), led thousands of women of her Abeokuta Women's Union in resistance against the British and the traditional ruler of the major southwestern Nigerian town of Abeokuta, the Alake Ademola II. Memorialized by the Nigerian Nobel Prize–winning author Wole Soyinka in his book *Ake* as the "wrapper wearers" (a reference to the traditional wrapped cloth worn by non-elite women), the women marched, sat in, attacked colonial and indigenous authorities, were arrested, and wrote

53

pieces supporting their cause in which they quoted both British and American statesmen on democracy. After her trip to China in 1956 the British declined to renew Ransome-Kuti's passport to keep her from traveling internationally to seek support for the women's cause. Although Western-educated and middle class, Ransome-Kuti took to wearing traditional wrappers and speaking in Yoruba (suggesting that if Europeans did not understand her they should acquire translators) when she led marches. When denied permits to march, the women began to refer to their marches as "picnics" and amassed in the thousands to protest. At one point in the demonstrations the women warned that "vagina's head will seek its vengeance."[91]

In 1949 women in Côte d'Ivoire partially spurred by being marginalized in the production of cotton, an activity in which they had played a central role, rebeled against French colonial authorities by invoking *adjanu,* a precolonial collective form of protest that mocked authorities through verbal insults and nudity, as had occurred in southeastern Nigeria. In addition to protesting the treatment of women, the adjanu also called for liberation of the male protesters incarcerated at Grand-Bassam.[92] In 1958 and 1959 a similar mass demonstration of more than seven thousand women, *anlu,* was called by Kom women in Cameroon to protect their crops and protest what they feared was the mounting alienation of land from women.[93] In his novel *God's Bits of Wood* (1982) Ousmane Sembene (also well known as a filmmaker) creatively narrates the story of the women of Senegal, who, in the late 1940s, went on a long march from the city of Thiès to Dakar to support striking male railway workers. Women supported the strike in other ways as well, such as providing the men with food and providing for the families of striking workers.

The Nigerian Women's Party, founded during the 1940s, appears to be the first all-women's party that fielded a slate of candidates for public office. In 1927 Oyinkan Abayomi (later to be Lady Abayomi) founded the British West Africa Educated Girls' Club, later renamed the Ladies' Progressive Club, a group that was behind the agitation that resulted in the establishment of Queen's College. On May 10, 1944, with twelve women she gathered in her home, she founded the Nigerian Women's Party (NWP). In its constitution the NWP aimed, in part, "To work for the amelioration of the condition of the women of Nigeria not merely by sympathy for their aspirations but by recognition of their equal status with men."[94] Although the party remained small compared to contemporary Nigerian women's organizations such as the Lagos Marketwomen's Association or the Abeokuta Women's Union, it pressed for girls' education and women's literacy classes, the employment of African women in the Nigerian civil service, and protection of the traditional rights of marketwomen.[95]

During the 1950s, women were very involved in all aspects of the well-chronicled "Mau-Mau" insurgency in Kenya, from funneling food, medicine, weapons, and information to men hidden in the forest; to performing the ceremonies by which people swore oaths to unite them; to being actual combatants.[96]

In the 1950s, South African women in Natal rebelled against forced removals from urban areas, which they saw as usurping their abilities to make decisions about their lives and threatening a new system of land allocation that would not recognize women's control over their own fields. Women burned fields, smashed trucks, and attacked other symbols of state power. At the same time, women in the Durban area resisted attempts to control domestic beer brewing by picketing and burning beer halls.[97] The most sustained and best-known protests of women in 1950s' South Africa were their protests against the Pass Laws. These laws required men and women to carry small, passport-sized booklets with their pictures in them. By means of these "passes" they were granted access by the apartheid government to move about in particular areas of the country and to hold specific jobs. On August 9, 1956, twenty thousand women protested these laws in Pretoria, South Africa, and their protest spread to other areas as well.

Through boycotts, marches, sit-ins, labor stoppages, refusals to pay taxes, mass demonstrations, attacks on symbols of colonial authority, collective ridicule, and in other ways, African women were active participants in protests against colonizers and those indigenes who supported and/or represented them. The nationalist movements that began to appear across the continent from the 1930s through the 1950s did not always admit women as full partners, however. Several organized separate bodies, women's wings, that were advisory to the main parties, including the African National Congress in South Africa, the Nigerian Youth Movement and the National Council of Nigeria and the Cameroons in Nigeria, and the Tanganyikan African National Union in present-day Tanzania.

Although several groups embraced causes that women championed such as woman suffrage (many colonies had limited male suffrage) and an end to the sexual harassment of women on European-run coffee plantations, it was generally not until the 1940s that male-run nationalist parties began to admit women into their ranks. The women were active nationalists before that, however, and admission into the main ranks of male-run nationalist parties was as much the result of women's agitation as it was progressive behavior on the part of men.

Although most independence struggles did not involve all-out war and were "settled" by the early 1960s, men and women alike were jailed and oth-

55

erwise harassed in all of them. In places such as Kenya, where the Mau-Mau insurgency was a truncated armed struggle, women and men lost their lives or were otherwise maimed. All independence struggles required the mobilization of women as well as men. Women drew on their traditional modes of organization and protest, all gender-based, to create hybrid organizations that were gender-based but used modes of protest such as petitions and suffrage that were introduced with colonialism. They also joined with men in organizations and activities that were gender-integrated and constantly agitated for roles in post-independence states that would recognize them as equals in the civic arena as well as in the family.

The process of armed struggled called into question not only the inequalities of the colonial period but also those of the precolonial period in areas where protracted armed struggles for independence occurred from the 1970s into the 1990s: Angola, Eritrea (somewhat of an anomaly here because Eritrea was struggling for independence from another African state, Ethiopia), Guinea-Bissau, Mozambique, Namibia, South Africa (although officially declared independent from Britain in 1910, I am referring to the end of apartheid), and Zimbabwe. Even more important, people engaged in discussions of how an independent new society would be organized.

Initially, there was resistance to women as armed combatants, and most women, even when traveling with guerrilla forces, were primarily intended to clean and cook for them. Over time, however, women became integrated in various ways into the armed forces of many national wars of liberation. Sometimes they were combatants, but often they were teachers, organizers, and spies.

Eventually, revolutionary groups such as the African Party for the Independence of Guinea-Bissau and Cape Verde (PAIGC) adopted the stance of "fighting two colonialisms" when it came to women—one against traditional patriarchy and one against colonial patriarchy.[98] Another revolutionary group, the Revolutionary Front for the Liberation of Mozambique (FRELIMO) at its 1968 Second Party Congress explicitly denounced polygyny, bride-price, and other practices it considered as exploiting women.

Women could also train male soldiers. In 1972 at the first congress of the newly formed Organization of Mozambican Women, the head and major theoretician of FRELIMO, Samora Machel, observed, "The emancipation of women is not an act of charity, the result of a humanitarian or compassionate attitude. The liberation of women is a fundamental necessity for the revolution, the guarantee of its continuity and the precondition for its victory."[99]

In several of these places (particularly Angola and Mozambique) the onset of independence was disrupted by the launching of civil wars spurred by disgruntled internal groups armed by states external to the continent in an extension of cold war–era politics. In others such as Zimbabwe and South Africa, a continued inequitable distribution of land inherited from the colonial era, among other factors, has created problems that have affected women more than men. In her 1996 biography the well-known South African activist Mamphela Ramphele wrote of her years as an activist struggling against apartheid: "The double jeopardy of being black and female in a racist society may well make one less afraid of the sanctions against success. A non-subservient black woman is by definition a transgressive—she is the ultimate outsider. But political activism, with its infusion of a purpose higher than oneself, and the steeling effect of having had to break most of the rules in a society desperately in need of transformation, have added an important depth to my life."[100]

Women's roles in anticolonial and nationalist struggles and liberation wars of the twentieth century have not left them equal to men in independent African states. The reality is that even if they were treated as men's equals, the poverty and political instability of many African states that affect all citizens regardless of gender or age would negatively impact their lives. In addition to the struggle for gender equality, African women are faced with struggling, along with men, for a global redistribution of wealth and power. Only the winning of both struggles can truly improve the lives of women and girls.[101]

Independence

During the first heady years of the 1960s when most African states had achieved independence there was great hope that people's lives would be transformed. It might, however, place things in perspective to realize that nearly three-quarters of a century after independence the United States was engaged in a civil war and still seeking to define its democracy. Within the next several decades African states (many of them the creations of colonial powers that threw together people of differing traditions and languages) will begin to mature politically, find their bearings economically, and continue to transform socially.

In 1967 Annie Jiagge, justice of the High Court of Ghana, wrote the original draft of the United Nations Declaration on Elimination of Discrimination against Women, adopted unanimously by the UN General Assembly in that same year. Ironically, in the vast majority of African states there was little distinction in the status of women between the later days of colonialism and the first several decades of independence. When it comes to agricultural training, for instance, despite the fact that women remained the primary agricultural producers, development schemes still offered training in new agricultural techniques to men, extended them credit for agricultural development,

57

and targeted aid for agriculture to them. As one scholar aptly sums up for Eastern and Southern Africa, "The consequences of 'development' policies are striking: women control less land, their land is less fertile and produces lower crop yields, legal and political barriers to women's land ownership continue, and new technology has often increased their workload without a tangible increase in benefits."[102] About West Africa another scholar writes, "In no states are women significantly represented in agricultural or technical training."[103] Even though there are studies several decades old that point this out, little headway seems to have been made in turning it around.

Wage-labor opportunities for women are far less available than for men in every sub-Saharan African state. There are women elementary and secondary school teachers, nurses, doctors, and lawyers, but their numbers are small, relatively speaking. Although everywhere women exhibit a tremendous thirst for education, their opportunities lag far behind those of men; the higher one goes up the ladder of education the fewer the number of women. Women in rural areas continue to farm and trade, and those in urban areas trade as well. Urban migration makes many unskilled women dependent on often-transitory relationships with married men (even when they are more mistresses than prostitutes) to supplement their incomes—a phenomenon called "outside wives" that creates discord among women in general.

Women's organizations, both within states and continentally, study gender disparity and rally to attempt to affect it in a positive way. The Association of African Women Organized for Research and Development (AAWORD), founded in 1977 and headquartered in Dakar, Senegal, has a continentwide membership that participates in international forums on women, holds continental conferences, and publishes on women's issues. The Women's Research and Documentation Center (WORDOC), founded in 1985 at the University of Ibadan in Nigeria, conducts research on Nigerian and West African women and actively promotes the presence of women in academic associations and the Nigerian workforce. Maendeleo Ya Wanawake (MYWO), founded in 1963 in Kenya, became so identified with the ruling KANU Party that it lost credibility for a while. Since 1997, however, MYWO has once again asserted its independence. African women academics have begun to publish in a variety of fields, including history, and the information and interpretations that they provide are valuable resources for other scholars.

Creative writing has become a major way for African women to make their voices heard. Authors such as Ama Ata Aidoo, Mariama Ba, Abena Busia, Tsitsi Dangarembga, Buchi Emecheta, Bessie Head, Flora Nwapa, Grace Ogot, and a host of others have provided a flourishing literature that allows access to women's experiences and thoughts. Literature is often a wonderful way to teach history.

Still, a number of things have affected the effective organization and influence of women. State corruption and political instability, increasing class stratification, unstable international prices for raw materials that cause state economies to fluctuate, often uncontrollably, and high international debt all coalesce to shrink opportunities for all Africans, especially women. Problems such as these, however, have often led states to scapegoat women as being part of the problem rather than part of the solution. In the 1970s in Zaire (now the Democratic Republic of the Congo or DRC) then-President Mobutu Sese Seko developed a policy known as *authenticité*. Claiming the policy as a return to "traditional African values," it basically sought to reinscribe authoritarian male leadership of both the country and the family. It was alleged that women's attempts to procure wage work militate against men's abilities to support themselves and their families.

Elements of the policy of authenticité even required women to have their husbands' permission to work outside their homes, often making them feel as though they were between a fictionalized, distorted "tradition" to which they were being held accountable and the reality of their daily lives, which required a twentieth-century perspective, education, and work effort. As one African woman scholar has noted, "Even women activists often live a double life, that of the liberated woman in the public sphere but succumbing to gender oppression at the domestic level."[104] In 1980s' Nigeria, the military state claimed that "indiscipline" on the part of marketwomen was responsible for high inflation and spiraling prices. The army even dispatched soldiers to the marketplaces to beat women traders and make them lower their prices.[105]

There have also been positive signs in states. In 1976 Muslim women in northern Nigeria received the right to vote. Although it was more than a quarter of a century after women received it in southern Nigeria, Muslim leaders began supporting the (albeit sex-segregated) education of women and girls, a very positive step over the past. Recently, however, with a resurgence in Islamic orthodoxy (or what is interpreted that way) in some northern Nigerian states, women are subject to being stoned to death for adultery and other oppressive interpretations of Shari'a. Since 1989 the Islamic military junta in Sudan has required that women be veiled and wear ankle-length dresses.[106] There are, however, small cohorts of educated Muslim women in northern Nigeria who through writings in the local press and radio broadcasts, as well as through schools they run in their homes, or by representing women accused under the new laws, have engaged a debate (often at great risk to themselves) about such interpretations of Shari'a.

For a time between the mid-1980s and the late 1990s in Nigeria the wives of the military heads of state Ibrahim Babangida (1985–93) and subsequently Sani Abacha (1994–98) were given wide latitude to discuss women's issues and convene women's conferences. The reality, however, was that these were oppressive regimes, and by allocating a "woman's voice" to their wives both leaders were providing a distraction from the voices of "grass-roots" women. Indeed, Babangida dispatched soldiers to beat marketwomen for raising their prices during a period of "structural adjustment," the name given to governmental attempts to forcibly restructure the economy, partially to meet demands of the World Bank.

Two other issues highlight the problems of women in independent Africa. First, there has been much discussion since the 1990s about an increase in human rights movements and democracy on the part of non-elites across the continent. Some see gender as highlighted in struggles for democracy— for instance, in the debate over female circumcision or, as it is more popularly known, "female genital mutilation" (FGM). A variety of surgeries are included under the designation "FGM," which has found ready publicity in the United States. Two political asylum cases involving African women have emphasized the issue. One was the case of Fauziya Kaaindja from Togo, whose 1996 petition was granted by the Immigration and Naturalization Service. The second is the 1999 case of Adelaide Abankwah of Ghana, who petitioned for asylum on the grounds that she feared being subjected to clitoridectomy (a form of FGM) if forcibly returned to Ghana.[107] *Genital Cutting and Transnational Sisterhood: Disputing U.S. Polemics,* edited by Stanlie M. James and Claire C. Robertson, does an excellent job of discussing FGM without sinking into the quagmire of defending it as a cultural practice (à la Jomo Kenyatta) or castigating African women for not "caring about" their daughters (à la Alice Walker). African women have themselves been at the forefront of working against FGM. Not all people practice it in any form, and some states (such as Nigeria) have outlawed it.

FGM continues to be a major discussion within the continent and between the continent and the outside world. Because the debate has been so embraced by Western feminists and is often objectified as a "savage" and "exotic" practice, discourse about it has easily played into old stereotypes about Africa. African women who work against FGM on a daily basis feel that such international discourse often makes their jobs harder and distorts attention away from many other things that African women struggle against.[108] Unclean water, malnutrition, poor medical care, and AIDS all require the same attention of the feminist movement in the West as FGM has received.

A second issue that is the other major international discourse about African women concerns AIDS. Women seem to be disproportionately affected with AIDS, and sometimes they are blamed for its spread. The problem of AIDS, of course, affects all Africans, men, women, and children alike. Wild rumors have spread about how to keep from contracting the disease, some involving having intercourse with virgins. The fight against AIDS has gendered aspects because women can pass it along during childbirth and because the poorest of women may be more vulnerable when they engage in prostitution to feed themselves and their children. The struggle for accurate testing, safe, available, and affordable drugs, and humanitarian policies in housing and other areas are real issues. Moreover, the presence of large numbers of populations with AIDS affects every other aspect of developing societies and economies. No one knows for sure why so many populations in Africa are affected. Rumors run wild about this also. Proper treatment for those who have AIDS in Africa is a problem for the entire world.

All is not bleak. I am constantly amazed by the creativity and inventiveness of people, especially women, as I travel on the African continent. I do not mean this in any simplistic way nor to diminish the pressures and deprivations under which people labor. African women are vibrant, capable, and well able to speak for themselves. Although they are sometimes victimized, they are not hapless victims absent agency. Throughout their history they have exercised agency, and they are well aware that not only does history make people but that people make history.

As we move into the twenty-first century, the scholarship on African gender history continues to thrive. Africans themselves are now producing much of it, although, unfortunately, many studies being produced on the continent of Africa are not immediately available in the West because of lack of resources for reproduction and distribution. Almost as soon as an overview such as this is produced, there is new literature that could augment it. Of course, the wider we cast the knowledge-gathering net, the clearer our understanding of all knowledge.

Notes

1. Burstein, ed., *Ancient African Civilizations*, 4.
2. Amadiume, *Reinventing Africa*, 4.
3. See, for example, Oyěwùmí's *The Invention of Women*, in which she argues that the Yoruba language is gender-neutral and that, along with age as a determinant of social status, this fact belies the notion that gender is a discriminatory form of social organization in Yoruba society.
4. Berger, "Women in East and Southern Africa," 41.
5. Shillington, *History of Africa*, 94.
6. Ibid., 16.
7. Ibid.
8. Berger, "Women in East and Southern Africa," 8.
9. Burstein, ed., *Ancient African Civilizations*, 33.
10. Berger, "Women in East and Southern Africa," 12.
11. Burstein, ed., *Ancient African Civilizations*, 7.

12. Shillington, *History of Africa,* 44.

13. Berger, "Women in East and Southern Africa," 13.

14. Burstein, ed., *Ancient African Civilizations,* 43.

15. Berger, "Women in East and Southern Africa," 14.

16. Ibid.

17. "Ancient Settlements Found in Eritrea," AOL news story, May 29, 1999.

18. Shillington, *History of Africa,* 14–16.

19. Berger, "Women in East and Southern Africa," 15–16.

20. Shillington, *History of Africa,* 58–60.

21. Berger, "Women in East and Southern Africa," 15.

22. Shillington, *History of Africa,* 146.

23. Berger, "Women in East and Southern Africa," 18.

24. Ibid., 19.

25. White, "Women in West and West-Central Africa," 64.

26. Berger, "Women in East and Southern Africa," 19.

27. See White, "Women in West and West-Central Africa," 65, for a full discussion of this practice.

28. Amadiume, *Reinventing Africa,* 16.

29. Ardener, *Perceiving Women,* 36; see also White, "Women in West and West-Central Africa," 103; Van Allen, "Sitting on a Man"; and Bastian, "Vultures of the Marketplace."

30. Rybalkina, "Women in African History," 85.

31. White, "Women in West and West-Central Africa," 66; see also Callaway, *Muslim Hausa Women in Nigeria.*

32. Tobrise, "Culture and Gender in Africa," 2.

33. White, "Women in West and West-Central Africa," 88–89.

34. See Amadiume, *Male Daughters,* for a full discussion of this practice.

35. See Awe, "The Iyalode," for a full historical discussion of this office.

36. Ibid.

37. White, "Women in West and West-Central Africa," 87.

38. Aidoo, "Asante Queen Mothers," 66; White, "Women in West-Central Africa," 87.

39. Berger, "Women in East and Southern Africa," 9.

40. White, "Women in West and West-Central Africa," 85–86.

41. Amadiume, *Reinventing Africa,* 18–19.

42. Berger, "Women in East and Southern Africa," 26.

43. Ibid., 29–30.

44. White, "Women in West and West-Central Africa," 79–80.

45. Callaway and Creevy, *The Heritage of Islam,* 43.

46. Coles and Mack, *Hausa Women,* 181.

47. Ibid.

48. White, "Women in West and West-Central Africa," 81.

49. Ibid., 81–83.

50. Ibid.; see also Callaway and Creevey, *The Heritage of Islam,* 42–43.

51. Callaway and Creevey, *The Heritage of Islam,* 46–53.

52. See Johnson, "Madam Alimotu Pelewura," for a biographical treatment of Pelewura.

53. Ibid.; see also Johnson, "Class and Gender."

54. Strobel, *Muslim Women in Mombasa,* 211.

55. Berger, "Women in East and Southern Africa," 22.

56. Robertson and Klein, *Women and Slavery in Africa.*

57. See the discussion in Inikori, "Export versus Domestic Demand."

58. See the discussion in Johnson-Odim, "From Both Sides Now," 95–96.

59. White, "Women in West and West-Central Africa," 68.

60. Ibid., 72–73.

61. For an autobiographical treatment of Madam Tinubu, see Biobaku, "Madam Tinubu."

62. "Introduction," in Amadiume, *Reinventing Africa;* Amadiume, *Male Daughters,* 64.

63. Amadiume, *Reinventing Africa,* 20–33; see also Amadiume, *Male Daughters.*

64. Johnson-Odim, "From Both Sides Now," 97.

65. Berger, "Women in East and Southern Africa," 29.

66. White, "Women in West and West-Central Africa," 77–78.

67. Berger, "Women in East and Southern Africa," 23.

68. White, "Women in West and West-Central Africa," 104.

69. Berger, "Women in East and Southern Africa," 27–30.

70. White, "Women in West and West-Central Africa," 102–3.

71. Johnson, "Madam Alimotu Pelewura," 3; see also Johnson-Odim, "Actions Louder Than Words," 84.

72. Johnson, "Grassroots Organizing," 147.

73. White, "Women in West and West-Central Africa," 100.

74. Johnson, "Oyinkan Abayomi," 159; see also Johnson, "Nigerian Women and British Colonialism."

75. Johnson-Odim, "Actions Louder Than Words," 87.

76. Berger, "Women in East and Southern Africa," 44.

77. Ibid., 22.

78. Presley, "Labor Unrest among Kikuyu Women in Colonial Kenya," 258–61.

79. Johnson-Odim, "Class and Gender," 240.

80. See, for example, the discussion in Mann, "The Dangers of Dependence."

81. Berger, "Women in East and Southern African," 40.

82. White, "Women in West and West-Central Africa," 79–80, 112.

83. Strobel, "Gender, Race, and Empire."

84. Johnson, "Class and Gender," 240, 247.

85. Berger, "Women in East and Southern Africa," 5, 35.

86. Toliver, "Aline Sitou Diatta," paper in author's possession.

87. There have been several treatments of this uprising. See, for example, Van Allen, "Aba Riots or Igbo Women's War" and Bastian, "Vulture of the Marketplace."

88. Johnson, "Madam Alimotu Pelewura."

89. Johnson, "Grassroots Organizing," 142.

90. Johnson, "Madam Alimotu Pelewura," 4.

91. Johnson-Odim, "On Behalf of Women," 147.

92. White, "Women in West and West-Central Africa," 103.

93. Ardener, *Perceiving Women,* 36–40.

94. Johnson, "Grassroots Organizing," 144.

95. Ibid.

96. Presley, *Kikuyu Women.*

97. Berger, "Women in East and Southern Africa," 48–56.

98. Urdang, *Fighting Two Colonialisms.*

99. Machel, *Mozambique,* 24.

100. Berger, "Women in East and Southern Africa," 59.

101. Johnson-Odim, "Third World Women and Feminism."
102. Berger, "Women in East and Southern Africa," 52.
103. White, "Women in West and West-Central Africa," 119.
104. Mlama, "The Cultural Context of Gender Equality," 5.
105. White, "Women in West and West-Central Africa," 125–26.
106. Berger, "Women in East and Southern Africa," 55.
107. "Woman Fearing Mutilation Has Asylum."
108. Johnson-Odim, "Third World Women and Feminism"; James and Robertson, eds., *Genital Cutting*.

Bibliography

This is by no means an exhaustive bibliography. Many of the sources included are those I have cited, although not all. Many of these sources, especially the essays by Berger and White, also have good bibliographies and/or endnotes that will provide useful leads to further information.

Aidoo, Agnes Ahosua. "Asanta Queen Mothers in Government and Politics in the Nine-teenth Century." In *The Black Woman Cross-Culturally*, edited by Filomena Chioma Steady, 65–72. Rochester, Vt.: Schenkman, 1985.

Allman, Jean. "Of 'Spinsters,' 'Concubines' and 'Wicked Women': Reflections on Gen-der and Social Change in Colonial Asante." *Gender and History* 3, no. 2 (1991): 176–89.

Amadiume, Ifi. *Male Daughters, Female Households: Gender and Sex in an African Society.* London: Zed Books, 1987.

———. *Reinventing Africa: Matriarchy, Religion and Culture.* London: Zed Books, 1997.

"Ancient Settlements Found in Eritrea." From archeological dig of Peter Schmidt, professor of archeology, University of Asmara at http://aolnews@aol.com.

Ardener, Shirley, ed. *Perceiving Women.* London: J. M. Dent and Sons, 1975.

———. "Sexual Insult and Female Militancy." In *Perceiving Women*, edited by Shirley Ardener, 29–53. London: J. M. Dent and Sons, 1975.

Awe, Bolanle. "The Iyalode in the Traditional Yoruba Political System." In *Sexual Stratifi-cation: A Cross-Cultural View*, edited by Alice Schlegel, 144–60. New York: Columbia University Press, 1977.

Bastian, Misty. "Vultures of the Marketplace: Southeastern Nigerian Women and Dis-cussions of the *Ogu Umunwaayi* (Women's War) of 1929." In Jean Allman, Susan Geiger and Nakanyike Musisi, *Women in African Colonial Histories*, 260–81. Blooming-ton: Indiana University Press, 2002.

Berger, Iris. "Women in East and Southern Africa." In Iris Berger and E. Frances White, *Restoring Women to History: Women in Sub-Saharan Africa*, 5–62. Vol. 1 in the series "Restoring Women to History," edited by Cheryl Johnson-Odim and Margaret Stro-bel. Bloomington: Indiana University Press, 1999.

Biobaku, S. O. "Madam Tinubu." In *Eminent Nigerians of the Nineteenth Century.* New York: Cambridge University Press, 1960.

Burstein, Stanley, ed. *Ancient African Civilizations: Kush and Axum.* Princeton: Markus Weiner, 1998.

Callaway, Barbara. *Muslim Hausa Women in Nigeria: Tradition and Change.* Syracuse: Syr-acuse University Press, 1987.

Callaway, Helen, and Lucy Creevey. *The Heritage of Islam: Women, Religion, and Politics in West Africa.* Boulder: Lynne Rienner, 1993.

Chauncey, George, Jr. "The Locus of Reproduction: Women's Labour in the Zambian Copperbelt, 1927–1953." *Journal of Southern African Studies* 22, no. 2 (1981): 189–200.

Coles, Catherine, and Beverly Mack, eds. *Hausa Women in the Twentieth Century.* Madison: University of Wisconsin Press, 1991.

Coquery-Vidrovitch, Catherine. *African Women: A Modern History.* Trans. Beth Raps. Boulder: Westview Press, 1997.

Crane, Louise, comp. *African Names: People and Places: A Teaching Manual.* Ed. Jane Ellen Mohraz. Urbana: African Studies Program, University of Illinois at Urbana-Champaign, 1982.

———. "Women's Role in Development in Africa." Curriculum Materials for Teachers. Urbana: African Studies Program, University of Illinois at Urbana-Champaign, 1984.

Geiger, Susan. "Women in Nationalist Struggle: TANU Activists in Dar es Salaam." *International Journal of African Historical Studies* 20, no. 1 (1987): 1–26.

Higginson, John. "Liberating the Captives: Independent Watchtower as an Avatar of Colonial Revolt in Southern Africa and Katanga, 1908–1941." *Journal of Social History* 26, no. 1 (1992): 55–60.

Hoffer, Carol P. "Mende and Sherbo Women in High Office." *Canadian Journal of African Studies* 4, no. 2 (1972): 151–64.

Ifeka-Moller, Caroline. "Female Militancy and Colonial Revolt: The Women's War of 1929, Eastern Nigeria." In *Perceiving Women,* edited by Shirley Ardener, 127–57. London: J. M. Dent, 1975.

Inikori, Joseph. "Export versus Domestic Demand: The Determinants of Sex Ratios in the Transatlantic Slave Trade." *Research in Economic History* 14 (1972): 117–66.

Isaacman, Allen, and Barbara Isaacman. "The Role of Women in the Liberation of Mozambique." *Urahamu* 13, no. 2–3 (1984): 128–85.

James, Stanlie M., and Claire C. Robertson, eds. *Genital Cutting and Transnational Sisterhood: Disputing U.S. Polemics.* Urbana: University of Illinois Press, 2002.

Johnson, Cheryl. "Class and Gender: A Consideration of Yoruba Women during the Colonial Period." In *Women and Class in Africa,* edited by Claire C. Robertson and Iris Berger, 237–54. New York: Africana Publishing, 1986.

———. "Female Leadership during the Colonial Period: Madam Pelewura and the Lagos Market Women." *Tarikh* 7, no. 1 (1981): 1–10.

———. "Grassroots Organizing: Women in Anti-Colonial Activity in Southwestern Nigeria." *African Studies Review* 25, no. 2 (1982): 137–57.

———. "Nigerian Women and British Colonialism." Ph.D. diss., Northwestern University, 1978.

Johnson-Odim, Cheryl. "Actions Louder Than Words: The Historical Task of Defining Feminist Consciousness in Colonial West Africa." In *Nation, Empire, Colony: Historicizing Gender and Race,* edited by Ruth Roach Pierson and Nupur Chaudhuri, 77–93. Bloomington: Indiana University Press, 1998.

———. "From Both Sides Now: Gendering the Black Atlantic." In *Women in African Scholarly Publishing,* edited by Cassandra Veney and Paul Tiyamke Zeleza, 91–107. Trenton: Africa World Press, 2001.

———. "On Behalf of Women and the Nation: Funmilayo Ransome-Kuti and the Struggle for Women's Equality and Nigerian Independence." In *Expanding the Boundaries of Women's History,* edited by Cheryl Johnson-Odim and Margaret Strobel, 144–57. Bloomington: Indiana University Press, 1992.

———. "Third World Women and Feminism." In *Third World Women and the Politics of Feminism*, edited by Chandra Talpade Mohanty, Ann Russo, and Lourdes Torres, 314–327. Bloomington: Indiana University Press, 1991.

———, and Margaret Strobel. "Conceptualizing the History of Women in Africa, Asia, Latin America and the Caribbean, and the Middle East." Introduction to the series "Restoring Women to History: Women in Sub-Saharan Africa" published by Indiana University Press, 1999. An earlier version appeared in the *Journal of Women's History* 1 (Spring 1989): 31–62.

———, and Nina Mba. *For Women and the Nation: Funmilayo Ransome-Kuti of Nigeria*. Urbana: University of Illinois Press, 1997.

Machel, Samora. *Mozambique: Sowing the Seeds of Revolution*. London: Committee for Freedom in Mozambique, Angola, and Guine, 1975.

Mann, Kristin. "The Dangers of Dependence: Christian Marriage among Elite Women in Lagos Colony, 1880–1915." *Journal of African History* 24 (1983): 37–56.

———. *Marrying Well: Marriage, Status and Social Change among the Educated Elite in Colonial Lagos*. New York: Cambridge University Press, 1985.

Mba, Nina Emma. *Nigerian Women Mobilized: Women's Political Activity in Southern Nigeria, 1900–1965*. Berkeley: Institute of International Studies, University of California, 1982.

Mlama, Penina. "The Cultural Context of Gender Inequity." Manuscript in author's possession, 1997.

Morrow, Lance F. "Women in Sub-Saharan Africa." In *The Cross-Cultural Study of Women*, edited by Margot Duley and Mary I. Edwards, 290–375. New York: Feminist Press, 1986.

Oyèrónté̩wùnmí, Oyèrónké. *The Invention of Women: Making an African Sense of Western Gender Discourses*. Minneapolis: University of Minnesota Press, 1997.

Presley, Cora Ann. *Kikuyu Women, the Mau Mau Rebellion, and Social Change in Kenya*. Boulder: Westview Press, 1992.

———. "Labor Unrest among Kikuyu Women in Colonial Kenya." In *Women and Class in Africa*, edited by Clare C. Robertson and Iris Berger, 255–73. New York: Africana Publishing, 1986.

Ramphele, Mamphela. *Across Boundaries: The Journey of a South African Woman Leader*. New York: Feminist Press, 1996.

Robertson, Claire C., and Iris Berger, eds. *Women and Class in Africa*. New York: Africana Publishing, 1986.

———, and Martin A. Klein, eds. *Women and Slavery in Africa*. Madison: University of Wisconsin Press, 1983.

Rybalkina, I. G. "Women in African History." *Africa* 29, nos. 3–4 (1990): 83–91.

Sacks, Karen. *Sister and Wives: The Past and Future of Sexual Equality*. Urbana: University of Illinois Press, 1982.

Sembene, Ousmane. *God's Bits of Wood*. London: Heinemann, 1982.

Shillington, Kevin. *History of Africa*. New York: St. Martin's Press, 1989.

Steady, Filomina Chioma, ed. *The Black Woman Cross-Culturally*. Rochester, Vt.: Schenkman, 1985.

Strobel, Margaret. "Gender, Race, and Empire in Nineteenth- and Twentieth-Century Africa and Asia." In *Becoming Visible: Women in European History*, 3d ed., edited by Renate Bridenthal, Susan Mosher Stuard, and Merry E. Wiesner. New York: Houghton Mifflin, 1998.

———. *Muslim Women in Mombasa, 1890–1975*. New Haven: Yale University Press, 1979.

Tobrise, Mael I. E. "Culture and Gender in Africa." Manuscript in author's possession, 1997.

Toliver, Wilmetta Jesvalyn. "Aline Sitoe Diatta: Addressing Historical Silences through Sengalese Culture." Manuscript in author's possession, 1997.

Turrittin, Jane. "Aoua Keita and the Nascent Women's Movement in the French Soudan." *African Studies Review* 36, no. 1 (1993): 59–90.

Urdang, Stephanie. *Fighting Two Colonialisms: Women in Guinea-Bissau.* New York: Monthly Review Press, 1979.

Van Allen, Judith. "'Aba Riots' or Igbo 'Women's War'? Ideology, Stratification, and the Invisibility of Women." In *Women in Africa: Studies in Social and Economic Change,* edited by Nancy J. Hafkin and Edna G. Bay, 59–85. Stanford: Stanford University Press, 1976.

White, E. Frances. "Women in West and West-Central Africa." In Iris Berger and E. Frances White, *Women in Sub-Saharan Africa: Restoring Women to History,* 63–129. Bloomington: Indiana University Press, 1999.

Wilks, Ivor. "She Who Blazed a Trail: Akayaawa Yikwan of Asante." In *Life Histories of African Women,* edited by Patricia W. Romero, 113–39. Atlantic Highlands: Ashfield Press, 1988.

"Woman Fearing Mutilation Has Asylum." Associated Press, Aug. 18, 1999.

2

Women in the Middle East
since the Rise of Islam

NIKKI R. KEDDIE

This chapter discusses women in the Middle East since the rise of Islam in the early seventh century c.e. It is selective, covering several areas and topics where good research has been done. It starts with the Near East before the rise of Islam, as many features of Islamic times arose not from Arabia but from pre-Islamic civilizations that were early conquered by Muslim armies. The change from a tribal society in Arabia to one with a state and written laws also altered the position of women. Their roles in the Middle East after the Islamic conquests reflected pre-Islamic Near Eastern and Arab cultures modified to meet the needs, laws, and customs of new Islamic states and societies as well as a variety of times, places, and religious and other ideas.

Like other civilizations, pre-Islamic Near Eastern civilizations were male-dominant, although ancient Egypt, before Greek and Roman control, was closer than other ancient civilizations to being gender-egalitarian. Some scholars see similarities in traditional gender attitudes and practices among all Mediterranean cultures, whereas others emphasize similar gender and family structures and attitudes in cultures from the Mediterranean to East Asia, with Northern Europe and Africa having different patterns.[1] The interaction of Arab tribal and Near Eastern imperial traditions made the Middle East somewhat different in gender attitudes and practices from both the European Mediterranean and East Asia, however much it shared some features with them. Islam was not the only variable, as the adoption of many pre-Islamic practices shows, but Islamic laws and beliefs were important in shaping gender beliefs and practices.

Some features seen as Islamic existed in many ancient civilizations of the Middle East and the Byzantine Empire. The creation of agriculture and the domestication of animals in the prehistoric Middle East produced enough economic surplus to support the specialized occupations found in cities, states, and empires. Distinctive female and male spheres precede cities, with women working in or near the home owing to frequent childbearing and care, but the rise of cities and states increased the separation of gender roles. Men monopolized public positions of power while women specialized in the domestic and childbearing sphere. In Near Eastern empires there was increasing control over women's actions and movement in public. The pre-Islamic Middle East and ancient Greece saw the spread of veiling and seclusion, especially of elite women. Assyrian law gave men proprietary rights over women and exclusive divorce rights, and it had rules on veiling. High-status women had to veil, whereas harlots and slaves were forbidden to do so, showing a differentiation by class and respectability that continued later. Large harems for the powerful, including slaves, eunuchs, and concubines, were found in various ancient Near Eastern empires.

The pre-Islamic religions of the area supported male-dominant attitudes and practices. Among them, Judaism and Christianity saw Eve as introducing evil into the world, and Judaism allowed polygamy and strong male privilege in marriage and divorce. These religions and attitudes influenced Islam, both in its origins and in its doctrinal and legal evolution, while other influences came from the practices of pre-Islamic Near East. Male control in the family and society was seen as functional in societies that had high infant death rates and valued frequent childbirth to ensure reproduction. In most premodern societies, women's primary role was seen as a childbearer. Men wanted to guarantee the family line by restricting access to women, and that encouraged practices and beliefs supporting male dominance. Although we may call all historical societies "patriarchal," that does not tell us about their varying specifics. Gender-inegalitarian ideas, including female inferiority and male dominance, are found in all civilizations, but the differences in ideology and practice over time and space are the stuff of history.

Among pre-Islamic Arabian tribes some groups had systems that counted descent and inheritance in the female line, but most tribes were patrilineal and most marriages were patrilocal, with wives living with their husbands' families. There was some variety in customs, with some groups reportedly allowing polyandry—more than one husband for a woman—and some allowing women freely to divorce their husbands. Most tribes were, however, patriarchal, and tribal men reacted strongly to threats to wives, daughters, and sisters (which among nomadic tribes included abduction). Preference for marriage between the children of brothers, or failing that between more distant cousins in the male line, may go back to pre-Islamic times, although it increased after the rise of Islam. Tribal organization included group power centering on male (agnatic) relatives, which continued strong in later Islamic law and society.

The role of the Prophet Muhammad and his revelations, later written in the Quran, in changing the position of women is a subject of controversy. The belief that Muhammad and the Quran brought major favorable change in the position of women has been challenged by some scholars, most of whom see the Quran as bringing reforms although not nearly to the point of equality. The Quran condemns infanticide and says that women should inherit (half of what men receive) and control property, including the dower that men gave upon marriage. Few sources describe the situation of urban Arab women in Mecca before the Quran, but some pre-Islamic Arab women already controlled property and women had a larger role in the public sphere than they did after the first generations of Islam.

Many now say that the decline of women's position after the earliest Islamic period was due to foreign and local patriarchal accretions, not to what the Quran enjoins. Some see the Quran as implicitly gender-egalitarian and interpret it to support this view. The emphasis on the Quran as a major determinant in the position of women overstates its role, but some in every period appeal to the Quran as the basis of their views on women. Both the pre-Islamic practices of most tribes and later Islamic law supported the domination of extended patrilineal kin groups, led by male elders, in which women and the young were subordinate.

The prophet Muhammad (ca. 570–632 C.E.) was an orphan in a minor branch of the dominant Quraish tribe in Mecca and at age twenty-five married a forty-year-old merchant, Khadija, for whom he worked. Until she died he was monogamous. At age forty he had his first revelation, followed by others, and Khadija became the first of a group of believers in the religion that became known as Islam (submission, that is, to God). The early revelations stressed strict monotheism and fear of the Day of Judgment in which all would go to paradise or hell; they also called for moral behavior, including good treatment of orphans, widows, and the unfortunate. Most Meccans, who had an economic interest in the old ways, including a major Meccan shrine to three goddesses, did not accept Islam. In 622 Muhammad moved to Medina, called there as an arbiter among tribal groups, including Jewish tribes. In time he became the real ruler of a new state centering in Medina, and his Medina revelations were often legal and became a key element in Islamic law. Muhammad conquered Mecca in 630 and most of Arabia before his death in 632, after which there were revolts in Arabia, with women prominent in some of them.

The Quran's revelations on women are today often divided into two groups. One addresses men and women and deals equally with both as believers, enjoined to act similarly regarding morality and modesty. The other group contains unequal rules for women, although less unequal than what later became Islamic law and practice. Among these are the right of a husband to beat a wife who persists in disobedience; the right of men to divorce by a thrice-stated declaration; the right of men to have up to four spouses; the need for women to have male guardians and be obedient to their male kin and husbands and agree to sex whenever the husband wants; and women's inheritance as half that of men. On inheritance, it is noted in compensation that women control their own property and that husbands must support their wives but not vice versa.

The only revelation suggesting any seclusion of women concerns Muhammad's wives, and it seems clear that women were not secluded in early Islamic times. One verse says that women should draw their cloaks about them when they go out, with no indication of a complete veil, and one asks them to veil their bosoms and cover their ornaments. If the whole body and face were meant there seems to be no reason to tell women to veil their bosoms, and the later idea that "ornaments" means everything but the hands, feet, and (possibly) the face is a forced one. Men were told to speak to Muhammad's wives only through a curtain, and that verse, like the previous one, was later taken to enjoin veiling for all women, at least from puberty to menopause.

There is ample evidence that women were publicly active in the earliest Islamic period as they had been in pre-Islamic Arabia, even supporting men in various ways in the frequent warfare. This public role decreased after the period of conquest of settled lands after Muhammad's death, when leaders of the Muslim community (caliphs) were chosen by an elite. By 656 the caliphs' armies had conquered all of the Iranian Empire and much of the Byzantine Near East, including greater Syria, Egypt, and much of North Africa. In these provinces most people belonged to different Christian sects than did the Byzantine rulers, and many were glad to escape Byzantine religious persecution by agreeing to give up their cities peacefully in return for freedom of religion. These promises were predominantly kept, as Islam decreed tolerance for "people of the book"—Christians, Jews, Sabeans, and (in most cases) Zoroastrians. Conversion in these areas occurred later and mostly voluntarily, and minority religions remained, although much reduced in size.

The second caliph, Umar, 634–644, carried out the major Islamic conquests and added to state controls and laws, including more stringent laws increasing punishments for women and restricting their movements. The next caliph, Uthman, 644–656, was more lenient. With the growth in the state's size and wealth, however, and in imitation of the practices of the conquered imperial elites, the tide turned toward a lowered position for women, who were already subject to male dominance.

Although women continued for a time to be active in religion, politics, and warfare, the last one to play a major political role in Islam's first centuries was A'isha, Muhammad's favorite wife, who aligned with one of the parties that arose after his death. One group believed that Muhammad's son-in-law and cousin, Ali, and his successors were the legitimate leaders of the Muslim community. Another group favored a caliph from the Umayyad family of caliph Uthman. When Uthman was murdered and Ali became the fourth caliph, A'isha became a highly visible rallying point for those favoring an Umayyad caliph and opposing Ali in Islam's first civil war. After A'isha and her allies were defeated in the Battle of the Camel, her failed leadership was used as a warning against women in politics. Traditions (*hadiths*) on this and other matters were collected and written down in the ninth century C.E. and reflected restrictive, often negative attitudes about women then and afterward.[2] Much of Islamic law and practice is based on such Traditions about the words and deeds of Muhammad, although the authenticity of most hadiths is doubted by many modern scholars.

The roles of women in pre-Islamic tribal society in Arabia and in the earliest days of Islam were more public than those of elite women of the conquered imperial territories. The social and gender stratification of conquered Islamic territories and the wealth that came to Islamic conquerors favored development of elite harems, domestic slavery, veiling and seclusion, and other features characteristic of Middle Eastern urban centers. The egalitarianism of tribal societies should not, however, be exaggerated. Many gender attitudes and practices of both the Middle East and other Mediterranean societies resulted from interactions of tribal nomadic societies with settled states. Practices and ideas common to many Mediterranean societies include the salience of tribal and patrilineal kinship structures and groupings, ecologically fragile environments, and concepts of honor centering on female virginity and chastity. When such practices and ideas are so widespread we may conclude that they existed also in a past for which there is less documentation than for recent times.

Three basic types of economic units were found in the Middle East: settled agriculture, nomadic pastoralism, and urban settlement. All were interdependent, and some groups were borderline. Both nomadism and agriculture developed out of a mixed agricultural-pastoral productive mode. Aridity or mountainous terrain favored nomadic pastoralists whose main product was herded animals and who were organized into kin-based clans and tribes. In the Middle East, agricultural settlements were more controlled by states than were armed and mounted nomads. States arose once an agricultural surplus supported social stratification and urban control of the countryside. Nomadic tribes often lived on the margins of state-controlled territories and were difficult to control. The organization and culture of agriculturalists, urban-dwellers, and nomadic tribes involved specific kinds of treatment of, and attitudes toward, women on the part of dominant males. All three groups were patriarchal but in different ways. Pre-Islamic Middle Eastern empires had urban elite harems, slavery, and veiling and seclusion. Nomads and agriculturalists had far less economic surplus and less gender segregation because all had to do physical tasks. Nomadic women were not secluded, there were no large harems, and women had a role in warfare and in public. Arab nomads, however, were very concerned about genealogical purity, and family and kin groups controlled women's sexuality and related actions.

It has been argued that a Mediterranean emphasis on female virginity and chastity as central to male honor is tied to the difficult terrain and mixed pastoral and agricultural settlement of the region and the prevalence of tribal groups. Tribal beliefs and practices and the struggle of all groups for scarce resources affected the position of women, and many of these effects continued through the centuries.[3] Pastoral tribes, because they had to move through large unbounded territories, had to fight for position, gain goods, and increase power through raids or warfare. The size and strength of kin groups were crucial. Even more than in nontribal areas, women were valued for the number of their sons, and purity of lineage was a special concern. The importance of lineage purity in both tribal and settled groups was tied to a belief that the honor of men depended on the chastity and fidelity of women, enforced by family sanctions that sometimes included killing women who strayed. Such beliefs are very old, and some similar beliefs and practices are found outside the Islamic world although stress on patrilineal endogamy is specific to Muslims.

Settled tribes made up most of the urban population in Arabia, and nomadic tribes were predominant in the armies that conquered the Middle East. Many remained and often settled in conquered areas. Tribes in some Islamic periods and places were powerful and admired, and their customs entered Middle Eastern culture. The influence of settled conquered people was also strong, including their religious beliefs and state ideologies and practices, so the Islamic synthesis that developed reflected both tribal-nomadic and settled cultures, often in uneasy symbiosis. The synthesis, over time, meant a less public role for women than existed in pre-Islamic Arabia and emphasis on partly tribal ideas of honor and protection of the lineage.

After Muhammad's death, under the first four "pious caliphs" (632–661) chosen by a Muslim elite, doctrinal disagreements grew. The most important dissenters said that leadership should pass to Muhammad's cousin and son-in-law Ali (Muhammad having no living sons) and then to Ali's male descendants. These were called the party (shi'a) of Ali, later the Shi'a. In this group Muhammad's daughter, Ali's wife Fatima, had a lofty role. She, Ali, their two sons, and Muhammad are the five holiest people of Shi'ism.

The main event in the age of the pious caliphs was the rapid conquest of a huge territory, which soon spread all the way from Spain in the West to Pakistan in the East. At first the conquering armies lived separately in what became new cities, but soon many of the conquered came in to offer goods and services and were absorbed as clients of the tribes. These clients were the first to want to convert to Islam, which gave them tax benefits. Gradually, more widespread conversion occurred, although Christian, Jewish, Zoroastrian, and Sabean "people of the book" remained tolerated. One sign that the position of women in these societies was not simply a by-product of Islamic doctrine is that their status and practices in such minority religious communities were quite similar to those among the Muslims although seclusion was less strict.

Good documentation about the Muslim world begins only in the ninth century C.E. Important for the history of women are collections of Islamic Traditions and exegeses of law, which helped to set Islamic, especially Middle Eastern, cultural assumptions about gender and reflected the times when they were written. After the first period women were excluded from institutionalized participation in public life, and many upper- and middle-class urban women were veiled and secluded. The rise in negative views of women's nature and influence was reflected in theological and legal interpretations of the Quran, in law, and in other writings.

Medieval Islamic society was more patriarchal in practice and male-supremacist in ideas than early Islamic Mecca and Medina. Influences on the unequal status of women from conquered areas included practices and religious and other ideas prevalent among the conquered people. Jewish and Christian biblical traditions, including symbolic images of the defective nature of women, were more hostile to women than were the contents of the Quran. Islamic writings came to embody ideals of patriarchal tribes and many from earlier Middle Eastern empires and religions. Many of these ideas stressed the themes of the weakness of women and its paradoxical partner, women as an evil, highly sexualized threat to the male and the proper ordering of society. These themes were read into Islamic scripture although some have biblical sources. This view of women prevailed when other Bible-related themes were rejected, suggesting that a negative view of women filled social needs. With modern social changes, many Muslims began to reject such Traditions and call for a return to the Quran, giving it new interpretations, and reject later accretions, although some gender images have a basis in the Quran and continue to survive in conservative exegeses.

One example is the changed interpretation of the story of Adam and Eve. The Quran speaks of Adam and his wife without naming her; it was to Adam that Satan (Iblis) whispered about the tree, causing the eating of forbidden fruit and the couple's expulsion. Both asked God for forgiveness, and in the Quran the man and woman are treated equally. Medieval Muslim interpretations used Judeao-Christian stories to change the story and create and stress Traditions that blame Eve, and by implication women, for the weakness and guile that let Satan bring on Adam's fall. God then condemned women to bleed each month and carry and deliver children in great pain and danger and also made women foolish.

Numerous hadiths on women's inferiority and evil were propagated and only began to be seriously questioned in modern times as reformers increasingly stressed the full personhood of women. Women were often seen as Satan's tools, cursed by moral, mental, and physical deficiencies. Men, having repented, became free of God's curse. One hadith attributed to the prophet said, "If I were to order anyone to prostrate himself before another but God, I would command the woman to prostrate herself before her husband because of the magnitude of his rights over her." The primal story of Adam and Eve came to be taken as proof of women's lower moral, mental, and physical nature, and the consensus of Islamic scholars (*ulama*) supported and perpetuated this teaching as a doctrine of Islam.[4] The idea of women as the "rope of Satan" is still found in some communities and has parallels in Christian, Jewish, and other traditions that influenced Islam. Such ideas justified the practices of discrimination against women that may have originated in desires to assure male control of the household and assure the certainty of paternity and purity of genealogical lines.

Along with misogynist interpretations of the Quran came interpretations of historical events, notably A'isha's failed leadership in the first civil war, used to show that women should not enter politics and public life. The first Shi'i imam, Ali, whose caliphate brought A'isha's enmity, is quoted in a book attributed to him as speaking against women, especially in public life. Some Traditions see women as *fitna* (a "source of temptation or chaos"), and some cite Muhammad as warning against female rule. Misogynist traditions regarding A'isha contributed to a negative view of women endorsed in many Islamic texts. That view, however, does not mean women were normally treated as evil. Most women lived in accordance with a pattern of male and age dominance and had important if delimited spheres of autonomy and power, especially within the household, where they became increasingly dominant with

75

age. Women not only managed households but also carried out various critical productive jobs.

Women in the Early Islamic Centuries

Many women were important and respected in the first decades after the rise of Islam. Despite A'isha's failure as a political leader, her positive role as Muhammad's favorite wife was stressed in many Traditions. She and other women among Muhammad's wives and followers remained for a time important as transmitters of Tradition and even to a degree participated in public life. One such woman was Zainab, the daughter of Ali and Fatima and sister of the third Shi'i imam, Husain, who challenged the Umayyad caliph for leadership of the Muslim community and, along with most of his followers, was killed in battle. Husain's martyrdom in 680 C.E. became the occasion for the major Shi'i mourning ceremonies over the centuries. Zainab is remembered as a heroine of the event, for protecting Husain's last living son from death and showing courage when brought as a prisoner before the Umayyad caliph Yazid in Damascus.

From the eighth century, caliphs began to seclude their wives and build up large harems of wives and slaves, practices also followed by some other rich people but not by ordinary folk. The later Umayyads emulated such Sasanian practices, including women's seclusion. These practices increased under the next caliphal dynasty, the Abbasids (750–1258). Under the late Umayyads and Abbasids most Arabs adopted many of the settled ways of the conquered people. Although the Arabic language prevailed in the Middle East outside Iran, the lifestyles of settled Arabs adapted to those of the settled empires. Women, including the wives and mothers of caliphs, were still often very influential but increasingly from behind the scenes.

This change was reflected in the development of Islamic law. After Muhammad's death, law was often adopted from the conquered areas, but those who wanted more extensive moral and legal guidance than found in the Quran increasingly relied on Traditions about his sayings and deeds that were presented as coming from his wives and companions through later generations of pious and learned persons, including women. Given the key role of Traditions, many laws and practices of the conquered areas were attributed to the Prophet.

Varying schools of Islamic law developed during the ninth century and reflected both the importance of the patrilineal kin group among the Arabs and the restrictive view of women of the time. Quranic verses were interpreted to mean strict veiling, and women's subordinate position in marriage and other rights became part of law. All schools of Sunni law continued the tribal practice of favoring male relatives (agnates), who had a privileged position in inheritance (except in Shi'i law). Women retained important ties to male agnates even after marriage, especially after the death or divorce of husbands. A legal system favoring extensive kin groups headed by male elders continued for centuries.

In part, increased gender stratification reflected the growing economic surplus and rise in cities. Marked gender segregation was found in urban society rather than in the rural or tribal lives of most people. Prosperity was also a major factor in the growth of slavery, male and, especially, female, that characterized the Middle East. Slavery and concubinage were recognized in the Quran, which, however, recommends good treatment of slaves and either freeing them or allowing them to purchase freedom. Some harsher treatment came after the conquests and a great increase in the number of slaves. Most were domestic or employed in commerce or as soldiers.

Slaves were, in theory and mostly in practice, taken from non-Muslims beyond the Islamic borders—including the Caucasus and Central Asia, Europe and, increasingly, Africa. Female slaves were largely domestic workers, sexual partners (their owners had this right), and entertainers. Slave girls and boys were trained to be singers, dancers, and musical performers. Under Islamic law, men could have sexual relations with female slaves; the child of a slave mother was free, and the mother was liberated either in the master's life or upon his death. Some slave women who were married to rulers or other powerful men became powerful themselves, as was also true of free women in similar circumstances. Women's influence was often constructed, however, as a factor in the decline or disarray of dynasties from the Abbasids through the Ottomans.

Most medieval writers found birth control, either by coitus interruptus or various barrier methods, permissible, although most agreed that free women would have to consent. This has been seen as a sign of woman's power, and, like many sources, it shows that women's as well as men's sexual nature and needs were recognized. Leila Ahmed argues, however, that permitting contraception reflected a situation where a man's children by slave wives were free and would inherit, something free wives and many husbands disliked.[5]

Slaves helped make possible the strict seclusion of female masters; many urban women of the middle to upper classes scarcely left home and were heavily covered when they did. Architecture reflected the needs of seclusion, with buildings built low so as not to overlook courtyards or the quarters where women lived separate from men. Aside from the rich and powerful, however, harems did not contain multiple wives, concubines, and slaves. Most marriages were monogamous, with multiple women mostly for a small elite. Only Catholicism among major religions enjoined monogamy, with Western Judaism following suit much later.

Most non-Muslims in Islamic societies had family and veiling-seclusion customs similar to those of Muslims, although usually less restrictive, and each community had particularities in its own family law. Urban seclusion did not mean that women were uninvolved in production. They performed many rural tasks and most of the work in the chief rural and urban handicraft, textiles.

Regarding property rights, although local customs varied here as on other matters, according to Islamic law women had a right to control their own property and were not obliged to contribute to household expenses; one of a husband's duties was to support his wife and family. This partly justified inheritance rules under which most inherited property was divided so males inherited twice as much as females. Women rarely inherited as law said they should in rural and tribal areas, where inheritance meant passing flocks or land out of a patrilineal family's control. Some property and rights were, however, given to daughters. One way to avoid the inheritance law was to give away property during one's lifetime. Another was to set up a *waqf* (perpetual endowment) to be administered by a man who had an Islamic education and functions (*ulim;* pl. *ulama*). The endowment, then, could benefit one's chosen descendants, be used for a charitable purpose, or both. It appears that more waqfs were used to cut out female inheritors than to favor them.[6] Women endowed waqfs, and there have been studies of the special features of women's waqfs, including those that went to charitable purposes and to building monuments.[7]

Under Islamic law, women were entitled to financial support and sex in marriage. Men were entitled to obedience and sex on demand and could divorce without a reason or court process. Women, however, could divorce only for limited reasons such as impotence, serious disease, and desertion and then only by court order. There was a form of divorce in which a wife agreed to give back the important dower paid by a husband if he agreed to the divorce. (Some husbands who wanted to divorce behaved badly so their wives would request such a divorce and forfeit their dower.) Divorced men had legal guardianship of the children, although divorced wives kept custody of them until ages that varied by their gender and the school of law.

Many aspects of male-female relations were not included in Islamic law but reflected strong persistent local, and often tribal, customs, including extreme concern over virginity and chastity. Suspicious conduct sometimes led to being killed by a male relative, more often a brother than a husband, but such "honor killing" was not sanctioned in Islamic law. Another custom in a minority of Islamic societies, mostly influenced by East Africa, was clitorectomy, which is not called for in the Quran or Islamic law although it often came to be considered Islamic where it was practiced.

The first Islamic centuries saw limits on the public role of women, increasing seclusion, and the development of a male-dominant legal system, which, however, also protected women's rights in several ways, including property ownership, certain divorce rights, protection against extreme abuse, and rights to support and sex from a husband. In the Quran men were told they could only have multiple wives if they treated all equally, but in law and custom that was taken to mean giving each wife equal quarters and equal access to marital sex.

For all the inequalities that Muslim women faced, as did, in varying forms, most women at this time, there were important areas for self-expression and cultural life, including ones involving family, friendships, and work. Popular religion, including the mysticism (closeness to the divine) known in the Muslim world as Sufism, had in most cases a greater role for women and their religious expression than did mainline Islam. The first person in Islam to be considered a saint was a female Sufi and poet, Rabi'a (d. 801). With the development of Sufi orders from the late Abbasid period, some had parallel women's groups. A few allowed women as equal members, although a few others barred them. Women also instructed women in Islam; in the Shi'i world such women were called mullas, like their male counterparts. Women's religious life included visits to saints' tombs, which provided a chance for outings and conversation. Other aspects of girls' and women's activities included education at home or in elementary Quran schools for some, with a few women achieving high levels of education. Social life included extensive visiting; contact with tradeswomen who came to homes; the important ritual of the public bath, where women gathered for hours to be cleaned and groomed and to talk; and all-female celebrations and entertainments.

In literature, although there were few female authors and poets like Rabi'a there was an oral literature among females as well as theater games and much depiction of women. In popular literature the most famous portrayals are in the *Thousand and One Nights,* collected after the Abbasid period but set in that period and including older stories, especially from Iran. In the frame story the characters, all with Persian names, include the brilliant storyteller Shahrazad, whose tales save the lives of untold young women who would otherwise be killed in vengeance for one wife's unfaithfulness.[8] Many stories present women as interesting and clever but frequently unfaithful and driven by sexual passion. Some literary work, including a number of outstanding Persian poems, has a more exalted view of women and unrequited or difficult love. From modern observation we can assume that women composed and recited poetry, and several names of female poets have been recorded.

TURKS, MONGOLS, AND MAMLUKS: NEW RULERS
AND GENDER ATTITUDES

The northern tribal people who increasingly ruled the Middle East from the eleventh century onward had more egalitarian gender practices concerning women than either the pre-Islamic Near Eastern empires or Arab and other indigenous tribes. This was part of an overall difference between the two groups of tribes that has been analyzed with emphasis on the different ecology and history of the northern invaders and their ability to set up long-lived empires.[9]

The nomadic Turks, who had earlier spread from Mongolia westward, first entered the Middle East as slave soldiers, a few of whom came to rule in some areas. Major migration into the Middle East of Turkish tribal people came with the political and economic decline of the Abbasids, which from the eleventh century on made possible the invasion and conquest of much of the Middle East by Turks, beginning with the Seljuqs. Among the Seljuqs and succeeding Turkish-ruled dynasties, elite women often played a powerful public role as relatives of rulers, participating in administration and warfare. Sometimes they became de facto rulers themselves.[10] In this they carried on the pre-Islamic traditions of the Turkish tribal group from which the Seljuq and the Ottoman dynasties arose. As Guity Nashat maintains:

> Initially Turkish and Mongolian women exerted direct influence over major decisions and could ascend the throne as regents. Royal wives played an active role in the internal politics of the Ilkhanid [Iran-Mongol] state and participated in the deliberations of the highest Mongol council, the Kuriltay, in the choice of the ruler. This lively participation was especially characteristic of the wives of the great Mongol Ilkhans, whose exploits are recounted in Rashid al-Din's . . . *Universal History*. . . . He justified his departure from the contemporary norms of Islamic society, which left women unmentioned, by explaining that the Mongols accord their women equal treatment.[11]

The Seljuqs and later rulers like the Egyptian-based Mamluks and the Mongols converted to Islam either before or after they entered the Middle East. In time, each group came to be, if settled, strict Muslims who largely conformed to Middle Eastern and Islamic settled norms regarding the position of women. Those Turkish and Kurdish popular religious groups who had special beliefs and practices (like the Bektashi Sufi order, the Alevis of Anatolia, and the Ahl-e Haqq of Iranian Kurdistan), continued to modern times to have largely equal participation of often unveiled women in their activities. Most conquered non-Turkic people were less affected in their gender relations by Turkish conquest than were some Turkic or Kurdish groups. Many Turks and others who remained nomads, however, retained powerful public positions for women, who could ride and fight and did most of the tribe's physical labor; leading women often took command in the absence of their husbands.

The famous fourteenth-century Arab traveler Ibn Batuta, starting from a North African world where women were veiled and secluded, noted with some distaste a few Islamic people outside the central Middle East. Among them, he observed, women had a freer, more assertive role. Of the Turks he observed:

> A remarkable thing which I saw . . . was the respect shown to women by the Turks, for they hold a more dignified position than the men. [There follows a description of the rich garments and respected treatment of a princess and her retinue.] I also saw the wives of the merchants and commonality. One of them will sit in a wagon which is being drawn by horses, attended by three or four maidens to carry her train, and on her head she wears a conical head-dress incrusted with pearls and surmounted by peacock feathers. The windows of the tent are open and her face is visible, for the Turkish women do not veil themselves. Sometimes a woman will be accompanied by her husband and anyone seeing him would take him for one of her servants; he has no garment other than a sheep's wool cloak and a high cap to match.[12]

Other sources tell of the participation of Turkish and Mongol women in battle and in rule, something found as late as the early modern Turkish-ruled Safavid and Ottoman empires. In later times strong women tended to exert influence from within the harem.

Turks (persons who spoke Turkic languages) came to rule Iran and Turkey via conquest beginning in the eleventh century, and the Mongol invasions of the early thirteenth century brought in more Turks than Mongols as soldiers. Like the Turks, Mongols were a tribal nomadic people among whom women had an important public role however negative other aspects of the destructive Mongol conquest were. In some places and periods military slaves, largely of Turkic origin, took over as rulers. The Mamluks, for example, ruled Egypt, Syria, and western Arabia from 1250 to 1517, and some women had important roles among them. Queen Shajarat al-Durr, of Turkic slave origin, the widow of an Ayyubid leader, was the first ruler of the Mamluk dynasty. Her role is subject to controversy. Earlier male historians suggest that she had little independent power or importance, but more recent feminist writers list her as one of the most important de facto women rulers in the Islamic world.[13] Other Mamluk ruling-class women also played important public roles. The Mamluks' tribal and ethnic background in populations where women's status was high was probably a factor, and constant warfare also created many widows well positioned to take over some of their husbands' power.

The Mamluk period saw many active, educated women, and admonitions from conservative ulama against women appearing too much and too freely in public indicate that those things were happening. One text enjoins women from mixing with men in the bazaar, from listening to sermons in mosques, from laxness in veiling, and from sociable trips.[14] At least in Egypt and probably elsewhere, such sources show, women often did not behave or dress in the way that conservative ulama approved. The greater role of women found in documents from Mamluk times onward was not only due to Turkish influence but also to a greater variety in practice in the Middle East than can be inferred from scantier references to women in earlier sources, some of which mention Egypt as a place where women had greater freedom.

In this period most urban women were apparently veiled and to a degree secluded, and women's main role was to marry and have children. There were some jobs for urban women, for example, as craft worker, peddler, bath attendant, and prostitute. Domestic service in middle-class and wealthy homes was also a major source of jobs, although much such work was done by slaves, male as well as female and increasingly of African origin. Women of all classes were central to the production of textiles and carpets, either in their homes or in small workshops. Rural and tribal women had a wide range of nondomestic work—raising and processing plant and animal food, spinning, and weaving. Because they worked outdoors, rural women were less veiled and secluded than urban ones. They did not, however, have better lives. Rural women were often poor, worked very hard in difficult conditions, and like rural men had minimal access to education. Urban women might have access to Islamic education, were more likely than rural women to inherit as Islamic law said they should, and were also more likely to refer to courts to protect their rights. Some had more, and more varied, consumption and leisure activities than did rural women.

The Ottomans (ca. 1400–1918) and the Safavids (1501–1722), two major dynasties of Turkish origin, dominated the Middle East in the early modern period. The Ottomans, beginning from a small group in Anatolia, in time conquered much of the Balkans, Anatolia, what remained of the Byzantine Empire, and most Arab lands. Theirs was the best-organized and longest-ruled empire in the Middle East. The Ottomans, like most Turks, were strict Sunni Muslims. The Safavids began in a Sunni Sufi order in Iranian Azerbaijan. Some of their fifteenth-century leaders gained followers in Eastern Anatolia among tribes that followed popular brands of Shi'ism, and the Safavids became Shi'is. In the early sixteenth century they conquered Iran and made it a Shi'i state, in part to distinguish themselves from their Sunni rivals in the West and East. The identification of Iran with Shi'ism dates from this dynasty.

During the first period of both Ottoman and Safavid rule, royal women retained some of the open power they had in earlier Turkic nomadic societies. In the sixteenth century a number of Ottoman and Safavid women were openly involved in politics in both the central and provincial courts. During later periods that power was more expressed from harems, but it remained important and often decisive, especially in the seventeenth-century Ottoman Empire. One study of the Ottoman harem has demonstrated how central that institution was to the administrative system. Queen mothers of sultans were especially powerful. Among the Ottomans after the early period, princes were brought up in royal harems and hence much influenced by the women there, especially their mothers and often eunuchs as well. The formerly dominant belief that "harem rule," especially in the seventeenth century, was disastrous for the Ottoman Empire is now challenged.[15] The central harem had a hierarchical organization and inner conflicts. Similar structures were found in provincial harems and in Safavid central and provincial harems, where leading women were far more influential on policy than past historians realized.[16]

Women throughout the Ottoman Turkish and Arab lands frequently came to, or sent representatives to, Islamic courts, and *qadis* (judges) tended to protect their Islamic legal rights to inheritance, property, and legal treatment regarding marriage and divorce. That does not mean the judgments were gender-egalitarian, but they did tend to protect women's legal and property rights and were not, in most cases, instruments to increase gender inequalities beyond those provided for in law.[17]

In families, age hierarchies were as important as gender hierarchies. Older women exercised control over young males and females, and young men were often almost as vulnerable as young women. As they matured, wives, especially if they had sons, received greater authority and responsibility. Short lifespans and male mortality sometimes made women de facto heads of households.[18]

Judith Tucker notes that legal cases in Ottoman Syria and Palestine seldom dealt with suspected sexual transgressions by girls or women, which were, despite contrary admonitions of Muslim jurists, most often dealt with by families.[19] Sexual transgressions were discussed in Muslim law, and although some sixteenth-century Ottoman laws covered sexual transgressions, other rulings explicitly or implicitly left punishments to family members.[20] Male relatives possibly rarely killed girls and women accused of transgressions, but such killings did provide warnings to others. Recent studies suggest that women had important legal protections if they went to Islamic courts, but the courts' judgments may have been less important in the lives of many women, especially those of the popular urban and rural classes, than were customary practices.

Mamluk, Safavid, and Ottoman documents show that upper-class women held urban land, controlled significant sums of money, and managed some businesses. Even those who were secluded could use agents to conduct business, and some were involved in property management, speculation, and providing capital for trade. Women in the Ottoman imperial harem financed important buildings, many of which were used for social services. Women were also involved in *waqf* endowments, which sometimes had female administrators and beneficiaries.[21] Less is known about poorer women, but they were unlikely to own land or flocks, much less have capital for endowments or businesses.

WESTERN VIEWS OF MIDDLE EASTERN MUSLIM WOMEN

Western attitudes toward Islam and the Middle East often condemned the treatment of women. Hostility in the Christian West to the Muslim Middle East goes back to the Middle Ages, when Muslims were seen as a military threat as well as followers of a false religion. From early modern times, polygamy, veiling, seclusion, and harems were frequently attacked; Muslim women were often seen as slaves; and there were fantasies about hypersexual harems. Muslims were militarily threatening well into the Ottoman period, and Western Christian characteristics such as military aggressiveness and religious intolerance were projected onto them. Most Europeans believed that Western women had a uniformly higher position in society than Muslim women, even though that was untrue in matters of property ownership, inheritance, and some possibility for divorce. Westerners also sometimes projected onto Muslims their own sexual fantasies.

Regarding the eighteenth-century Ottoman Empire, Ladies Mary Montagu and Elizabeth Craven had a very different view. Although the men who wrote about Near Eastern women seldom had contact with them, Lady Mary entered into upper-class harem activities. She compared Ottoman women's position favorably to that of Western women, especially as they owned and controlled property, had social lives that she saw as free, and could use the head-to-toe outer garment as a means to hide sexual affairs.[22] Elizabeth Craven said, "I think I never saw a country where women enjoy so much liberty, and free from all reproach, as in Turkey. . . . The Turks in their conduct towards our sex are an example to all other nations."[23] These women were reacting to discrimination against women in England, however, and their enthusiasm was not an objective evaluation of the position of average Ottoman women.

The nineteenth century saw the flowering of Western negative stereotypes about the Muslim Middle East that have come to be known, following the major book of that name by Edward Said, as Orientalism.[24] Said's book brilliantly and usefully points up a number of phenomena and also has problematic aspects, including blaming Orientalist scholars for ideas of Western superiority. These were more based on economic and military developments that allowed western countries to conquer or dominate non-western areas, on continued religious prejudice, and on the nineteenth-century rise of "scientific racism" (which put black people on an even lower rung than "Orientals"). Scholars who saw Muslims as inferior were expressing widely held views that were expressed even more strongly and influentially by politicians, travelers, missionaries, journalists, and other writers. Some professional Orientalists helped spread attitudes of superiority, but their role in this was relatively small, and they were reflecting as much as causing Western attitudes. Anti-Islamic prejudices continued to be strong as were other prejudices against Asians and Africans, but they should not be lumped together and blamed especially on scholars.

Although Said does not significantly discuss gender, his book has influenced several works analyzing the sexual images of the Orient found in the modern West. "Orientalist" artists and writers, far more than scholars, perpetuated highly sexualized images of Middle Eastern women. Beyond that directly sexual aspect, westerners tended to view Middle Eastern Muslim women as being totally oppressed and having no spheres of independence. In addition to art and literature, the writing of Protestant missionaries, colonial officials like Lord Cromer, and travelers provided major sources of Western attitudes toward Muslim women and men.

The (sometimes prejudiced) writing of Orientalist scholars has been more subject to intellectual criticism than has nonscholarly writing, however, because scholars claimed to have the credentials and documentation to tell the world what Islam really was. Said's critique of Orientalism is more valid for modern Western views of Arabs than for views of, say, Iranians or Indians, who were in part admired by Orientalists, largely because they spoke languages related to European languages. Greater negativity toward Arabs included a strong tendency to attack their attitudes and practices toward women, which was part of French and British colonial strategy in areas they ruled or dominated in the Middle East and North Africa, all of which were Arab (i.e., mainly Arabic-speaking) areas.

1798–1914 European contacts with the Middle East in warfare, diplomacy, and trade were never interrupted but became more important with the rise of capitalism from the fifteenth century on, as well as modern warfare, European expansion, and extensive trade. Western contacts increased with growing military and political involvements from Napoleon's 1798 invasion of Egypt on and as European industrial production grew and trade increased. Among indigenous populations some local Christians and Jews became prominent in economic and other relations with Europeans. They began to have Western-influenced schools, often sponsored by Western Christian or Jewish groups, which in time included girls as well as boys. Although many of the new schools were also open to Muslims, a far lower percentage of the total Muslim population attended.

Because of educational and cultural contact with the West, minority communities saw growing differentiation from the majority of Muslims in the role of women and the numbers of educated women, whereas previously such differences had been smaller. In the nineteenth and twentieth centuries there was also increasing cultural differentiation among Muslims, between the majority of the population and those middle- and upper-class groups that had social and economic ties to the West and often Western-style educations. The majority tended to have gender relations called "traditional" and often associated with "Islam," whereas the latter group increasingly adopted modes influenced by those in the West.

In Istanbul and its immediate surroundings, certain Westernizing trends that affected women and the family began as early as the eighteenth century; in other areas, such changes came later and at different rates in different places. Cities near the Mediterranean had the most European trade and interaction with the West, while places like Afghanistan or Arabia were affected less and later. Moreover, influences differed greatly by class and mode of production.

The usual (although contested) dividing line taken for important Western influence and control is Napoleon's 1798 invasion of Egypt. Napoleon introduced unveiling and Western treatment of some women, but after he left there was a backlash against this and against the women involved. For a time the presence of Western foreigners reinforced veiling and seclusion, much as the coming of strangers to rural localities continues to do.

Napoleon's advance greatly weakened the former military rulers of Egypt under Ottoman suzerainty. That paved the way for an Ottoman military officer, Muhammad Ali (r. 1805–48) to destroy their remaining forces and take control of Egypt and later Syria. Muhammad Ali saw the importance of Western military strength and tried to build a modern army supported by modern industries, translation bureaus, and medical and technical schools. His policies impacted women in various ways. Some entire families had to do forced labor, women whose husbands underwent long-term conscription had to work more on the land, and some women worked in Muhammad Ali's factories. His school for women health practicioners was at first unable to attract free women and enlisted women of African slave origin, but it came to enroll free women and was the first government school to educate girls and women. There were some new jobs for them, but, overall, women were pushed out of positions as active owners and traders of goods and property. Many peasant women had to work harder for less return.[25]

Elsewhere in the Middle East there were less abrupt changes in women's lives. Growing European economic domination meant that the rest of the world increasingly exported raw materials, of which cotton and oil are two Middle Eastern examples, and imported factory-made goods from the West. In the early nineteenth century, European powers used victories or crises to make Egypt, Iran, and the Ottomans sign trade treaties incorporating free entry of European goods and very low tariffs. This not only hurt chances of industrialization but also, given the low prices of European goods, meant that most handicrafts declined. The resultant economic disruptions affected both men and women although there were a few contrary trends of increasing demand for a few handicrafts, notably some textiles and especially, after around 1875, carpets, which employed many women and girls in workshops and at home, especially in Iran and Anatolia. Women and children were increasingly employed in textiles in Syria, Anatolia, North Africa, and elsewhere. Handwork wages were very low and conditions often bad, even if women worked at home. The role of women in craft and industrial workshops grew and helped support families but was more limited in the Middle East than in Europe or Japan because there were cultural barriers, especially for Muslim women, which were sometimes overcome only by extreme economic necessity.[26]

Most major historical changes have both positive and negative aspects and affect different groups differently. Some scholars note that earlier women in extended families had more family help with housework and children and a more inter-class social life than do most women today, with the women's part of the household including servants with whom family women were on close terms. Women of different classes mixed more—residentially, in baths, and in visits and trips to shrines—than they do now when women have private baths, no slaves, servants, or clients, and many do not go to shrines. It seems misplaced to overstate the virtues of the old days, when women servants and family clients often received more personal support than popular-class women did later but were still mostly locked into poverty and service or slavery. In both East and West, some changes that came with capitalism have been very hard on many women, especially those of the popular classes. Change was, however, critical to the eventual spread of women's education, published writing, public activity, legal gains, lowered birth rates, choice in marriage, advances in health and hygiene, and other phenomena that meant more freedom of choice for many women, even though many have not yet seen substantial benefits, even from the change from extended to nuclear families.[27] Certain values were stronger in the past than they are now, but overstating their virtues while neglecting their negatives can play into the hands of those who still do not want more choices and legal equality with men made available to women.

Many westerners and some Middle Easterners have thought that local culture and traditions were so overwhelmingly negative that they had to be subverted or overturned for Middle Eastern countries to flourish and for women to have positive lives. This view was found in different degrees among nineteenth- and early-twentieth-century writers, both eastern and western, who often highlighted the position of women as the worst thing about the Middle East. This view was especially characteristic of British and French colonial officials. It blended old prejudices against Islam, nineteenth-century "scientific racism," and a Eurocentric view that non-Western countries could only advance if they totally Westernized.

The ills of Muslim women and the rightness of (inegalitarian but different) Western gender relations were standard themes of colonial ideology.[28] Nonetheless, it remains true that Middle Eastern women were subordinate and often mistreated and that the evolution of women's rights in the West provided the only obvious model for reform for many. The Westernizing approach of many intellectuals was not always explicit, but it continued at least implicitly when Iranian, Turkish, and various local Arab nationalisms became prominent among thinkers and rulers in the twentieth century. Some nationalists, notably Turkish and Iranian ones, constructed national traditions full of Western values, blamed foreigners or Islam for decline, and disdained current customs and Islamic practices. Most Arab nationalisms were different in that Islam was treated as part of Arab nationalism, and negative features were most often seen as distortions of Islam, but even Arab nationalisms read modern Western values into the Arab-Muslim past.

Most nineteenth- and twentieth-century changes in women's status and in ideas about women were not due to colonial rule. Many similar changes occurred in countries that were colonized and those that were not. Current criticisms of imitating Western ways and ideas often fail to note that these ideas are not intrinsically Western and did not develop in Western countries until changes in social and economic realities made them appropriate. What was key was the appropriateness to a certain stage of capitalist or partly capitalist society of "Western" ideas of marital choice, stress on the marital more than the agnatic family, women's public roles, and, for a time, focus on "scientific" domesticity and child-rearing. Such ideas were not widely borrowed until they were locally useful and were not borrowed in classes that did not find them appropriate.

Capitalist society, developed first in the West, involved the increasing separation of economic activity from the home and restructuring women's roles in domesticity and child-rearing. Western ideas of domesticity were seen as appropriate in the rest of the world once capitalist development began there, and with later socioeconomic development in both West and East women's nondomestic employment came to be valued. No doubt Western power and prestige encouraged intellectuals to adopt Western ideas, but those ideas became influential only when local developments made them useful.

Economic and cultural relations with the modern West affected the position of women. In the Middle East, Egypt and the western parts of the Ottoman Empire saw the earliest modern socioeconomic change, arising in large part from trade with Europe. In this area the sexual division of labor grew among the laboring classes, with men employed in producing cash crops and in trade and workshops and women left more to the domestic sphere and various unpaid or ill-paid employment and crafts, especially textile work.

The effects of Western contacts were as strong in Istanbul, western Anatolia, Lebanon, and a few other Mediterranean centers as in Egypt, but the history of women in modern Egypt has been far more studied, and hence perforce is often taken as exemplary of these changes. The head of Muhammad Ali's educational mission to Paris, Rifa'a al-Tahtawi, in a book about France recommended that girls receive the same education as boys because that was done in strong nations. The Egyptian Educational Council recommended public education for girls in the late 1830s, but aside from the 1832 school for women health practitioners nothing was done until the 1870s. In Egypt and elsewhere, upper-class girls increasingly received Westernized educations at home, and missionary schools pioneered in modern education for both genders. Missionaries in Middle Eastern countries were forbidden to convert Muslims, but some Muslims came to their schools, and local Christian communities started to set up their own schools, including the Egyptian Copts, Greek (Orthodox), and Armenians. The French-based Alliance Israélite Universelle set up schools for Jewish children from Morocco to Iran, which some non-Jews attended, and the French government also subsidized schools. Many of these came to include girls, often in separate schools.

In Egypt, Khedive Isma'il (r. 1863–79) created a committee that began modernized schools for boys and girls, and Tahtawi wrote a textbook that stated women should be educated and advocated equality in marriage. Isma'il established a few primary and secondary schools for girls, but a financial crisis, Isma'il's abdication, and especially the British occupation of 1882 slowed educational expansion. Muslim societies and missionary schools had more girls enrolled than did government schools in the early twentieth century.

An Islamic modernist thinker and educator, Muhammad 'Abduh, was the first influential Arab Muslim to argue that Islam was basically gender-egalitarian and that unequal treatment of women came from later corruptions of the religion. Some other liberal intellectuals agreed. By the late nineteenth century, women in Egypt, Istanbul, and elsewhere were launching magazines and publishing articles, and a growing number of families were adopting or adapting European ways.

Some men and women in Egypt, the Ottoman Empire, and Iran were changing the position and roles of women, in part because large, expensive harems and slavery were not compatible with the development of the capitalist system and hence were in decline. The advantages of modern methods of health, hygiene, and child-rearing became increasingly clear and began to be promoted. For this, new models for women were needed, and some men and women began to advocate new health measures and cleanliness, especially for infants and children. Such ideas slowly spread, and the call for careful housekeeping and hygiene in writing by and for women led to healthier families and was in its day modern, however old-fashioned and constraining it may seem in an age when women's careers are given greater priority.[29]

Modernizing governmental reforms in the nineteenth and twentieth centuries often impacted women. The Ottoman Sultan Selim III began an abortive program of military reforms in 1789, but a true reform program, like that of Muhammad Ali in Egypt, could not begin until Sultan Mahmud II destroyed the old military janissary corps in 1826. Mahmud was followed by ministers who led in various reforms until a constitution was declared in 1876, and even the next, conservative, sultan, Abdulhamid II, did not entirely reverse the reform current. Reform was slower in Iran, which was less affected by European contacts, but in all these areas educational, public health, and economic measures affected the position of women as well as gender attitudes among the educated.

Direct colonization, which began with the French conquest of Algeria from 1830, also affected women. Most of the Middle East remained formally part of the Ottoman Empire until after World War I but was subject to huge Western economic and political interference. British and French rulers were highly critical of "Muslim" treatment of women but did little to advance women's education in their territories and refrained from interfering with Muslim family law.[30] Modernized law codes were adopted in civil and commercial law in Egypt and the Ottoman Empire, but the parts of Muslim law that pertained to women, family, and inheritance remained in force so that, in practice, Islamic law became synonymous with these spheres. The ease with which some Islamic law could be abolished, contrasted with the continued difficulty of reforming laws affecting gender, shows the cultural centrality of gender and family issues. Many men whose lives were disrupted or made harder by the Western impact clung to old ways regarding women and the family.

In this period women participated in politics, often from behind the scenes, as with the continued strong influence of several Ottoman and Iranian rulers' wives and mothers. Women from various classes were active in bread riots and also in rural and urban revolts in Egypt, Algeria, and elsewhere. In Iran the Babi messianic religious movement that began in the 1840s and adopted a radical program, including revolts, had an outstanding radical woman preacher and poet, Qurrat al-Ain, who sometimes spoke unveiled. The majority of Babis chose to follow a new prophet from the 1860s, who began the Baha'i religion, which adopted liberal views in many spheres, including women's rights. Women participated in the several national revolts and rebellions in Iran between 1891 and 1979. In the 1891 revolt against a British tobacco monopoly, the shah's wives refused to smoke when the leading Shi'i cleric declared a boycott. In the constitutional revolution of 1905–11, women set up revolutionary and nationalist organizations and took important actions in favor of the constitutionalists and against foreign encroachments.[31] Elsewhere middle- and upper-class women participated in various nationalist movements aimed at ending European rule or control and setting up modern national states. In Turkey the writer and speaker Halide Edip turned her eloquent work to nationalist and reform causes, beginning with the successful Young Turk revolt against Abdul Hamid in 1908 and continuing with the defense of Turkish territory against dismemberment by Western allies after World War I and advocacy of social reform. Other Turkish and Arab women were also politically active.

Despite the small number of women who then attended schools, many girls, especially in the upper classes, received a partly modern education at home. In Egypt and the Ottoman Empire women of the ruling family played a prominent role in a few mixed-gender salons. The women's press included articles on bettering the conditions of women, including the pros and cons of veiling and reports of mistreatment of women.[32] Some women began to demand reforms in family law and increased access to education, work, and political rights.

Those who advocated imitating Western steps toward gender equality, like Tahtawi, were less controversial before westerners became colonial rulers. Once the British took over Egypt in 1882, advocacy of Western ways became more controversial among those who stressed national independence, which they tied to a defense of certain traditions. In Egypt there thus developed differences both among male thinkers and politicians and among women writers and activists. The most prominent writer on women was the Egyptian Qasim Amin. In his *Liberation of Women* (1899), a book widely translated and read in the Middle East, Amin supports Western ways and strongly criticizes Egyptian ones, with special criticism of the ulama and of women's ignorance. The main recommendation he made that elicited much hostile reaction was to end veiling and seclusion, an idea that has, in its veiling component, remained a critical area of contestation. Amin's recommendation for unveiling was rejected not only by many ulama and conservatives but also by some women writers who promoted women's rights.

For a century the question of veiling has had a central place in debates about women in the Muslim world. The practice of veiling formerly included covering at least the lower part of the face as well as the whole body except for hands and feet, while recently it has evolved to forms of dress, often called *hijab,* that leave the face uncovered although not the hair or neck. Traditionally, it was mainly urban women who veiled, although others covered their hair and bodies in different, often colorful and less concealing, ways. Veiling was meant to keep women unseen by unrelated men and was part of a complex of practices that included seclusion. Those who thought women could be liberated by putting them in Western dress and imitating Western ways, however understandable their views, often ignored local sensibilities, exaggerated the importance of dress, and gave too little heed to other changes in beliefs and mores and educational, legal, and political reforms. It is, however, relevant that the veil attacked by Amin and others was not the hijab found on many modern women today but part of a complex set of beliefs that mandated that women should be hidden, should not play public roles, and should have key decisions made for them by men.

Leila Ahmed is critical of Amin in ways not accepted by all. Her views point up the complex nature of debates over the veil in the period of Western domination and resistance to it:

> Amin's book . . . marks the entry of the colonial narrative of women and Islam—in which the veil and the treatment of women epitomized Islamic inferiority—into mainstream Arabic discourse. And the opposition it generated similarly marks the emergence of an Arabic narrative developed in resistance to the colonial narrative. . . . The veil came to symbolize in the resistance narrative, not the inferiority of the culture and the need to cast aside its customs in favor of those of the West, but, on the contrary, the dignity and validity of all native customs, and in particular those customs coming under fiercest colonial attack—the customs relating to women—and the need to tenaciously affirm them as a means of resistance to western domination . . . it is Western discourse that in the first place determined the new meanings of the veil and gave rise to its emergence as a symbol of resistance.[33]

There was, however, a different discourse that said that the veil, like male privileges in marriage, divorce, and elsewhere, were distortions of Islam, and veiling and male privilege had a growing number of critics. Some were Westernizers who were often accused of complicity with Western powers, but some spoke rather of restoring the egalitarian values of early Islam. There was an overall class distinction between largely upper-middle-class or intellectual

Westernizers and their petty bourgeois or popular-class opponents. As governments Westernized without becoming democratic or egalitarian their opponents often stressed values they found in original Islam. Some such opponents were conservatives, but others, like the nineteenth-century Young Ottomans, were not. Those today who criticize secular reformers and feminists for going too far in imitating the West may have a point, but in a past when Western ways to many represented a host of desired achievements—industrial and military strength, citizen participation in government, increased citizen and gender equality, and reduced privileges for elites—it was inevitable that many reformers should want to imitate the West. Islam and tradition were associated with old regimes and ways of life, and it was not until those old regimes were overthrown that new versions of Islam could become widespread.

Educated women increasingly expressed themselves in the arts and literature and began a women's press, initially centering in Cairo and Istanbul. Popular-class women's culture included performances for other women, although some performers continued to be slaves or, if they performed for men, prostitutes. Family life saw a gradual decline in harems and seclusion for the rich. There was a trend toward brides and grooms having more choice in marriage and for strengthening the role of husbands compared to that of the natal family, a trend that was contradictory in its impact on women, depending on how supportive or dominating husbands were as compared to natal male relatives. One scholar has found in the Tunisian archives evidence of a kind of jail for disobedient wives where they were sent until ready to be obedient.[34] Some wives, however, were protected from gross mistreatment by recourse to Islamic courts or by taking refuge with their natal family until the husband promised to reform.

From the late nineteenth century, new circumstances and ideas led to a decline in large harems and slavery, a rise in marriage age, and the beginnings of choice in marriage. The decline in large, autonomous households was partly due to the strengthening of state and local governments, both colonial and indigenous, which took over some functions formerly performed by households. The pioneer in change was Istanbul, where a demographic and social study shows that in the late nineteenth century most people lived in monogamous households of four to five people, had few children, and married in their late teens or later, making Istanbul demographically comparable to West European countries.[35] We have no similar studies for other Middle Eastern cities, but these trends showed up, although later, in many of them. Central parts of the Ottoman Empire began modernizing during the eighteenth century, and changes in the family and elsewhere mean that parts of Turkey saw significant changes for women and families well before the reforms of Atatürk during the 1920s and 1930s.

One aspect of the move to small households was a decline in slavery, which by the nineteenth century was mostly composed of black domestics. Slave trading was outlawed between the 1850s and the 1890s in the Ottoman Empire, Egypt, and Iran. Abolition came later, but once bans on slave trading were enforced slavery declined rapidly; manumission continued to be widespread, and children of free men and slave women were free. Large harems, based on polygamy, concubines, slave servants, and eunuchs, were increasingly seen as outdated and unsuited to new conditions.[36]

Hence, between 1798 and 1914 dramatic political and economic changes in the area that led to Western dominance and dependent economic relations with the West created changes in the position of women, which varied greatly by class and region but opened the door to improved health, education, and public roles. At the same time they created hardships for many popular-class women.

1914 TO TODAY   The period since 1914 has seen further major political and socioeconomic changes that had varying impacts on women. Among these was the post–World War I dissolution of the Ottoman Empire, which had already lost Algeria, Eastern Europe, and (de facto) Egypt. The successor states were Turkey, whose borders were set after a nationalist struggle led by Mustafa Kemal, later called Atatürk, and the Arab states of Asia, which became mandates controlled by Great Britain (Iraq, Transjordan, and Palestine) and France (Syria and Lebanon). These Arab states had nationalist movements in which women participated, and most gained independence in the 1930s and 1940s. Palestine saw U.N.-sponsored partition and Israeli expansion after warfare and the rest taken over from 1948 to 1961 by Jordan (West Bank) and Egypt (Gaza). The lands of the Arabian Peninsula—Saudi Arabia, Yemen, Oman, and the Gulf sheikhdoms—were independent but far more traditional. Egypt, first a British protectorate, gained considerable independence from 1922 on as a result of nationalist movements and total independence with the officers' coup in 1952 and the abolition of the monarchy. Iran became more independent and centralized after a 1921 coup and the subsequent rise of Reza Shah Pahlavi. Tunisia and Morocco received independence from France in the 1950s, whereas Algeria, with a heavy population of settlers, had a long struggle (in which women played a key role) for independence. Palestine, declared a homeland for the Jews in the Balfour declaration and the League of Nations covenant, became the scene of competing nationalisms before and after its division by the United Nations in 1947. In recent decades the main governmental changes have followed antimonarchist revolutions in Iraq in 1959 and Iran in 1979, the occupation of Arab Palestine by Israel in 1967, and of Iraq by the United States in 2003.

94

Some women's involvement in politics began before World War I with participation in the Iranian Revolution of 1905–11, in the successful Young Turk movement that began in 1908, and in women's organizations and press, especially in Egypt and Turkey. The war and its aftermath increased nationalist struggles for independence, and women participated in many of them. Although the interwar period saw the growth of women's organizations, especially in Egypt where some took an openly feminist stance, most activist women agreed to concentrate on goals of national liberation, even if that often meant toning down demands for such aims as reforming family law, gaining the vote, more public positions, and greater gender equality. There were, however, groups that put forth demands for greater women's rights, and the very participation of women in nationalist struggles and movements gave them greater experience, visibility, and respect as public persons.

Most women's organizations, some of which began before World War I, had primarily educational and charitable goals. They pioneered in creating institutions that had not existed before or had, in completely different form, been monopolized by religious groups. Before 1914 there were very few state girls' schools; girls' schooling was largely pioneered by foreign organizations, including missionary ones. From the late nineteenth century, first Christian and then Muslim or mixed women's groups and individuals formed girls' schools, which often provided a model and impetus for states to launch programs for girls' education. Turkey, already ahead in state-sponsored girls' schooling, extended it greatly under Atatürk, and other states made varying efforts in the interwar period. The new universities set up in this period in Turkey, Iran, Egypt, and elsewhere were overwhelmingly coeducational. Most nationalists promoted education for women to be good mothers and fulfill certain public roles. Various religious and traditional forces strongly opposed girls' education, especially after puberty, saying that girls did not need education, which might threaten their chastity and keep them from needed tasks at home. The women's groups promoting education, and the schools they founded, were thus often involved in difficult struggles.

Women's organizations mainly attracted upper- and upper-middle-class women, and their charitable and social work in part embodied traditional views of charity and noblesse oblige. Yet they were innovative and important in setting up education and workshops promoting domestic skills, hygiene, and crafts, which improved health and gave some women saleable skills. Some women combined work on such issues with efforts for greater gender equality. Among them were the pioneering Egyptian feminist Huda Sha'rawi, chief founder in 1923 of the Egyptian Feminist Union, and Iran's Sedigheh Daulatabadi, who created a number of feminist organizations and publications. Women's groups contributed to the women's press, sponsored lectures and cultural events for women, and gave them greater, more organized public presence than before. Their efforts in health, education, social sciences, and job promotion had direct and pioneering impact and encouraged governments to do more in these fields.

New roles for women, stressed in the writing and teaching of women's groups in Egypt and elsewhere, were congruent with the changeover from large elite households, harems, and slaves. The new domesticity stressed in many lectures and publications was also useful in creating more autonomous nuclear families. Women of classes that formerly looked down on manual work and had few ideas of hygiene became educated—and educated others—on how to manage a new type of household. As usual, gains involved losses, and in some ways modern domesticity in both East and West was a straightjacket, binding women to long hours of cleaning, cooking, and child-rearing and placing new limits on their proper behavior and language.

The tendency today to see scientific domesticity and other ideas proposed by educated women as a blind copying of the West omits the strong indigenous elements intertwined in all modernizations and local socioeconomic changes that made certain ideas appropriate to capitalism everywhere. Beth Baron was the first to present the domesticity debate as one of major importance for recent women's history, which cannot be limited to a study of feminist movements and struggles. Baron recognizes the dialectical, contradictory nature of the domesticity project, a point developed further by Afsaneh Najmabadi and others in *Remaking Women: Feminism and Modernity in the Middle East*, edited by Lila Abu-Lughod.[37] That book also expands on another point noted in Baron's writings: The growing role of the conjugal compared to the natal family, with more power for husbands and less for birth relatives, could be constraining as well as liberating for women.

An important and complex aspect of changing women's roles in the past two centuries was the opening of new occupations to women, which was often liberating for middle-class women but less so and often a negative experience for popular-class ones. The first new occupations open to women were usually teaching and nursing. In most countries access to other professions, including medicine, dentistry, and the arts (literature, music, and the theater), was more gradual. In several countries women were increasingly welcomed in governmental and private offices and sometimes filled political positions. For popular-class women, factory, workshop, and paid agriculture jobs were often low-paid, exploitative, and not liberating. Women still make up a smaller proportion of the labor force in the Middle East than in other parts of the world, even allowing for official figures' understating women's labor force participation.[38]

Women were, in ways that varied by place and circumstance, active in numerous nationalist movements that characterized the period from 1918 until the 1970s. Nationalism focused on unifying and modernizing states that were legally free and on gaining independence in those that were not (e.g., in the first post-1914 decades, most Arab states). Nationalists wished to play down or overcome internal divisions of class, status, tribe, ethnic group, and religion. Many nationalist men similarly endorsed greater gender equality, in part to mobilize and ultimately treat everyone within the national borders as citizens, although few favored total gender equality. The chief difference in program was between colonized or partly colonized (Arab) countries and legally free Turkey and Iran.

Turkey, which had already experienced considerable nineteenth-century reform, changed radically after Atatürk led an armed nationalist struggle that ended the division of Anatolia imposed by World War I allies and abolished the sultanate and caliphate, creating a new republic that broke with the past. Atatürk's modernizing program included ending the shari'a and enacting a modern family code, based on the Swiss civil code, in 1926 that ended polygamy, repudiation, and male custody and inheritance privileges, although men remained heads of households with some powers over their wives. Women got the vote in municipal elections in 1930 and in national ones in 1934, long before they did in France, Italy, or Switzerland. Unveiling and the adoption of Western dress were strongly promoted for women, and there was municipal legislation on the issue and limits on women's dress in government institutions, including schools and universities.

Although legal changes took time to be nationally enforced, with de facto polygamy and unregistered and underage marriages continuing in the hinterland, the trend was unmistakable. Scholars and others have begun to see negatives in Atatürk's reforms and in the secular and centralizing nationalist policies of many Turkish governments, noting that Islamic and ethnic sensibilities were suppressed. Recent cultural battles have occurred around some women's hijab at the university and elsewhere. No country has found an ideal, conflict-free way to reform gender issues that are deeply embedded in culture and in power relations among different groups and classes. Reformers in much of the Middle East are confronted by the continued local power of old regimes, tribes, and conservative ulama, and their attempts to take power from these groups include cultural attacks. It is impossible to have gender policies that all groups favor. These issues continue in the contemporary Middle East, where some present new Islamic politics as a (usually nonegalitarian) solution to gender and other problems although others do not.

Turkey and Iran were the primary independent Middle Eastern states after 1918, and Iran, like Turkey, saw a nationalist government under a military man come to power. Reza Khan, the military leader of a coup against the old regime in 1921 after an abortive campaign for a republic deposed the Qajars and crowned himself shah. As part of his modernizing and centralizing measures, Reza Shah extended public education, including university education, for boys and girls; created Iranian Boy and Girl Scouts; and, from 1936, enforced unveiling. In Iran, less modernized than Turkey, that policy was traumatic for many women, some of whom stopped leaving their homes until it was de facto abandoned after Reza Shah's 1941 abdication. Earlier, Iran had a nascent women's press and a series of women's organizations, and there, as in Turkey after the new nationalist regimes took power, women's organizations were increasingly brought under central government control.[39]

It was not until much later that Iran had the legal reforms regarding women's rights that are of much greater importance to their lives than are dress codes. Reza Shah's codified family law was based on the shari'a. Only under his son, Muhammad Reza Shah, were women given the vote in 1963. In 1967 there was, under pressure from politically active women, a Family Protection Law that greatly limited polygamy and made divorce and custody rights equal and subject to court control. As had been done under Habib Bourguiba in Tunisia in 1956 after independence from France, the new law was proclaimed to be Islamic—based on a better interpretation of Islam. In the case of Iran, that did not prevent it from being repudiated after the Ayatollah Khomeini came to power in 1979, although women's struggles and social realities meant that several of its provisions were essentially reenacted.[40] Various independent Arab regimes adopted less comprehensive reforms. The necessity of independence for reform was suggested by Bourguiba's support for traditional law and veiling until independence was gained; immediately thereafter he adopted a radically changed personal status code.

The policies of Atatürk, the Pahlavi shahs, and Bourguiba, which included encouragement of all levels of education, public roles, and many professions for women, are often called state feminism, and although there is no alternative term, this may wrongly suggest that women's rights were the central element in these leaders' thinking. They were, in fact, primarily concerned with unifying and modernizing their countries and increasing the power and spheres of their governments. For these aims, curbing the power and autonomy of previously powerful groups and institutions, including foreigners, tribes, ethnic groups, and religious leaders and institutions, was of key importance. Many such groups had a vested interest in old forms of patriarchy. Those Middle Eastern governments that worked with such groups rather than suppressing them introduced few reforms in the condition of women, a point clearly argued by Mounira Charrad to explain the dramatic difference between postindependence Tunisia, on the one hand, and Morocco and Algeria, which saw very little personal status reform until the Moroccan reforms of 2003 and 2004, on the other.[41]

As for countries not led by "state feminists," Egypt has had the strongest, longest, and most varied women's movement in the Middle East; women's rights groups there have encouraged significant social change in fields like health, education, family practices, and women's employment. Yet in terms of changing the laws affecting women Egypt has done less than Tunisia, Turkey, or Iran. The centralizing nationalist Gamal Abdel Nasser met feminist demands for the vote and eligibility for election, but he did not reform family law, which was partially, and rather tentatively, reformed under his successor, Anwar Sadat. Although legal rights are not absolute indicators of women's status, the inability of Iran's clerical rulers to make their post-1979 reversal of such rights stick is one indication that legal changes are significant. Egyptian women's movements organized major demonstrations for both nationalist and feminist goals, worked both within and outside political groups and parties, and carried on education and propaganda. They had important impacts on education, job training, changing the image of women, and expanding public roles and employment for them as well as on the achievement of woman suffrage and eligibility for election in 1956. Margot Badran presents a comprehensive survey of women's activism in Egypt in the twentieth century until suppression of independent women's organizations and their merger into state-controlled organizations from 1956.[42]

Egypt's uniquely varied women's movement was not only due to its early exposure to the West and to capitalist forces but also to its having had the longest modern period of any Middle Eastern country when independent feminist organization was possible, from before World War I until 1956. In most of the Middle East, feminist organization was constrained by colonial rule or indigenous governments. Egypt was unique in having a major feminist organization of international importance and affiliations, the Egyptian Feminist Union (EFU), headed for decades by the pioneer of Egyptian feminism Huda Sha'rawi, a woman of elite origin and multifaceted activities. Sha'rawi and the EFU campaigned on a range of issues and engaged in extensive social service and educational activities.

There were also Egyptian feminists who had a more radical outlook, for example Doria Shafik or the leftist Inji Aflatun. The conflict with Islamism (Islamic politics), including Islamist women, began in the interwar period with the rise of the Muslim Brotherhood and its women's affiliates and continued thereafter in Egypt and elsewhere. Shafik, who achieved a *doctorat d'état* from the Sorbonne, founded the second important Egyptian feminist organization, the Bint al-Nil Union. She was a controversial figure who had tense relations with several women's leaders and was often seen as being too French, too Western, and too upper bourgeois despite her strong nationalist record. After she launched a hunger strike in 1957 she was confined to house arrest for three years, then entered partly self-imposed isolation, and committed suicide in 1975.[43]

Activist women had a wide range of views, from giving priority to feminism to following ideologies in which women's issues were either secondary, like nationalism and socialism, or were interpreted in nonfeminist and often anti-Western ways, including conservative and Islamist ideologies. Such contradictions were found also in other countries, and feminists often had to make tactical decisions about how strongly to push demands for greater gender equality.

Women in twentieth-century Syria and Lebanon followed a distinct trajectory. A book by Elizabeth Thompson that covers women, local and colonial power structures, and major opposition movements, accords the study of women its proper place as a central issue in politics and society, which both affects and is affected by other groups and issues.[44]

The women's movement in Syria and Lebanon was never strong enough to be a serious challenge to dominant colonial and local patriarchal structures and forces, including a growing hostile populist Islamic movement. As in many countries, the movement for women's rights was a movement of elite, educated women, whereas most popular-class women were not involved. Other actors often made alliances at the expense of women or women's demands. The communist parties of Syria and Lebanon and trade unions gave effective support to the growing body of women workers even though communists, like nationalists, backed down on earlier espousal of women's political demands. As elsewhere, many women participated courageously in nationalist independence struggles, but when independence came the nationalist elite did very little for them. (Earlier struggles were important, however, in encouraging post–World War II Syrian regimes to promote greater rights and public roles for women.)

In colonized areas like Syria, Lebanon, and North Africa, as long as the main struggle was against foreign rule, nationalists wanted to distinguish themselves from Europeans and were less open to a "Western-style" approach to women than were noncolonial Iran and Turkey. But particular situations are contradictory and complex. After independence, for example, colonized Tunisia behaved like some noncolonized countries, whereas since the 1979 revolution noncolonized Iran saw an anti-Westernizing backlash while in recent decades Syria moved toward secular governments that backed greater women's rights. Coverage of the role of leftist political and trade union groups in women's history would be useful for more scholars of Middle Eastern women, whose emphasis has been more on the deficiencies of the left than on significant positive contributions.

Palestine has seen many wrenching historical changes since World War

I, with wars leading from Ottoman rule to British mandate, to partition, Israeli annexation or occupation, and the two Palestinian Intifadas. Several authors, notably Anneleis Moors and Ellen Fleischmann, trace women's role in Palestine. Moors shows how legal and judicial protections for women, often emphasized in recent works based on Ottoman judicial records, predominantly benefit certain classes of women and how court judgments are often not enforced. Modern developments have affected the classes differently, with many urban women benefiting from educational opportunities to get professional jobs that afford some economic independence. Rural women, however, have seen their role in agriculture decline, which often makes them more dependent on men and less in control of property than before. The trend toward greater importance for the conjugal family and less for the natal family has led to more pooling of conjugal property and more choice of marriage partners.[45] Similar socioeconomic difficulties for rural and tribal women and gains and losses brought by increasing importance of the nuclear conjugal family are found elsewhere. Palestinian women have had a leading role in nationalist struggles, bringing them new public roles and causing many of them to postpone feminist demands.

In North Africa, tribal groups were historically very powerful, and governments were limited in their control of tribes, especially those far from governmental centers. In a book on Tunisia, Algeria, and Morocco, Monica Charrad analyzes the main features of Islamic family law, not with the common stress on individual women's rights but as reflecting the interests of the extended male family line as far more important than those of the conjugal family.[46] She interprets wives' property being kept separate from husbands'— and women using the names of their fathers rather than their husbands—as signs of the stronger role of the agnatic family. This is also reflected in the ease of divorce and a return to the agnatic family by divorced or widowed women. Much of this is applicable in other Middle Eastern areas, as is the discussion of tribal law and custom, which, although varied, is predominantly even more favorable to the agnatic patriarchal family than is Islamic law.

Charrad shows that only a state like Tunisia that could put down tribal power and centralize rule could rid itself of most patriarchal features of law. The emphasis on tribal power should be applied to much of the Middle East and supplemented by a stress on religious forces composing those involved in traditional religious institutions and those attracted to newer Islamic politics. Although Islamic political organizations and movements began in the interwar period, until the 1970s they were less important on both a popular and governmental level than were nationalist ones. During the earlier period essentially secular leftist and communist organizations also played a prominent role in countries that included Iran, Egypt, Syria, and Iraq. Since then,

Islamist movements have become increasingly important, incorporating many young people, women, and former nationalists or communists. Although Islamists rule only in Iran of the countries considered here, they also rule in Sudan, are strong in Pakistan, and have growing policy influence in Egypt and some other countries. Saudi Arabia combines an older form of monarchical-Islamic rule with financial encouragement of Islamic tendencies abroad.

Contemporary Islamic political movements have largely called for the use of Islamic law as the legislative basis for government activity, often claiming that only the shari'a, in theory of divine origin, can be true law in an Islamic society, and parliaments and governments can only approve regulations. The movement toward declaring the shari'a to be the basis of all legislation rests on the idea that shari'a means Islamic law, whereas it means "the way" and is, more accurately, all obligations of all Muslims, whether enforceable in a law court or not. It was never before modern time a state law code but rested on flexible judgments by Muslim judges based on continual debate and discussion among legal scholars over the centuries.[47]

Islamic law was codified for the first time in the Ottoman Empire in 1870, and much of that codification passed to the Ottoman successor states of Iraq, Syria, Palestine, and Transjordan. In these laws, most criminal and civil law was removed in favor of Western-style law codes. What remained covered the matters of most concern to women and the family—marriage, divorce, child custody, and inheritance laws. Some Islamist women say that a proper interpretation of Islam would bring egalitarian interpretations of the shari'a, but in practice most legal steps that have been taken in the name of "restoring" the shari'a have been antiegalitarian.

Women's roles and status in recent decades have expanded in many ways but have been affected by the partially contradictory rise of Islamic politics. This has numerous causes, including failures of all governments, even secular ones, to meet people's needs, growing economic and cultural crises, and the persistence of struggles against Western powers and Israel, seen as a colonial implantation. Although Islamic politics involve many tendencies, from right to left they are similar in wanting states to implement Islamic beliefs and practices, including the shari'a and often literal application of the punishments in the Quran and in post-Quaranic law.[48] The Quran is mostly read as endorsing polygamy, male control (including, in marriage, veiling), and strong punishment for adultery although Islamist women interpret it differently. Read literally, the Quran does not require veiling, and its requirement of four eyewitnesses to adultery should make convictions almost impossible. On these questions, however, most Islamists follow Tradition rather than literal scripture.

With the spread of Islamic political ideologies, many defenders of women's rights in the Muslim world have reinterpreted the Quran and early Islam, and many who may be internally secularists now use Islamic arguments. Male-supremacist interpretations are, however, more in line with most literal texts and remain dominant in the religious establishment and in most lay circles. The advances made by women after the early years of the Islamic Republic of Iran are relevant to the questions faced by Muslim women elsewhere. These advances, however, are less due to Islamic feminists' convincing others of new interpretations of the Quran and Islam than to effective pressure of women and their allies around current issues and to the needs of modern society for educated, working women and for lower birth rates. Active participation in the 1978–79 revolution of women from left to right, with the hope of most that conditions would improve, was followed by the shock to many of the annulment of the Family Protection Law of 1967/75, imposition of "Islamic dress," and removal of women from many spheres of life and work.

Since the 1980s in Iran some rights and roles have gradually been regained, and there have been advances in education, health, and family planning. In Iran as elsewhere there is an "Islamic feminist" trend that promotes women's rights in Islamic terms and interprets Islam in more gender-egalitarian ways and also effective resistance of many women to reversals of rights. Women had a major role in the elections of the reformist president Mohammad Khatami in 1997 and 2001, and even with press crackdowns and jailings since 2000 they continued to advance in sports, the arts, greater public freedom, and most professions.

Among the issues under discussion are whether Islam can become egalitarian for women and whether states that call themselves Islamic, such as Iran, Pakistan, Saudi Arabia, and Sudan, can fully implement women's rights. These questions are contested rather than resolved because they are highly political and relate to the future, which is not knowable. The question of whether Islam can be gender-egalitarian is now rarely stressed among scholars, who tend to see general statements about Islam as a reification of something that has varied by time and place.

Despite such avoidance of global statements about Islam, it is true that Islamic countries stand lower than economically equivalent non-Muslim countries in the usual indexes of women's welfare from international agencies and that this is probably connected with widespread beliefs and practices. Although all revealed religions have male-supremacist content, appeals to inegalitarian revealed texts are more common in Islamic areas now than elsewhere. Most governments that call themselves Islamic have a lower legal status for women than governments that did or do not stress Islam. Critics of Islamic politics may say that there is no reasonable way to interpret the Quran, hadith, or shari'a as being gender-egalitarian. Islamist feminists counter in part by citing Quranic nonlegal verses addressed equally to males and females and say that these rather than legal rulings give the true message of Islam.

The controversy is part of a contestation on whether a universalism about human rights is the best approach for scholars or whether it is better to deal with cultural contexts and refrain from head-on criticism of areas whose rights limitations may be based on widely believed cultural concepts. This conflict is acute for the Islamic Middle East because, first, the Quran and Traditions contain inegalitarian elements, and a greater proportion of Muslims than of Christians and Jews practice literalism regarding their revealed text and the laws derived from it. Such strictness has been more widespread in the Middle East than in areas that were converted later and not by conquest. Second, the long record of Western hostility to Islam and of imperialism brought a stronger counterreaction to modern Western ideas than in non-Muslim areas. Such factors, along with the failures of many Westernizing nationalist governments and others in democracy and in economic development and equity, encouraged the rise in Islamic politics among men and women. In this context some see the emphasis on universal human rights, or publicity given to bad treatment of women in Muslim countries, as a new imperialist "civilizing mission." That is especially true because many westerners did (and do) exaggerate the bad position of women in Islamic countries. Varieties of cultural relativism, which today may be called multiculturalism, are thus prevalent among liberal and leftist scholars today although they ironically also appeal to some who favor traditional Islamic practices.

Islamists in many countries take advantage of the "two cultures" gap—those in popular and traditional middle classes tended to follow many traditions, including veiling and other limits on women, while the new middle and upper classes, with Western-oriented educations and jobs, accepted modern models for women's rights and status. Most such models were not intrinsically Western but the result of socioeconomic changes and women's and men's struggles that happened to occur first in the West but then elsewhere in varying forms. This was not how they were often perceived, however. Islamists also gained support among some Westernized students, intellectuals, and others because of the association of authoritarian secular regimes, which increasingly lost support, with the West. Islamism came, from the 1970s onward, to be seen as the most politically potent counter-ideology, rejecting both failed secular Westernizing rule and imperialism. Many liberals and leftists allied with Islamists. Some women adopted the hijab as a form of protest, and some saw positive aspects to it, such as reducing class differences in female display and sexual harassment and ending sexual distractions at work.[49]

In Iran, Khomeini's ideas were not traditional, and he supported women's activism in his cause and reversed his former opposition to women voting. Nonetheless, adherence to traditional or popular-class standards regarding women was part of Khomeinism, as of Islamist ideologies outside Iran. Just as the position of women had been a central question for early oppositional nationalists, so, with a new and powerful framing, Islamists saw it as central to resistance to imperialism and restoration of morality. The hijab came to be a major symbol showing that Islamist movements and states were truly Islamic.

A nuanced perspective sees that women's roles and status at any stage of history reflect historical, social, and cultural circumstances, including class and gender systems that favor and are favored by those with wealth and power. Many women in any period derive advantages from practices such as the protection family, kin, and contact with many other women offer, but that does not mean old customs are the best in modern circumstances. Advances in health, education, and professional possibilities for many women have been accompanied by increased sexual and workplace exploitation and sometimes decreased economic roles for others, but that does not mean the potentialities afforded by modern changes should be rejected rather than expanded. Women and men are sometimes criticized for aping Western practices in the family as elsewhere without scholarly recognition that this was not just the result of blind imitation but involved practices suitable to new socioeconomic conditions, first experienced by the urban middle and upper classes but later spreading to others. Needed are more studies of the relation of gender and family structures to modes of production and governance and their necessary change, involving both gains and losses, with the development of dependent capitalism and new types of states and state policies.

The tendency of some to idealize past conditions, whether from the earliest Islamic period or periods preceding imperialism, while being critical of modern developments risks playing into the hands of patriarchal Islamists who also idealize the past. Relativism is useful insofar as it means situating practices and ideas in specific contexts—socioeconomic, political, and ideological. Understanding, however, the reasons why certain ideas and practices became prevalent should not preclude criticisms of such practices that take into account egalitarian views appropriate to more modern societies.

There is huge variation, by class and region, in the complexities of Middle Eastern women's lives, ranging from Turkey and Tunisia on the modernizing side to Saudi Arabia on the other. As a gross generalization, women's education, job and professional possibilities, and access to health services, including birth control and children's health, with improvements in health and declining birthrates, has increased in nearly all countries, often with major governmental input. Legal gains have continued in some countries but have been challenged by Islamists and others and in most countries husbands and male kin retain significant legal power over girls and women and greater rights than women in marriage, divorce, custody, inheritance, and freedom of movement. International bodies, including U.N. agencies and international conferences, have encouraged attention to women's issues and organization. Moreover, local organizations are now working effectively on a wide variety of issues, including, in some countries, such formerly taboo issues as honor killing and clitorectomy. In several countries there has been a growth, encouraged by international agencies, of nongovernmental organizations focusing on women's issues, which has brought gains but has meant that some governments have turned over some of their health, welfare, and educational functions to the NGOs.

In general, women's power and agency was always greater than most outsiders imagined, and women's socioeconomic role in a variety of jobs and professions and in the home today is more independent than a simple reading of laws might make one think. Yet this is primarily true of urban women who have some education, and a significant number of rural, tribal, and popular-class women have harder lives and fewer economic roles and possibilities than before. An overarching problem is the continued strength of ideas and customs that privilege men, whether based in religion or other aspects of culture, mean second-class status in various spheres for many women, and subject some to violence and other forms of mistreatment. Although women's situation is not nearly as bad overall as it is often depicted, and women have advanced toward greater equality and independence, there remains much to be done—and many people recognize that and are acting upon it.

Islamist movements have been contradictory in their impact, giving some formerly secluded girls and women a chance to be educated, meet together, work along with males if in hijab, and even develop their own interpretations of Islam. At the same time, they generally uphold male supremacist ideas. It is for the future to tell whether feminist interpretations of Islam will increase in importance and influence and formerly important secularist ideas and movements will see revivals, perhaps in new forms such as those that recognize the Quran's moral and ethical statements but not its legalistic ones or Islam's political supremacy.

Notes

Thanks to Beth Baron, Azita Karimkhany, and Ehud Taledano for help on this essay.

1. Deniz Kandiyoti, "Islam and Patriarchy: A Comparative Perspective," in *Women in Middle Eastern History: Shifting Boundaries in Sex and Gender,* ed. Nikki R. Keddie and Beth Baron (New Haven: Yale University Press, 1991), 23–42.

2. Denise A. Spellberg, *Politics, Gender, and the Islamic Past: The Legacy of A' isha bint Abi Bakr* (New York: Columbia University Press, 1994).

3. Jane Schneider, "Of Vigilance and Virgins: Honor, Shame, and Access to Resources in Mediterranean Societies," *Ethnology* 10 (Jan. 1971): 1–24. Several articles by anthropologists discussing Schneider's theses followed.

4. Barbara Freyer Stowasser, *Women in the Qur' an, Traditions, and Interpretation* (New York: Oxford University Press, 1993), ch. 2.

5. Leila Ahmed, *Women and Gender in Islam: Historical Roots of a Modern Debate* (New Haven: Yale University Press, 1992), 92; B. F. Musallam, *Sex and Society in Islam: Birth Control before the Nineteenth Century* (New York: Cambridge University Press, 1983).

6. Mounira M. Charrad, *States and Women's Rights: The Making of Postcolonial Tunisia, Algeria, and Morocco* (Berkeley: University of California Press, 2001), 44.

7. Ülkü Ü. Bates, "Women as Patrons of Architecture in Turkey," in *Women in the Muslim World*, ed. Lois Beck and Nikki Keddie (Cambridge: Harvard University Press, 1978), 245–60; D. Fairchild Ruggles, ed., *Women, Patronage, and Self-Representation in Islamic Societies* (Albany: SUNY Press, 2000), chs. 1–7.

8. Fedwa Malti-Douglas, *Woman's Body, Woman's Word: Gender and Discourse in Arabo-Islamic Writing* (Princeton: Princeton University Press, 1991); Fedwa Malti-Douglas, "Shahrazad Feminist," in *The Thousand and One Nights in Arabic Literature and Society*, ed. Richard G. Hovannisian and Georges Sabagh (New York: Cambridge University Press, 1997), 40–55.

9. Thomas J. Barfield, "Tribe and State Relations: The Inner Asian Perspective," in *Tribes and State Formation in the Middle East*, ed. Philip S. Khoury and Joseph Kostiner (Berkeley: University of California Press, 1990); Thomas J. Barfield, "Turk, Persian and Arab: Changing Relationships between Tribes and State in Iran and along Its Frontiers," in *Iran and the Surrounding World 1501–2001: Interactions in Culture and Cultural Politics*, ed. Nikki R. Keddie and Rudi Matthee (Seattle: University of Washington Press, 2002), 61–86.

10. On elite women in the Seljuq and subsequent periods, see Ann K. S. Lambton, *Continuity and Change in Medieval Persia: Aspects of Administrative, Economic, and Social History, Eleventh–Fourteenth Century* (Albany: SUNY Press, 1988).

11. Guity Nashat and Judith E. Tucker, *Women in the Middle East and North Africa: Restoring Women to History* (Bloomington: University of Indiana Press, 1999), 58.

12. Ibn Batuta, *Travels in Asia and Africa 1325–1354*, trans. and selected by H. A. R. Gibb (1929, repr. London: Darf Publishers, 1983), 146–47.

13. David J. Duncan, "Scholarly Views of Shajarat al-Durr: A Need for Consensus," 1999, at http://www.ucc.ie/chronicon/duncfra.htm.

14. See the following articles about the Mamluks in *Women in Middle Eastern History*, ed. Keddie and Baron: Huda Lutfi, "Manners and Customs of Fourteenth-Century Cairene Women: Female Anarchy versus Male Shar'i order in Muslim Prescriptive Treatises" (99–121); Carl F. Petry, "Class Solidarity versus Gender Gain: Women as Custodians of Property in Later Medieval Egypt" (122–42); and Jonathan P. Berkey, "Women and Islamic Education in the Mamluk Period" (143–57).

15. Leslie P. Peirce, *The Imperial Harem: Women and Sovereignty in the Ottoman Empire* (New York: Oxford University Press, 1993).

16. Maria Szuppe, "The 'Jewels of Wonder': Learned Ladies and Princess Politicians in the Provinces of Early Safavid Iran," in *Women in the Medieval Islamic World*, ed. Gavin R. G. Hambly (New York: St. Martin's Press, 1998), 325–47. Other chapters in this volume that have important new analyses of women in Turkish-ruled areas include

Priscilla P. Soucek, "Tīīmūrid Women: A Cultural Perspective" (199–226) and Kathryn Babayan, "The 'Aqāīd al-Nisā: A Glimpse at Safavid Women in Local Isfahānī Culture" (349–81). See also Rudi Matthee, "Prostitutes, Courtesans, and Dancing Girls: Women Entertainers in Safavid Iran," in *Iran and Beyond: Essays in Middle Eastern History in Honor of Nikki R. Keddie*, ed. Rudi Matthee and Beth Baron (Costa Mesa: Mazda, 2000), 121–50.

17. Among the books using legal and endowment documents for the Ottoman period are Margaret L. Meriwether, *The Kin Who Count: Family and Society in Ottoman Aleppo, 1770–1840* (Austin: University of Texas Press, 1999); Judith E. Tucker, *In the House of the Law: Gender and Islamic Law in Ottoman Syria and Palestine* (Berkeley: University of California Press, 1998); Madeline C. Zilfi, ed., *Women in the Ottoman Empire: Middle Eastern Women in the Early Modern Era* (Leiden: Brill, 1997); and Afaf Marsot, *Women and Men in Late Eighteenth Century Egypt* (Austin: University of Texas Press, 1995). See also the chapters in *Women, the Family, and Divorce Laws in Islamic History*, ed. Amira El-Azhary Sonbol (Syracuse: Syracuse University Press, 1996) by F. Zarinebaf-Shahr, Abdal-Rehim Abdal Rahman Abdal-Rehim, Iris Agmon, Nelly Hanna, Mary Ann Fay, Dina Rizk Khouri, Najwa al-Qattan, Amira El Azhoury Sonbol, Dalenda Largueche, and Madeline C. Zilfi.

18. Meriwether, *Kin Who Count*, 211.

19. Tucker, *In the House of the Law*, ch. 5.

20. Fariba Zarinebaf-Shahr, "Women and the Public Eye in Eighteenth-Century Istanbul," in *Women in the Medieval Islamic World*, ed. Gavin R. G. Hambly (New York: St. Martin's Press, 1998), 301–24; Leslie P. Peirce, *Morality Tales: Law and Gender in the Ottoman Court of Aintab* (Berkeley: University of California Press, 2003).

21. Judith E. Tucker, "Women in the Middle East and North Africa: The Nineteenth and Twentieth Centuries," in Guity Nashat and Judith E. Tucker, *Women in the Middle East and North Africa* (Bloomington: Indiana University Press, 1999), 80–81.

22. Billie Melman, *Women's Orients: English Women and the Middle East, 1718–1918: Sexuality, Religion and Work*, 2d ed. (Ann Arbor: University of Michigan Press, 1995), ch. 3. Melman covers the variability of English women's views and also their connection to the situation in England. Men's views were, overall, more negative and stereotyped.

23. Quoted in Nashat and Tucker, *Women in the Middle East and North Africa*, 72.

24. Among the critics of Said's classic *Orientalism* is Sadik Jalal al-'Azm, "Orientalism and Orientalism in Reverse," reprinted with other items in *Orientalism: A Reader*, ed. Alexander Lyon Macfie (New York: NYU Press, 2000), 217–38. I also have an unpublished conference paper, "Thoughts on the Twentieth Anniversary of Orientalism and the Rise of Postmodernism" (1998).

25. Judith E. Tucker, *Women in Nineteenth Century Egypt* (New York: Cambridge University Press, 1985); and in Nashat and Tucker, *Women in the Middle East and North Africa*, 76–77; Marsot, *Women and Men in Late Eighteenth Century Egypt*.

26. Personal correspondence with Donald Quataert; Donald Quataert, "Ottoman Women, Households, and Textile Manufacturing, 1800–1914," in *Women in Middle Eastern History: Shifting Boundaries in Sex and Gender*, ed. Nikki R. Keddie and Beth Baron (New Haven: Yale University Press, 1991), 161–76; Leonard M. Helfgott, *Ties That Bind: A Social History of the Iranian Carpet* (Washington, D.C.: Smithsonian Institution Press, 1994).

27. On the new burdens placed on women by job-holding and doing all the work in

nuclear households, see Sana al-Khayyat, *Honour and Shame: Women in Modern Iraq* (London: Saqi Books, 1990).

28. See the penetrating discussion in Ahmed, *Women and Gender in Islam*, ch. 8.

29. Beth Baron, *The Women's Awakening in Egypt: Culture, Society, and the Press* (New Haven: Yale University Press, 1994).

30. On the impact of colonialism, see especially Julia Clancy-Smith, *Rebel and Saint: Muslim Notables, Populist Protest, Colonial Encounters—Algeria and Tunisia, 1800–1904* (Berkeley: University of California Press, 1997), and Julia Clancy-Smith and Frances Gouda, eds., *Domesticating the Empire: Race, Gender, and Family Life in French and Dutch Colonialism* (Charlottesville: University Press of Virginia, 1998).

31. Janet Afary, *The Iranian Constitutional Revolution, 1906–1911: Grassroots Democracy, Social Democracy, and the Origins of Feminism;* Mangol Bayat-Philipp, "Women and Revolution in Iran, 1905–1911," in *Women in the Muslim World*, ed. Lois Beck and Nikki Keddie (Cambridge: Harvard University Press, 1978).

32. Baron, *The Women's Awakening;* Jasamin Rostam-Kolayi, "The Women's Press, Modern Education, and the State in Early Twentieth-Century Iran, 1900–1930s," Ph.D. diss., University of California, Los Angeles, 2000.

33. Ahmed, *Women and Gender in Islam*, 163–64. For a general discussion of the tendency of intellectuals in colonies first to accept, but increasingly to react against, Western ideas, see Nikki R. Keddie, "Western Views versus Western Values: Suggestions for a Comparative Study of Asian Intellectual History," *Diogenes* 26 (1957): 71–96.

34. Dalenda Largueche, "Confined, Battered, and Repudiated Women in Tunis since the Eighteenth Century," in *Women, the Family, and Divorce Laws in Islamic History*, ed. Amira El-Azhary Sonbol (Syracuse: Syracuse University Press, 1996), 259–89.

35. Alan Duben and Cem Behar, *Istanbul Households: Marriage, Family and Fertility, 1880–1940* (New York: Cambridge University Press, 1991).

36. Beth Baron, *Egypt as a Woman: Nationalist Gender and Politics* (Berkeley: University of California Press, 2005).

37. Lila Abu-Lughod, ed., *Remaking Women: Feminism and Modernity in the Middle East* (Princeton: Princeton University Press, 1998); Baron, *The Women's Awakening*.

38. Nadia Hijab, *Womanpower: The Arab Debate on Women at Work* (New York: Cambridge University Press, 1988); Jenny B. White, *Money Makes Us Relatives: Women's Labor in Urban Turkey* (Austin: University of Texas Press, 1994).

39. Parvin Paidar, *Women and the Political Process in Twentieth-Century Iran* (New York: Cambridge University Press, 1995), pt. 1; Eliz Sanasarian, *The Women's Rights Movement in Iran: Mutiny, Appeasement, and Repression from 1900 to Khomeini* (New York: Praeger Publishers, 1982).

40. The most comprehensive of the many works on modern Iranian women is Paidar, *Women and the Political Process;* see also Nikki R. Keddie, "Women in Iran since 1979," *Social Research* 67 (Summer 2000): 405–38 (issue on "Iran since the Revolution").

41. Charrad, *States and Women's Rights*.

42. Margot Badran, *Feminists, Islam, and Nation: Gender and the Making of Modern Egypt* (Princeton: Princeton University Press, 1995).

43. Cynthia Nelson, *Doria Shafik, Egyptian Feminist: A Woman Apart* (Gainesville: University Press of Florida, 1996).

44. Elizabeth Thompson, *Colonial Citizens: Republican Rights, Paternal Privilege, and Gender in French Syria and Lebanon* (New York: Columbia University Press, 2000).

45. Annelies Moors, *Women, Property and Islam: Palestinian Experiences, 1920–1990*

(New York: Cambridge University Press, 1995); Ellen L. Fleischmann, *The Nation and Its "New" Women: Feminism, Nationalism, Colonialism, and the Palestinian Women's Movement, 1920–1948* (Berkeley: University of California Press, 2002).

46. Charrad, *States and Women's Rights.*

47. Stephen Humphreys, *Between Memory and Desire: The Middle East in a Troubled Age* (Berkeley: University of California Press, 1999), ch. 10.

48. On women and the new religious politics, see the relevant chapters on the Muslim world by Valentine M. Moghadam and others in the *Journal of Women's History*'s special issue on "Women and Twentieth-Century Religious Politics: Beyond Fundamentalism," ed. Nikki R. Keddie and Jasamin Rostam-Kolayi, 10 (Winter 1999), and Keddie's article in it, "The New Religious Politics and Women Worldwide: A Comparative Study" (11–33).

49. Quotations from working women on these points are found especially in Maryam Poya, *Women, Work and Islamism: Ideology and Resistance in Iran* (London: Zed, 1999).

3

Women in Early and Modern Europe: A Transnational Approach

JUDITH P. ZINSSER AND BONNIE S. ANDERSON

Every European historian has taken a course entitled "Western Civ." Some of us did it twice, once in high school and once in college. Instructors told a story of men's actions and masculine achievements. When they taught the period from 1500 to the present they mentioned a few queens and social reformers, not to give a fuller picture of Western Europe's history but because these women's actions mirrored those of men and reflected what was valued as "achievement" in a man's world. Most women, however, disappeared, made invisible by supposedly gender-neutral, "apolitical" words and phrases like "the peasant's revolt" or "the rise of the middle classes."

Unfortunately, even in our more feminist-conscious world, none of the leading European history textbooks gives a more inclusive history of Europe's past. One of the best sellers integrates women in sections on "social history" but then omits most of their political, economic, intellectual, and spiritual contributions. Another details laws and customs that constrained and denigrated wives, mothers, and daughters but neglects what women actually did. Readers thus see women as victims rather than active agents.

Even when these textbooks describe exceptional heroines who succeeded in men's roles, misplaced humor perpetuates negative stereotypes about their lives and undermines respect for their accomplishments. One text has a glossy insert about "Catherine before She Was Great." Imagine an equivalent section on "Ivan before He Was Terrible." In short, standard textbooks in European history fail to integrate women. At best it is an "add women and don't stir" phenomenon. No Western civilization text presents the past with women and men acting together in all eras, regions, and contexts—political, economic, social, religious, and intellectual.[1]

New Questions

In the initial stages of planning *A History of Their Own: Women in Europe from Prehistory to the Present* we realized that the first obstacle to the formation of an inclusive picture of early modern and modern European history is the traditional chronological divisions of Western Europe's past.[2] Usual periods like Renaissance and Reformation or the Era of Revolution highlight transformations in men's lives and from men's perspectives.

Renaissance historian Joan Kelly first explained the loss of European women's experiences and the perpetuation of negative views of women's qualities and capabilities through the use of male-defined eras.[3] "There was no Renaissance for women, at least not during the Renaissance," she argued in 1984, because the criteria for inclusion in this historical epoch valued experiences and achievements only possible for men.

In the Renaissance, as in the Enlightenment and the Industrial Revolution, new groups of men acquired educations, became citizens, and participated in all aspects of these eras. The same opportunities existed for only a small percentage of elite women, and even they continued to feel the effects of women's disadvantaged status, which limited their roles and diminished their significance. Male-centered categories and criteria of achievement erased women's accomplishments because their successes did not match those of men. This disparity between women's very real contributions to the richness of Europe's past and their absence from the historical record led us and other historians of women to abandon traditional periodization and seek an organization and a set of categories and criteria that would reflect women's experiences and highlight the significance of their activities.

To bring women to the center of the narrative and present the history of Europe from their vantage points requires historians to be intellectual radicals. Only a radical examination of the premises underlying our construction of past realities explains the omission of women and the means to their inclusion. We developed new questions to guide our research and analysis. What had ordinary women done in the past? How had they lived? What tasks filled their days? What motivated their actions and determined their attitudes? What might explain the startling contrasts between women's and men's lives in the same eras? How had women come to be, in the phrasing of the United Nations Decade for Women Report of 1985, the "disadvantaged, invisible majority"? Why had laws, economic systems, religion, and politics excluded European women from the most valued areas and activities of life? How had cultural attitudes evolved to define women and qualities identified as "feminine" as innately inferior and subordinate all things female to men and all things male? Why had men created or acquiesced to this unequal system of social relationships?

We also asked whether there have been commonalities in European women's lives. What if anything linked a craftswoman selling her wares in sixteenth-century Nuremberg to a peasant raising her children in seventeenth-century Sicily to a university graduate contemplating a profession in late-nineteenth-century England? Perhaps most important, why had women accepted or been forced to accept limitations that devalued their activities, denigrated their nature, and subordinated them to men?

We were interested in the "exceptions"—women who achieved prominence in traditional male realms. Why did Queen Isabella of Castile, Christina of Sweden, Marie Curie, and Margaret Thatcher gain prominence? And what about women like Christine de Pizan, the fifteenth-century writer and courtier who first protested against women's disadvantaged and denigrated status? Why did some identify with other women and start to question all women's subordination? How and why did feminism begin, and where might it lead as it calls into question the basic values of European culture and society?

These questions can form the basis of a course in European women's history just as they provided the basis of our narrative in *A History of Their Own*. Ideally, such an approach makes women the center of study, presents early modern and modern history from women's perspectives, and chronicles their active agency in their cultures. In addition, this approach addresses questions raised by the theoretical works of Natalie Zemon Davis and Joan W. Scott, who both have argued persuasively for the significance of "gender" in analyses of history.[4]

Historians of gender explore how perceived sexual differences between women and men become culturally and politically significant.[5] By saying "perceived sexual differences," historians emphasize that European culture has exaggerated the significance of sexual difference. Women and men are more similar than different. Understanding the history of European women (and men), therefore, involves studying how terms like "female" and "male," "feminine" and "masculine" have been defined and manipulated to perpetuate attitudes, practices, and institutions that favor all things male and masculine. How have these meanings and differences been articulated and made part of institutional structures and strategies? How have gendered identities operated as forces within European societies?[6]

New Periodization

These questions lead to new ways of organizing historical narratives. The French multivolume history under the general editorship of Georges Duby and Michelle Perrot, *A History of Women in the West,* rejects traditional periodization and uses a topical approach reflecting women's various activities within European cultures. Olwen Hufton's *The Prospect before Her* divides early modern women's histories according to their relationships to men: daughter, wife, mother, mistress, widow. Merry E. Wiesner's survey *Women and Gender in Early Modern Europe* uses such perceptions of women as "Body," "Mind," and "Spirit" as organizing categories.[7]

In *A History of Their Own,* we turned to anthropology, with its emphasis on "place" and "function," for organizing concepts. We looked at women's "places" within geographic and institutional contexts and concentrated on the "functions" they performed there. Thus, we focused on specific categories of women. "Women of the Fields," for example, discussed Europe's peasant women, and "Women of the Churches" described those active in Europe's religious institutions.

These organizing principles place women at the center of a transnational European history narrative. Familiar historical events, significant in traditional accounts of the early modern and modern centuries, often appear more than once as different groups of women experience them. Industrialization, for example, affected women differently in different places, and so it appears in sections about elite women, peasant women, and the women of modern cities. In addition, as traditional historical periods and events recede in significance, others grow in importance. Factors often ignored in histories of men, whether contraception or clothing, diseases or the design of homes, prove crucial in women's lives.

Inherited Traditions and Continuities
in European Women's Lives

So much of European beliefs, history, art, and values comes from the matrix of the ancient world that to ignore this legacy distorts women's lives. Without exploration of some of the traditions that have been perpetuated in European cultures, both we and our students will remain confused about basic premises because we all have been influenced by distorting preconceptions about relations between women and men in the past.

Most people assume that conditions between men and women in the past were "separate but equal"—their lives, labor, costumes, and behavior might

differ but a traditional balance existed between the two. Early European societies, however, were warrior cultures in which the subordination of women
was well established, and that subordination was promulgated throughout the
ancient world, which institutionalized the system in its laws, art, religions, and
customs as well as in everyday attitudes and beliefs. The pantheon of Greek
and Roman gods, for example, contains powerful and important female deities: Aphrodite (Venus), Hera (Juno), Athena (Minerva), and Artemis (Diana). None, however, possessed the omnicompetence or dominion of the male
deities Zeus (Jupiter) or Apollo. Much ancient literature of Western culture,
whether Greek, Roman, Germanic, or Celtic, justifies misogyny—the hatred
and fear of women. While conditions worsened for women compared to men
in the early modern and much of the modern periods, women have been
subordinated to men in all but a few human cultures. Instances of relative
equality have been rare and usually have disappeared once agriculture was
established. To highlight connections between the ancient past and the
present, students can read classical texts of Europe's early history that influenced the early modern era, like the *Odyssey* of the Greeks, the *Tain Bo* of
the Irish Celts, Soranus' second-century *Gynecology*, or the late fifth century
Burgundian Code.[8]

In the ancient world, Hebrew women were considered to be exception-
ally well treated, and many positive traditions about women from Judaism have
been transmitted to European culture through the acceptance of sacred Jewish texts as the Old Testament of the Christian Bible. From the commandment
to "honor thy father and thy mother" to praise of the good wife in the Book
of Proverbs, Judaism established that virginal daughters, chaste wives, and busy
homemakers should be respected and praised. In addition, however, a number of core Jewish beliefs subordinated women to men. The conviction that
menstruation pollutes, the greater "uncleanliness" of birthing a daughter than
a son, and strictures that a woman's word stands only if a man does not con-
tradict her denigrated women and helped to establish a tradition of female
subordination.

Early Christianity empowered women. Jesus' relatively egalitarian treatment of the female sex as related in the four Gospels of the New Testament
provided an important positive legacy. Parables stressed women's equality
before God. In the first centuries after the death of Jesus, Christianity gave
women new roles as martyrs, proselytizers, deaconesses, holy ascetics, saints,
missionaries, and founders and leaders of religious communities.

As the Christian church established itself, however, negative beliefs about
women prevailed. Beginning in the fourth century, church fathers emphasized
female evil and inferiority, stigmatizing Eve as the source of "original sin."
Women were excluded from the priesthood, and God's injunction to Eve from

Genesis 3:16, that "your desire shall be for your husband and he shall rule over thee," was repeatedly cited to justify subordination of all women. A series of teachings by male religious authorities and papal decrees placed control of women's fertility and sexuality in the power of the church. The paradoxical figure of Mary, both Virgin and Mother, gave women a mixed message. Although she retained female spiritual power, as the subordinated wife and mother she also embodied the traditional ideals of obedience and sexual purity.[9] By the early modern and modern periods Christian churches had become important institutions perpetuating traditions of female subordination.

Historians of women have carefully researched the differences in women's lives based on geography, culture, and class. Despite obvious changes from one century to another and across these categories, however, change has not meant transformation. As medieval historian Judith Bennett argues, gendered patterns of dominance and subordination continue as a "patriarchal equilibrium" is reestablished in each new era.[10]

Until the last decades of the twentieth century all women were defined by their relationships to men. Within the male-dominated family, a woman is first identified as her father's daughter, then as her husband's wife or widow or her son's mother. The "family" protected by law and custom, the union of a woman and a man for the purpose of procreation, presumed the heterosexuality of both partners and prescribed their primary functions and roles. Even those women who lived more autonomous lives in female spiritual communities were defined by their rejection of earthly marriage and described as "brides of Christ."

Child rearing and household maintenance have been seen throughout Europe's history as preordained, biologically appropriate tasks for women. That is, they have been gendered. Whether women hired servants to do this work or performed it themselves, they have been judged on how they have fulfilled their roles as wives and mothers—far more than men have been judged as husbands and fathers.

Defining women's primary duties as care of the family and the home has never precluded other work. In all historical eras, the vast majority of European women have labored at other chores and assumed other responsibilities. They have done piecework in the home and earned wages in shops and textile mills to generate outside income. This "double burden" of caring for a family and home and earning additional income has characterized the lives of most European women, differentiated them from men, and made the continuance of their families possible.

In addition, "women's work," whether in the home or outside of it, has traditionally been valued less and considered less important than men's work. Raising children and maintaining the home have been taken for granted and not valued as much as labor performed by men, whatever it may be. Paid labor available to women has usually been less prestigious than men's, has traditionally required less formal training, and has been more vulnerable to fluctuations in the economy. As a result, when they have been paid for work, women have consistently received between one-half to two-thirds of what men earn. This set of economic factors has continuously limited women's options and opportunities.

Female subordination has been institutionalized in Europe, but times of change have tended to allow women to come to the fore and assume new roles, often those traditionally reserved for men. Throughout the reformations of the sixteenth and seventeenth centuries, during the revolutions of 1789, 1848, and 1917 and in the upheavals caused by the two world wars, women assumed new roles, from prophesying the downfall of kings to writing declarations of rights to flying fighter planes. Conversely, times of consolidation and institutionalization have reestablished male authority over female activities, glorified images of the dutiful wife and mother, and limited women's opportunities to achieve in any other roles. Associated with order, tradition, and orthodoxy, female subordination has seemed "natural," safe, and familiar. In all these ways, gender has shaped European women's lives throughout the centuries.

Early Modern European Women's History, 1500–1800

GOALS, QUESTIONS, AND EMPHASIS

From the early fifteenth century, opportunities offered by changes in circumstances for women during the Protestant and Catholic reformations, in the early phases of commercial capitalism, and in the elegant royal courts of Europe caused individuals and groups of women to act in new ways and achieve like their male contemporaries. Overall, however, their status in relation to men remained the same. For nuns, silk weavers, court musicians, or early feminists who had access to the new learning of the Renaissance and the scientific revolution, change did not mean transformation or signal the end of gendered dominance or subordination. Instead, a successive layering of justifications for women's subordination pushed all women into their accustomed place. New religious doctrines and institutions, new restrictive laws, new economic strictures, and new secular pronouncements, all made in the name of reason and science, stated old verities in new ways. By the beginning of the nineteenth century the denigration of women and of qualities identified as "feminine" had reached its nadir.[11]

WOMEN AND RELIGIONS

Christianity is responsible for some inherited traditions that have proven positive for women. Instructors can explore this heritage in a unit on women who chose the religious life or were active for their faith in the early modern period. As in the medieval era, mysticism—an appeal to direct revelation from God—offered women authority even against the institutionalized male hierarchy of the Catholic Church. The transcript of the trial of Benedetta Carlini given in *Immodest Acts: The Life of a Lesbian Nun in Renaissance Italy* and St. Teresa of Avila's *Book of Her Life* offer rich portrayals of visionary women.[12] Both sources illustrate the constraints for women within the established church, the opportunities for autonomy within the convent, and the special status of the visionary, which challenged the power of the male hierarchy, especially the priest's exclusive right to act as confessor. *Immodest Acts* also invites discussion of historical and contemporary attitudes toward women's sexuality.

The Protestant and Catholic reformations of the sixteenth and seventeenth centuries presented European women of all classes with a range of roles and opportunities similar to those enjoyed in the first century after the death of Jesus.[13] Queens, princesses, and noblewomen used their resources as landholders to advance and protect Christian sects they favored. Townswomen tore down the "idols" of the old faith and went to the stake as martyrs. Women of different classes preached, prophesied, and helped administer their congregations. Catholics like St. Angela Merici founded new orders that acted in the world rather than behind the cloistered walls of the nunnery. The Ursulines taught, the Sisters of Charity nursed the sick.[14] The more radical Protestant sects asserted the spiritual equality of all believers, whether female or male. Some, such as Quaker leader Margaret Fell, argued for the end of women's subordination in all aspects of life.[15] Fell was second only to George Fox as a leader of their new sect.

By the end of the seventeenth century, however, even the Quakers had succumbed to ancient traditions that gave women separate tasks within the faith and made them second to men. In the Catholic Church and in Protestant sects, clerics and communities of believers gradually reestablished or created new institutional structures giving paramount authority to men. Sermons, prayer books, and doctrinal pronouncements reaffirmed woman's inferior status and limited her activities to traditionally appropriate roles—the wife and mother, obedient companion, and pious helpmate in the male-headed household.

The widespread accusations of witchcraft against European women, particularly women peasants, coincided with this retrenchment. For almost 250 years, from Spain to Russia, Sweden to Sicily to the British Isles, learned and privileged men of all Christian sects accused women of heretical devil worship. Between the late fifteenth and the end of the seventeenth century at least a hundred thousand European women died in the persecutions.[16] Villagers identified the witches, usually old women without families, who readily admitted their power to do good or harm. Sometimes voluntarily, more often under torture, they answered yes to questions about heretical practices and worship of the devil.

There is now a vast literature on the prosecutions for witchcraft. *Servants of Satan: The Age of the Witch Hunts* by Joseph Klaits gives a clear and authoritative analysis of the complexities of this gendered crusade. For a sense of the vastness of the persecutions see *Early Modern European Witchcraft: Centres and Peripheries,* a collection of essays edited by Bengt Ankarloo and Gustav Henningsen. For the procedures and the way it might have felt for a peasant woman, see the questions compiled and then published for prosecutors in the early-seventeenth-century demonology prepared by Henri Boguet, judge for the Archbishopric of Saint-Claude, after he had rooted out the heresy in Burgundy.[17]

TOWNSWOMEN

Since the 1920s historians have argued about the lives of women in the expanding economy of Europe's walled towns. Did crafts- and merchantwomen enjoy a "golden age" of opportunity and authority that they lost with the establishment of mercantile capitalism and the decline of the guilds? No, according to recent feminist histories of Italian, German, French, and English townswomen's lives.[18] Overall economic change did not transform the basic relationship of the female subordinate to the male.[19] Instead, the cultural attitudes coincident with the expanding economic world of the sixteenth through the eighteenth centuries painted ever more horrible images of the woman outside of male authority. The Renaissance humanism of the universities and urban courts posited yet more learned explanations of and justifications for the inferiority of women, who were presumed to be emotional creatures incapable of restraint without the guiding hand of male reason.[20]

Guild regulations from the thirteenth and fourteenth centuries that had guaranteed women access to certain crafts were swept away in the attacks on those protecting craftsmen. Others allowing women to inherit guild privileges from their husbands or fathers disappeared in the increasing competition. Changes in the production of cloth and foodstuffs kept women at the least-skilled levels. The constants of women's labor continued: They held the jobs that required the least training, gained little prestige, received the lowest pay, and were the most vulnerable to fluctuations in the local economy. On women's crafts and occupations during this period see two collections, *Women and*

Work in Pre-Industrial Europe, edited by Barbara A. Hanawalt, and *European Women and Preindustrial Craft,* edited by Daryl M. Hafter. Much new scholarship on prostitution, although not specifically on these centuries, also describes the occupation of last resort for early modern Europe's townswomen.[21]

The advent of commercial capitalism offered opportunities. *The Memoirs of Glückel of Hameln,* written by a Jewish townswoman living at the end of the seventeenth century, is the first known memoir by a European woman.[22] It tells not only of women's household responsibilities but also of Glückel's success as a trader, both before and after her husband's death. The letters of fifteenth-century Florentine Alessandra Strozzi, another successful businesswoman, show how she also guarded her own and her husband's fortune despite deaths and the exile of male family members.[23]

These two women's lives demonstrate, however, that whatever authority they exercised in the new economic circumstances of their day, it had no permanent effect on female status or roles. Successful in business themselves, they made no effort to educate their daughters to a similar life, and they gave over the wealth they accumulated to a new husband or to eldest sons. These women maneuvered within society's constraints without challenging them. Significantly, the culture of towns in the early modern period produced some of the most virulent misogyny in Europe's history.[24] Popular tales like those collected by Boccaccio for his Decameron mocked and denigrated women of all classes and categories. Vain, spendthrift wives, screaming hags, insatiable young seductresses, and lying adulteresses populate tales, sermons, and popular broadsides. Portrayals of the ideal woman went to the other extreme. "Poor Griselda," the perfect, long-suffering, obedient wife, appeared just as frequently in popular stories.

WOMEN OF THE ROYAL COURTS

Like the women entrepreneurs of the towns from the early fifteenth through the eighteenth centuries, women in the courts of Burgundy, the Renaissance Italian city-states, and the royal courts of Europe's dynastic monarchs exercised political authority and assumed men's roles. They acted as regents for their husbands and sons or reigned as monarchs in their own name. Biographies now exist for most of the principal women rulers of the early modern era. There are studies of how noblewomen exercised direct and indirect authority and how they advanced their families through court activities and the networks they maintained.[25] Their letters, memoirs, and political testaments are being translated and published.

In this privileged world, all women functioned as members of families. Parents negotiated marriages to accumulate property and consolidate power. A royal or noble woman acquired this power on behalf of men or in the absence of male heirs. To ensure peace and the continuation of their privileges, families allowed the "unnatural" rule by a woman. Often, as in the cases of Elizabeth I of England, Christina of Sweden, and Maria Theresa of Austria, the alternative appeared to be civil war. Women rulers carefully crafted a public image and followed strategies that reconciled the contradictions between their sex and the role they had assumed.[26] None made a case for women's equal abilities, passed laws, or established institutions to foster long-term change. Instead, each governed as an exception, the extraordinary wife, mother, or daughter. With their deaths, power returned to its "rightful" place—into the hands of royal and noble men.

From the fifteenth to the eighteenth centuries, the courts offered women opportunities other than those of courtier and reigning sovereign. Italian courtesans like Venetian Veronica Franco entertained elite men in their salons and wrote and published their own poetry and music.[27] In the seventeenth century, Louis XIV of France institutionalized the role of favored royal mistress. In the middle of the eighteenth century, the *maîtresse en titre,* Mme. de Pompadour, became one of King Louis XV's principal advisers. The great courts of Europe employed women trained to play the organ and piano, sing and dance in operas, and paint royal and noble portraits. A number of collections and surveys describe the activities of women composers, including Mozart's sister.[28] Sources for the life of a major women painter of these centuries, Marie-Louise-Elizabeth Vigée-Lebrun, have been translated and published.

Europe's courts also produced the first professional women writers. Christine de Pizan dedicated *The Treasures of the City of Ladies* to Marguerite of Burgundy. In return she received money and gifts to sustain her household. The first French novel, the Comtesse de La Fayette's *Princess of Clèves,* presents the attitude toward love and marriage in the seventeenth century and suggests continuities in Western culture.[29]

LEARNED WOMEN AND THE BEGINNINGS OF FEMINISM

Women who acquired a "man's" education in these centuries created the first written records of women's opposition to subordination and denigration. From Christine de Pizan in the early fifteenth century to María de Zayas in seventeenth-century Spain, learned women spoke out against the constraints and attitudes that denied their intelligence and capacities. Male scholars engaged in this *querelle des femmes* (debate over women), arguing on both sides. Many examples of these women's writings have now been published in English. Katharina M. Wilson and Frank J. Warnke's *Women Writers of the Seventeenth Century* has selections from all over Europe.[30] Most often, these early feminists argued for women's capacities but not for changes in their central roles within the family. Thus, they inadvertently promoted what we now call the "double burden"—the woman functioning as wife and mother first, outside the family second. Even the angriest of the early advocates, like Mary Wollstonecraft in *A Vindication of the Rights of Woman* (1792), justified education because of the ways it would better prepare a young woman for her primary responsibilities within marriage.[31]

PEASANT WOMEN AND THE PERSISTENCE OF TRADITIONS

The lives of the overwhelming majority of Europe's women (up to 95 percent into the 1780s), the peasants, throw all women's strengths and vulnerabilities into high relief. The realities of life in the countryside in a preindustrial world were harsh. Major catastrophes occurred about every twenty-five years. Into the eighteenth century, armies took livestock, grain, and vegetables and left death, mutilation, and devastation. Half of the children did not live to twenty; little girls died at a higher rate than little boys.

Europe's peasant women coped however they could, despite impossible circumstances and choices. They married later and restricted births in times of hardship; they worked for wages; they bartered or sold produce grown in their household gardens; they cooked the family's meals and made the family's clothes; and they sewed the shrouds and said the prayers for the family dead. The roles and images of women in familiar folktales suggest the realities of peasant women's lives and the values they passed to subsequent generations. "The True Bride" appears in many variations and tells of a young woman, rather than a young man, who must perform tasks in order to win her beloved.

Since the early 1990s historians of Russia's peasantry have discovered many valuable sources for the study of these women.[32] In the early twentieth century, Olga Semyonova Tian-Shanskaia, a daughter of the landowning elite, described the subsistence conditions under which peasant women lived, the customary violence from men, the rituals and festivals that punctuated their year.[33] Tian-Shanskaia's account emphasized the continuities in peasant women's lives across time and across ethnic and political boundaries. She also documented what anthropologists call "strategies of resistance," the subtle ways in which peasant women countered male hegemony by indirect and passive means.[34]

Modern European Women's History, 1700 to the Present

GOALS, STRUCTURE, AND INTRODUCTION

Distinguishing among the roles and functions of three very different groups of women—privileged women, poor urban women, and feminists—aids in presenting the modern period from a female perspective. Privileged women came from the middle and upper classes but rarely controlled their family's wealth or power. Often active primarily in the domestic spaces of the salon and parlor, they negotiated their families' social connections, devoted themselves to the care of their children and homes, and created paths that led out of the parlor and into the public world.

Poor urban women constitute the second general category of women studied. The lives of working-class women who moved to the cities differed so greatly from those of peasant women that they constitute separate experiences, even though the same woman may have lived first in the countryside and later in the city. The lives of poor urban and privileged women became more similar in the twentieth century, so their lives can then be considered together. The third category, feminists, come from all social classes and all periods since the Renaissance but are united by their minority beliefs. They rejected traditions justifying women's subordination as natural, God-given, and universal and worked to enable all women to claim more opportunities and rights, including changes in every aspect of life.[35]

The vast majority of Europe's women and men lived as peasants until the twentieth century, and the transformations of women's lives in the modern era cannot be understood without this context. Ann Cornelisen's *Women of the Shadows* provides an excellent portrait of this change by detailing the lives of women in a southern Italian village in the 1960s.[36] Anne Barstow's *Witchcraze: A New History of the European Witch Hunts* gives a vivid account of the impact of the witchcraft persecutions on women's lives both at the time and thereafter. In addition, before the events of the modern era are dealt with, it is important to establish some of the continuities in European women's lives—the inherited traditions that influenced European cultural attitudes about women into the present (pages 114–17).

PRIVILEGED WOMEN OF THE EIGHTEENTH AND NINETEENTH CENTURIES

Much recent historical literature has been devoted to the lives of relatively privileged women. The stigmatization of female political power on all social levels took place during "the age of democratic revolutions" in the late eighteenth and early nineteenth centuries.[37] Beginning in 1793, when the revolutionary French government outlawed any political participation by women, including attending clubs and petitioning parliament, women's political power diminished just as men's was expanding. Intensified by the promulgation of the Code Napoleon, which officially made the man the head of the family and classified women as legally incompetent, along with children, criminals, and the insane, this era reduced women's options and rights in favor of domesticity. Faced with a newly defined concept of modernity that sought to cleanse political life by eliminating "female influence," activist women generally re-treated from both the public arena and the salon and prescribed domesticity for all who could afford it.[38]

Instructors can present the establishment of bourgeois hegemony—"the rise of the middle class"—from the female perspective. Income generated from commercial and early industrial capitalism enabled increasing numbers of families to hire a "maid-of-all-work." For men, the dividing line between middle and working class was usually measured by income; for women, it lay in the difference between being a servant and being able to employ one. As an employer, a woman, however lowly, became a "mistress." Domestic life changed as households ceased manufacturing food, clothing, and other items, severing the traditional connection between production and the home. As in the past, women were expected to advance their family's fortune by making advantageous marital and social alliances. Now, in addition, they were to im-prove their family's status by devoting themselves to mothering, by altering the family's behavior and acquiring new possessions to signify a rise in social status. This process has been vividly drawn in Leonore Davidoff and Cathe-rine Hall's *Family Fortunes: Men and Women of the English Middle Class, 1780–1850,* Marion Kaplan's *The Making of the Jewish Middle Class: Women, Family, and Identity in Imperial Germany,* and Bonnie G. Smith's *Ladies of the Leisure Class: The Bourgeoises of Northern France in the Nineteenth Century.*[39]

The traditional double standard of sexual morality, in which women are condemned for behavior allowed or praised in men, intensified in this era—one Scotswoman wrote that she had been shocked at eighty by literature that she had enjoyed hearing read aloud as a young woman in polite London so-ciety of the 1760s.[40] In northern Europe especially, women of the privileged classes were supposed to be "above" sexuality. Sexual innocence and chastity had become important markers of social status. Some women always contest-ed this ideal, however. Writers and artists such as George Sand and Elizabeth Barrett Browning criticized the stigma attached to unwed mothers and pros-titutes. In addition, some daughters of the privileged classes began to demand more scope and opportunity in their lives. Women entered public life first in philanthropic and charitable works and then in traditionally female fields like teaching and nursing. A great deal of literature has been devoted to the con-struction of the new domestic feminine ideal and its expansion or repudia-tion by privileged women in the later years of the nineteenth century.[41]

POOR URBAN WOMEN OF THE EIGHTEENTH
AND NINETEENTH CENTURIES

Scholars have paid increasing attention to the effects of both urbanization and industrialization on women in Europe.[42] The movement of people from the countryside into growing European metropolises dramatically transformed their experience. Urban squalor challenged the former peasant women who moved to cities. From women's perspective, the well-studied "population explosion" of the early nineteenth century assumes a wholly new significance, becoming a litany of heroic feats of poor mothers to raise larger numbers of children under adverse conditions. This was also an era when illegitimacy rates increased. With no village community pressing for marriage, more young women found themselves pregnant and alone as their male partners disappeared to a neighboring town or refused to accept responsibility for the child. Works that dramatically portray women's struggles in these new conditions include Rachel G. Fuchs's *Poor and Pregnant in Paris: Strategies for Survival in the Nineteenth Century* and Ellen Ross's *Love and Toil: Motherhood in Outcast London, 1870–1918*.[43]

Industrialization, so important in structuring men's lives in this era, had less effect on women than urbanization. Several scholars demonstrate the perpetuation of patterns of female subordination into the modern industrial era despite significant economic, social, and political changes in European men's circumstances and rights: Anna Clark in *The Struggle for the Breeches: Gender and the Making of the British Working Class*, Laura Lee Downs in *Manufacturing Inequality: Gender Division in the French and British Metalworking Industries, 1914–1919*, and Barbara Franzoi in *At the Very Least She Pays the Rent: Women and German Industrialization, 1871–1914*.[44]

As more men went to work in factories, women took their places as household servants. Domestic service traditionally employed as many men as women, but by the twentieth century such work had become more than 90 percent female. Unmarried women often sought factory jobs if they lived in industrial areas, but married women and women with children did piecework in the home, a field that also expanded tremendously as industry grew. Traditionally ill-paid and resistant to collective bargaining, piecework never provided enough income to live on. Well into the twentieth century, governments regulated industries employing large numbers of women but refused to interfere with women's domestic production. To male legislators, work in the home, however exploitative and dangerous, seemed "natural" for women.

Increasing numbers of poor urban women worked as prostitutes. The growth and regulation of prostitution in the nineteenth century has been the subject of a number of studies, among them Laurie Bernstein's *Sonia's Daughters: Prostitutes and Their Regulation in Imperial Russia*, Alain Corbin's *Women for Hire: Prostitution and Sexuality in France after 1850*, and Judith Walkowitz's *Prostitution and Victorian Society: Women, Class, and the State*.[45] Government registration, forced police and medical inspections, and confinement to locked "prison-hospitals" if symptoms of venereal disease were found transformed what had often been a temporary occupation into a permanent and denigrating way of life.

Urban women's experiences can illuminate new aspects of revolutions and reforms. Initially active in the opening phases of the revolutions of 1789, 1848, and 1870, women as a group were soon excluded from any participation in political life by male revolutionaries. Gay L. Gullickson's *Unruly Women of Paris: Images of the Commune,* Sara E. Melzer and Leslie W. Rabine's *Rebel Daughters: Women and the French Revolution,* and Marilyn Yalom's *Blood Sisters: The French Revolution in Women's Memory* explore the stigmatization of female revolutionaries.[46]

Maternity benefits and "protective" labor legislation for women have also have been the subject of a number of recent historical studies. Throughout Europe pro-natalist male legislators, eager to raise the birth rate and thus increase their nation's population, enacted maternity legislation. Protective labor legislation, often protested by the very women it sought to aid, barred women from all work at night, from mining, and from any kind of labor deemed too dangerous for women to perform. Studies such as *Maternity and Gender Politics: Women and the Rise of the European Welfare State, 1880s to 1950* and *Mothers of a New World: Maternalist Politics and the Origins of the Welfare States* explore the origins and ideologies of welfare states.[47] Improvements in poor urban women's lives by the first quarter of the twentieth century came not from such legislation but from the eradication of infectious diseases, the rising standard of living, and a subsequent decline in infant mortality and family size.

THE TWENTIETH CENTURY

By 1900 the demographic and economic factors that separated women in past eras diminished. Family size decreased at all social levels, and job opportunities widened for all women. In the twentieth century, women's lives differed most dramatically because of the national and political system under which they lived rather than their economic status within that culture. Three different political systems provide examples of these differences: the Western democracies, the Soviet Union, and Nazi Germany.

Women's experiences in World War I have been closely studied, especially in Britain. Driving ambulances and streetcars, working in munitions factories and in offices, women on all social levels proved their ability to perform labor they had been educated to believe was beyond them. The granting of voting rights to women in Northern Europe after World War I attests to governments' recognition of women's abilities and to the realization that the female vote would not upset traditional politics. Nonetheless, the end of the war saw a return to tradition in most European nations. Women were removed from the work force as quickly as they had been added to it as Britain, France, and Germany passed laws that rewarded motherhood and forced women to retire when they married.[48]

The exception to this pattern of development was the Union of Soviet Socialist Republics, where the Russian Revolution of 1917 instituted a new ideal of behavior and new opportunities for women. Active in the bread riots and demonstrations that forced the czar's abdication in February 1917, Russian women petitioned for their own organizations and for the vote. The new communist government instituted programs designed to foster female equality: intensive education for girls, abortion rights, divorce, and the right to labor. Although gains were certainly made, especially in state provision of childcare and education, they were limited by Soviet women's coerced participation in a labor force shaped for male workers. The strictures of a single-party political system, compounded by Stalin's seizure of virtually all power, further limited Soviet lives throughout the 1930s and 1940s. Stalin's 1930 elimination of all separate women's organizations and his subsequent outlawing of abortion and severe curtailing of the right to divorce especially affected women. Nonetheless, the Communist Party line continually proclaimed that female equality had been achieved and tolerated no opposition to that perspective. Two anthologies exploring these topics are *Women and Society in Russia and the Soviet Union* edited by Linda Edmondson and *Russia's Women: Accommodation, Resistance, Transformation* edited by Barbara Evans Clements, Barbara Alpern Engel, and Christine D. Worobec.[49]

In Western Europe, the assumption that women achieved equality by gaining the right to vote after World War I did not prevent the resurgence of many repressive traditions during the interwar years.[50] Achieving the illusion of freedom by adopting the new styles of the era—short hair, short skirts, and cosmetics—women were treated increasingly unequally as economic depression affected European societies, beginning with Britain in the early 1920s. Fired first, denied unemployment benefits, and criticized for "taking jobs from men," women found a reassertion of patriarchal values not only in government policies but also in intellectual life. The new "science" of psychology continued to universalize male experience, seeing women as "incomplete men" whose "penis envy" prevented their full development to adulthood. Although individual European women benefitted from psychological analysis, the restatement of traditional attitudes subordinating women limited such gains for them as well as for all women in Western societies.

FASCISM AND WORLD WAR II

Conditions worsened as fascist governments came to power in the 1930s. Often wrongly blamed for the rise of Hitler in Germany, women in fascist societies lost civil rights as new policies restricting their lives were implemented in Italy, Spain, and Portugal as well as Germany. Studies include Victoria De Grazia's *How Fascism Ruled Women, Italy, 1922–1945,* Marion Kaplan's *From Dignity to Despair: Jewish Life in Nazi Germany,* and Alison Owings's *Frauen: German Women Recall the Third Reich.*[51] Fascist ideology required domesticity for all women, and women were removed from the universities as well as the labor force (at least until the exigencies caused by World War II). Current scholarship focuses on whether women of preferred racial groups were victimized by or complicit with fascist regimes; on whether women and men responded differently as racial discrimination became state policy; and on how women developed strategies for surviving war, occupation, and genocide.

World War II was a "total war" in Europe—one that engaged civilian populations as well as military professionals. It shaped female experience from 1939 to 1945. As in World War I, women took men's places in factories and offices, and women of all classes played an active part as war engulfed the European continent. Recent work on Jews and Christians in Germany and the rest of Europe has sought to distinguish between female and male experience during the years of genocide. Dealing with the imposition of racial policy in everyday life, German Jewish women often wished to emigrate early but frequently were dissuaded by men convinced that normal conditions would return. When families sent members to safety, however, men were usually chosen first. Within slave labor and death camps, women tended to survive by forming artificial families that sustained them by sharing food, cleaning their living quarters, and providing comfort and support.

After the war, nations attempted to restore "normal" life, defined in this era—as in the 1920s—as encouraging women to resume their traditional roles of wife, mother, and housekeeper. A rise in the birth rates, reinforced by state payments and the reintegration of men into the labor force, returned many women in Western Europe to domesticity, regardless of their preferences. In the East, the greater disruption of the war plus the imposition of Soviet-style communism in eastern Germany, Poland, Czechoslovakia, Bulgaria, and Rumania, led to a different pattern. Expected to be part of the labor force, women in the Eastern bloc found themselves juggling the burdens of work, child care, and household maintenance because state services rarely provided sufficient support. In the few pieces of critical fiction published in these years, women complain of the tyranny of the clock—of the pressures caused by having too much to do over the course of a day.

FEMINISM

Those who developed a feminist perspective, ideology, and politics since the fifteenth century have been so exceptional in European culture that they are best understood as constituting a separate category within women's history.

Reacting against the patriarchal traditions handed down from antiquity, European feminists from as early as the fifteenth century created a dissenting literature. They argued that women were as fully human as men and thus entitled to "justice"—to relatively equal treatment in education, family life, and marriage. With the democratic revolutions of the late eighteenth century, feminists throughout the Western community claimed equal political rights. The clash between these demands and the new politics of the nineteenth century, which excluded women completely, has been the subject of recent scholarship.

Barbara Taylor, in *Eve and the New Jerusalem: Socialism and Feminism in the Nineteenth Century,* and Clare Goldberg Moses and Leslie Wahl Rabine, in *Feminism, Socialism, and French Romanticism,* explore the radical feminism that developed in the early Owenite and Saint-Simonian socialist movements.[52] First with the support of the men in these groups, later often in opposition to these "brothers" who sought to limit their activities, feminists organized early women's movements within their own societies and internationally. Flourishing between the 1830s and the 1850s, they expanded their demands on behalf of women, articulating new issues such as the connection of prostitution to the lack of jobs for women and the necessity of public care for children, the sick, and the elderly. In the repression that followed the failure of the revolutions of 1848, many feminists went to prison, and all were silenced.

Early feminists claimed a great deal more for women than the suffrage and equal rights societies that coalesced in the 1870s and 1880s. These largely bourgeois women's movements focused on the vote and succeeded in Northern, Protestant Europe after World War I and in Southern, Catholic Europe after World War II. Having accomplished their goal, and believing there was no further need for special advocacy for women, these groups had virtually disappeared by the 1950s.

European socialist women developed a parallel but separate women's movement within their national parties. Socialist parties became legal by the late nineteenth century and ruled their nations in the twentieth. Demanding not only the vote but also education, job opportunities, and sexual freedom, socialist feminists succeeded in placing women's issues on the agenda as a major goal to be accomplished after the revolution. They achieved the same kind of nominal equality as in the Western democracies. Told, however, that they had been given all that was necessary to make them equal to men, and discouraged from any independent political action after World War II, these socialist and communist women ceased to press for further feminist demands.

In the early 1970s the women's liberation movement in Europe made a tremendous impact. Inspired by the development of the feminist movement of the 1960s in the United States, European women's movements often outdid the Americans in resistance to patriarchal institutions and the magnitude of their claims for women's rights. Rapidly overturning traditional bans on contraception, abortion, and divorce, feminists in nations from Spain to West Germany organized politically in the 1970s and 1980s and raised new issues such as violence against women, female sexual slavery, and the commodification of women's reproductive capacity as "surrogate mothers."

Women in formerly communist states have lost the privileges afforded them by communist governments, from legalized abortion to female parliamentary quotas. They also lost jobs disproportionately and currently constitute 60 percent of Europe's unemployed. In the West, the weakening of the welfare state and the increasing feminization of poverty have eroded women's gains. Still, by every measure from education level to life expectancy, Europe's women lead the world. Many of those achievements are the results of feminism.

Globalizing European Women's History, 1500 to the Present

From 1500 to the present, European women have been part of global networks of trade, communication, migration, and hegemony. Like European men, they have been instrumental in such worldwide phenomena as the formation of nation states, the development of international economic systems, colonialism, and decolonization. Researchers have examined women's experiences both in their analyses of global networks and comparative studies of societies and economic systems. This section draws on this research and offers approaches and resources for placing European women's history into transnational and comparative frameworks.

Globalizing the narrative of European women's history can be done in a variety of ways. We recommend three basic approaches. The most ambitious is to take a familiar unit of men's European history and recast it in the context of "global phenomena." Study, for example, women's participation in the history of the nation-state or the interdependent world economy of the past five centuries. A second way to give an international or global dimension is to explore an era or topic comparatively, across cultures. Numerous histories of prostitution in different parts of the world exist and can be used for comparisons by era or by topic.

Finally, some historical phenomena are transnational by definition: the "European diaspora" is the most obvious. This movement of Europe's women and men to all parts of the world offers many resources for study of women's perspectives and activities in a global context. Since the sixteenth century,

European women have described their lives in foreign ports and in new settlements. They have written as merchant wives, as conquerors, as travelers, and as willing or enslaved labor migrants. Any one of these primary sources, or the innovative analytical studies of these European women's encounters with new environments and the people of other empires and nations, gives a global dimension to their experiences and to the traditional narrative of European history.

GLOBAL PHENOMENA FROM WOMEN'S PERSPECTIVES: NATION-STATES, INTERNATIONAL REFORM MOVEMENTS, AND ECONOMIC SYSTEMS

Women have been active in creating and sustaining national and international political systems, the activism that flowed across nation-states, and economic structures. These phenomena, in turn, have been premised on gendered ideologies.

The significance of gender in nation-state formation has a rich bibliography, written by women's historians and political scientists. *Women and Politics: An International Perspective* by Vicky Randall and *Women and the State: International Perspectives* edited by Shirin M. Rai and Geraldine Lievesley are useful introductions to the complexities of women's place in political life.[53] Ida Blom's 1995 review essay, "Feminism and Nationalism in the Early Twentieth Century: A Cross-Cultural Perspective," explores not only women's contributions in politics and the direct impact of feminism on the nation-state but also the ways in which gender played a role in the theoretical and legal definition of the nation and its citizens. *Feminism and Nationalism in the Third World* by Kumari Jayawardena offers useful information for comparison.[54]

Some feminist scholars have used the absence of women in the traditional history of international relations as a starting point for investigating whether the field of international politics has been founded on—and helped perpetuate—normative ideas about gender. Amy Swerdlow's 1995 review essay "Engendering International Relations Theory: The Feminist Standpoint" describes how underlying premises exclude women altogether from studies of international politics.[55]

International reform organizations, many of them created by women since the nineteenth century, also provide established historical topics that can give a global gender dimension. From the early antislavery societies to the Women's Christian Temperance Union and the international woman suffrage societies, this activism and reform has been charted in a number of studies, such as Moira Ferguson's *Subject to Others: British Women Writers and Colonial Slavery, 1670–1834* and Kathryn Kish Sklar, Susan Strasser, and Anja Schueler's *Social Justice Feminists in the United States and Germany: A Dialogue in Documents, 1880–1933.*[56] For books describing the creation and work of new women's advocacy organizations in the nineteenth and twentieth centuries, see Bonnie S. Anderson's *Joyous Greetings: The First International Women's Movement* and Leila J. Rupp's *Worlds of Women: The Making of an International Women's Movement.* Further, Carol Riegelman Lubin and Anne Winslow have studied women in the International Labor Organization; Winslow also edited *Women, Politics, and the United Nations.* Building on their activism during the United Nations Decade for Women (1975–85), European women have formed cross-national alliances to define and protect women's human rights, especially against all forms of violence specifically directed at women. See the collections *Human Rights of Women* edited by Rebecca Cook and *Women's Rights, Human Rights: International Feminist Perspectives* edited by Julie Peters and Andrea Volper.[57]

No single work currently allows charting women's participation in regional and global economies from the sixteenth to the nineteenth centuries, but a number place European women's economic experiences in the twentieth century into a worldwide context. Marianne H. Marchand and Jane L. Papart's *Feminism/Postmodernism/Development* explores the problems of gender inherent in the language of "development" and emphasizes the international and national divisions among women that complicate efforts to collaborate on economic issues. Two studies that analyze women's economic experiences in selected countries of Europe, Africa, Asia, and Latin America are Hilda Kahne and Janet Z. Giele, *Women's Work and Women's Lives: The Continuing Struggle Worldwide* and Nahid Aslanbigui, Steven Pressman, and Gale Summerfeld's *Women in the Age of Economic Transformation: Gender Impact of Reforms in Post-Socialist and Developing Countries.*[58]

COMPARATIVE TOPICS IN WOMEN'S HISTORY

Although few works of synthesis exist comparing women's experiences across oceans and continents in the early modern period, monographs on two topics exist and can be used to explore transnational attitudes about women and sexuality: the witchcraft heresy and prostitution. Carol F. Karlsen has a short section on the European persecutions in her study of Salem, Massachusetts, *The Devil in the Shape of a Woman,* and Vern L. Bullough and Lilli Sentz have edited the international *Prostitution: A Guide to Sources, 1960–1990.*[59] Comparative political topics have been covered in review articles and essay collections, which suggest useful resources and models of analytical approaches. Jeffrey N. Wasserstrom's "Gender and Revolution in Europe and Asia, Part 2: Recent Works and Frameworks for Comparative Analysis," compares women's participation in political revolutions, and *Women and Sovereignty* edited by Louis Olga Fradenberg comparatively assesses women rulers across the centuries.[60]

In contrast, many comparative studies exist for the modern period of European women's history. Some of the most innovative histories of women and gender in the nineteenth and twentieth centuries have focused on social welfare and labor legislation in Europe and North America. Two useful review essays explore this phenomenon: Renate Howe, "Gender and the Welfare State: Comparative Perspectives," and Seth Koven, "The Ambivalence of Agency: Women, Families, and Social Policy in France, Britain, and the United States." Koven has also edited a collection with Sonya Michel, *Mothers of a New World: Maternalist Politics and the Origins of Welfare*. A useful comparative examination of women and labor legislation is *Protecting Women: Labor Legislation in Europe, the United States, and Australia, 1880–1920*, edited by Ulla Wikander, Alice Kessler-Harris, and Jane Lewis. In the last quarter of the twentieth century, so-called protection of women justified increasing government involvement in regulating women's sexuality. Faye D. Ginsburg and Rayna Rapp have edited an excellent collection of comparative articles on this subject, *Conceiving the New World Order: The Global Politics of Reproduction*.[61]

Historians, political scientists, and women's studies scholars have written about feminism cross-culturally. To gain a sense of the field as it began, see the first publication of the International Federation of Research in Women's History, *Writing Women's History: International Perspectives*. For this 1991 volume, feminist historians from different parts of the world provided personal or bibliographical essays on the state of women's history and the feminist movements in their regions. For case studies reaching back to the nineteenth century, see *Suffrage and Beyond: International Feminist Perspectives* edited by Caroline Daley and Melanie Nolan.[62] Feminist cooperative efforts have highlighted different priorities and strategies. On these differences, see the very inclusive *Challenge of Local Feminisms: Women's Movements in Global Perspective* edited by Amrita Basu and the more provocative *Reorienting Western Feminisms: Women's Diversity in a Postcolonial World* by Chilla Bulbeck. Robin Morgan's anthology *Sisterhood Is Global: The International Women's Movement Anthology* chronicles similarities and differences around the world just before the 1985 United Nations International Women's Conference in Nairobi.[63]

CROSS-CULTURAL PHENOMENA: EXPANSION, DIASPORA, IMPERIALISM

European women have participated in all phases of Europe's encounters with other cultures as travelers and settlers and as agents of colonialism and reform. Exploring European women's experiences outside Europe illuminates new facets of such familiar phenomena as the European conquest of the Americas, the growth of European economic and political strength from the seventeenth to the nineteenth centuries, and immigration to North America in the modern era. Published primary sources, including travel literature and personal narratives, can supplement the secondary literature with vivid descriptions of both Europeans and the women and men they encountered abroad.

A great deal of research focuses on women's roles in the conquest and exploration of North America. Some work emphasizes women and the Luso-Hispanic diaspora. One early example is the now-classic *Women in Iberian Expansion Overseas, 1415–1815: Some Facts, Fancies, and Personalities* by the Brazilian scholar C. R. Boxer. More recent studies include Juan Francisco Maura's *Women in the Conquest of the Americas* (newly translated and published in English) and a collection of sources, *Untold Sisters: Hispanic Nuns in Their Own Words, Sixteenth-Eighteenth Centuries* edited by Electa Arenal and Stacey Schlau.[64] These are noteworthy recent additions to scholarship highlighting the early history of European women in the colonization of North America. In *Between Worlds: Interpreters, Guides, and Survivors,* Frances Karttunen tells of women intermediaries between indigenous cultures and early settlers. Karen Anderson describes the treatment of both Native American and European women in *Chain Her by One Foot: The Subjugation of Women in Seventeenth-Century New France.* Natalie Zemon Davis includes the study of Marie de l'Incarnation and the activities of the Ursulines in colonial Quebec in *Women on the Margins: Three Seventeenth-Century Lives.*[65]

The significance of women and gender in European imperialism has received attention from historians and literary scholars. Women travelers, particularly from the British Isles, left fascinating accounts of their adventures in sub-Saharan Africa and West Asia. Peter Hulme's review essay "Out of England: Women, Travel and Empire" provides examples, and Sara Mills's *Discourses of Difference: An Analysis of Women's Travel Writing and Colonialism* explores differences between European women's and men's responses to new cultures. Although most scholarship on missionaries describes work sponsored by religious groups from the United States, two books investigate Europe's Catholic and Protestant missionary women. JoAnn McNamara's *Sisters in Arms: Catholic Nuns through Two Millennia* describes the activities of European nursing and teaching orders in many parts of the world during the twentieth century. *Women and Missions Past and Present: Anthropological and Historical Perceptions,* a collection edited by Fiona Bowie, Debora Kirkwood, and Shirley Ardener, explores mission schools.[66]

The Women's Studies International Forum has produced two issues on European women's direct involvement in Europe's imperial ventures and with gender and imperialism: "Women, Imperialism and Identity" in 1998 and a

1990 collection published as *Western Women and Imperialism: Complicity and Resistance*. Two review essays provide more recent titles dealing with gender and European women in imperialism: "Beyond Complicity versus Resistance: Recent Work on Gender and European Imperialism" by Malia B. Formes and "Orientalism's Other, Other Orientalisms: Women in the Scheme of Empire" by Thomas J. Prasch.[67]

A great deal of research has focused on British women in India. Two studies that explore the interplay between European women's feminism and imperialism are Vron Ware's *Beyond the Pale: Women, Racism, and History* and Antoinette Burton's *Burdens of History: British Feminists, Indian Women, and Imperial Culture: 1865–1915*. In *The White Woman's Other Burden: Western Women in South Asia during British Colonial Rule*, Kumari Jayawardena provides life histories of women from Europe and the United States determined to "liberate" their South Asian counterparts. Other colonial enterprises are described in Billie Melman, *Women's Orients: English Women and the Middle East, 1718–1918* and the excellent collection edited by Julia Clancy-Smith and Frances Gouda, *Domesticating the Empire: Race, Gender, and Family Life in French and Dutch Colonialism*.[68]

European women and men have emigrated, establishing families on new continents and raising children who would identify themselves less with their parents' homeland than with the cultures and languages of their new country. Because of differing employment opportunities and family responsibilities, women have experienced migration differently from men. For a general perspective on European migration, both within Europe and to other parts of the world in the early modern and modern periods, see *European Migrants: Global and Local Perspectives* edited by Dirk Hoerder and Leslie Page Moch. U.S. immigration historians have written extensively about women's experiences and have included sections about life in the "old world" in their studies. Three examples are Donna Gabaccia, *From the Other Side: Women, Gender, and Immigrant Life in the U.S., 1820–1990;* Christiane Harzig et al., editors, *Peasant Maids, City Women, From the European Countryside to Urban America;* and Bruce Stave, John F. Sutherland, and Aldo Salerno, editors, *From the Old Country: An Oral History of the European Migration to America*. Eva Hoffman's *Lost in Translation: A Life in a New Language* provides a personal account of immigration from Poland to Canada and the process of adjusting to a new culture and new languages.[69]

Migration patterns are influenced by structures of regional and global economies and inequalities. To demonstrate how these international relationships, along with the decolonization movements of the 1960s, have changed Europe's own population and created new racial, ethnic, religious, economic, social, and political tensions, the voices and experiences of women from

Africa and Asia who have lived in Europe need to be included. For example, Jane Kramer's *Unsettling Europe* describes a Ugandan–South Asian family in England and a Euro-Algerian family in France in the 1970s. See also two West African novels, Emecheta's *Second Class Citizen* about a Nigerian woman in England and Ama Ata Aidoo's *Our Sister Killjoy; or, Reflections from a Black-Eyed Squint*, which concerns a Ghanaian in Germany.[70]

For the field of European women's history in the early modern and modern eras, review articles, case studies and primary source collections, memoirs, novels, poetry, and short story anthologies appear in ever greater numbers each year. Having identified new frameworks, analytical approaches, and possible topics, they can be used to create new narratives of women's experiences within the European context or across traditional boundaries and barriers, whether geographical, cultural, or historiographical.

Notes

1. For examples of current textbooks see Lynn Hunt, Theodore R. Martin, Barbara H. Rosenwein, R. Po-Chia Hsia, and Bonnie G. Smith, *The Challenge of the West: Peoples and Cultures from the Stone Age to the Global Age* (Lexington: D. C. Heath, 1995); Donald Kagan, Steven Ozment, and Frank M. Turner, *The Western Heritage*, 7th ed. (Upper Saddle River: Prentice-Hall, 2001); Mark Kishlansky, Patrick Geary, and Patricia O'Brien, *Civilization in the West*, 5th ed. (New York: Longman, 2003); and Jackson J. Spielvogel, *Western Civilization*, 5th ed. (Belmont, Calif.: Wadsworth/Thomson Publishing, 2003).

2. Judith P. Zinsser and Bonnie S. Anderson, *A History of Their Own: Women in Europe from Prehistory to the Present*, 2d ed. (New York: Oxford University Press, 2000).

3. For Joan Kelly's original formulation see "Did Women Have a Renaissance?" in *Women, History and Theory: The Essays of Joan Kelly* (Chicago: University of Chicago Press, 1984), 19–50. For a more recent discussion see Amanda Vickery, "Golden Age to Separate Spheres? A Review of the Categories and Chronology of Women's History," *Historical Journal* 36 (1993): 383–414.

4. Natalie Zemon Davis, "Women's History in Transition: The European Case," *Feminist Studies* 3, nos. 3–4 (1976): 83–103; Joan W. Scott, "Gender: A Useful Category of Historical Analysis," in *Gender and the Politics of History* (New York: Columbia University Press, 1988), 28–50. See also Joan Kelly, "The Social Relations of the Sexes: Methodological Implications of Women's History" and "The Doubled Vision of Feminist Theory" in *Women, History and Theory: The Essays of Joan Kelly* (Chicago: University of Chicago Press, 1984), 1–18. These and other key articles are in *Gender and History in Western Europe*, ed. Robert Shoemaker and Mary Vincent (New York: Oxford University Press, 1999).

5. Ava Baron, "Gender and Labor History: Learning from the Past, Looking to the Future," in *Work Engendered: Toward a New History of American Labor*, ed. Ava Baron (Ithaca: Cornell University Press, 1991), 21, 26, 31–32.

6. Sarah Hanley, "The Monarchic State in Early Modern France: Marital Regime Politics and Male Right, 1500–1800," in *Politics, Ideology, and the Law in Early Modern*

Europe, ed. Adrianna E. Bakos (Rochester: University of Rochester Press, 1994), 107–26; Joan W. Scott, "The Woman Worker," in *Emerging Feminism from Revolution to World War*, ed. Geneviève Fraisse and Michelle Perrot, vol. 4 of *A History of Women in the West*, ed. Georges Duby and Michelle Perrot (Cambridge: Harvard University Press, 1993), 399–426; Sylvia Schafer, "When the Child Is the Father of the Man: Work, Sexual Difference and the Guardian-State in Third Republic France," *History and Theory* 31 (1992): 98–115; Ann-Louise Shapiro, ed., *Feminists Revision History* (New Brunswick: Rutgers University Press, 1994).

7. Georges Duby and Michelle Perrot, eds., *A History of Women in the West* (Cambridge: Harvard University Press, 1993); Olwen Hufton, *The Prospect before Her: A History of Women in Western Europe, 1500–1800* (New York: Alfred A. Knopf, 1996); Merry E. Wiesner, *Women and Gender in Early Modern Europe* (New York: Cambridge University Press, 1993).

8. Consider also Njal's *Saga* (Icelandic) and Ovid's *Art of Love* (first century B.C.E.). All of these cited works have good English translations and have been published in paperback.

9. Marina Warner, *Alone of All Her Sex: The Myth and Cult of the Virgin Mary* (New York: Pocket Books, 1978).

10. Judith M. Bennett, "Theoretical Issues: Confronting Continuity," *Journal of Women's History* 9 (Autumn 1997): 73–94. In the same issue, see also Gerda Lerner on continuities in women's history (114–18).

11. Narrative surveys of this period include Wiesner, *Women and Gender in Early Modern Europe*, and Hufton, *The Prospect before Her*. A valuable collection of articles appears in Natalie Zemon Davis, ed., *Renaissance and Enlightenment Paradoxes*, vol. 3 of *A History of Women in the West*, ed. Georges Duby and Michelle Perrot (Cambridge: Harvard University Press, 1994). For more specific studies see Margaret L. King, *Women of the Renaissance* (Chicago: University of Chicago Press, 1991); Wendy Gibson, *Women in Seventeenth-Century France* (Basingstoke, U.K.: Macmillan, 1989); and Heide Wunder, *He Is the Sun, She Is the Moon: Women in Early Modern Germany*, trans. Thomas Dunlap (Cambridge: Harvard University Press, 1998). For sources see *Women Writers of the Renaissance and Reformation*, ed. Katharina M. Wilson (Athens: University of Georgia Press, 1986). The course description that follows uses the argument and structure of Anderson and Zinsser's *A History of Their Own*. See the sections entitled "Women of the Fields," "Women of the Churches," "Women of the Walled Towns" in volume 1 and "Women of the Courts" in volume 2.

12. Judith C. Brown, ed., *Immodest Acts: The Life of a Lesbian Nun in Renaissance Italy* (New York: Oxford University Press, 1986); St. Teresa of Avila, *The Collected Works*, vol. 1, trans. Kieran Kavanaugh and Otilio Rodriquez (Washington, D.C.: Institute of Carmelite Studies, 1976).

13. Sherrin Marshall, ed., *Women in Reformation and Counter-Reformation Europe: Public and Private Worlds* (Bloomington: Indiana University Press, 1989). For more specific studies see Lyndal Roper, *The Holy Household: Women and Morals in Reformation Augsburg* (New York: Oxford University Press, 1991), and *Profiles of Anabaptist Women: Sixteenth-Century Reforming Pioneers*, ed. C. Arnold Snyder and Linda A. Huebert Hecht (Waterloo, Ont.: Wilfrid Laurier University Press, 1996).

14. The Paulist Press publishes the correspondence of Francis de Sales with Jane Chantal and of Vincent de Paul with Louise de Marillac, the foundresses of two new orders in France.

15. The full text is available from the Pembroke Writers Project of Brown University or in *First Feminists: British Women Writers, 1578–1799,* ed. Moira Ferguson (Bloomington: University of Indiana Press, 1985). See also *The Examinations of Anne Askew: The English Martyr,* ed. Elaine V. Beilin (New York: Oxford University Press, 1996).

16. For estimates see Anne Llewellyn Barstow, *Witchcraze: A New History of the European Witch Hunts* (San Francisco: Pandora Press, 1994), Appendix B, 179–81. On the extent of scholarship, see the review essay by Elsbeth Whitney, "The Witch 'She'/ the Historian 'He': Gender and the Historiography of the European Witch-Hunts," *Journal of Women's History* 7, no. 3 (1995–96): 77–101; the Web site at http://www.psmedia.com/witchcraft.htm; and the six-volume series of articles edited by Bengt Ankarloo and Stuart Clark in *Witchcraft and Magic in Europe: The Eighteenth and Nineteenth Centuries* (Philadelphia: University of Pennsylvania Press, 1999).

17. Joseph Klaits, *Servants of Satan: The Age of the Witch Hunts* (Bloomington: Indiana University Press, 1987); Bengt Ankarloo and Gustav Henningsen, eds., *Early Modern European Witchcraft: Centres and Peripheries* (New York: Oxford University Press, 1993); Henri Boguet, *An Examen of Witches* [Discours des sorciers], trans. E. Allen Ashwin and ed. Montague Summers (Great Britain: John Rodker, 1929), 211–38. For a study of the demonologies see Stuart Clark, *Thinking with Demons: The Idea of Witchcraft in Early Modern Europe* (New York: Oxford University Press, 1997).

18. Alice Clark, *Working Life of Women in the Seventeenth Century,* with an introduction by Amy Louise Erickson (1919, repr. New York: Routledge, 1992). For works countering Clark's thesis see Judith M. Bennett, *Ale, Beer, and Brewsters in England: Women's Work in a Changing World, 1300–1600* (New York: Oxford University Press, 1996); Judith C. Brown and Jordan Goodman, "Women and Industry in Florence," *Journal of Economic History* 40 (March 1980): 73–80; and Martha C. Howell, *Women, Production, and Patriarchy in Late Medieval Cities* (Chicago: University of Chicago Press, 1986).

19. Two occupations illustrate this phenomenon, one traditionally assigned to women and the other, a new craft. In the early modern period midwives, like other traditional female healers, saw their knowledge ridiculed, their practice limited, and their access to new information and training restricted or forbidden. See *The Art of Midwifery: Early Modern Midwives in Europe,* ed. Hilary Marland (New York: Routledge, 1993). Initially, Renaissance artists worked out of guilds and workshops, which allowed some women to excel before new constraints evolved. Mary D. Garrard, *Artemisia Gentileschi* (Princeton: Princeton University Press, 1989); James A. Welu, ed., *Judith Leyster: A Dutch Master and Her World* (New Haven: Yale University Press, 1993).

20. For learned men's views and women's responses see Ian Maclean, *The Renaissance Notion of Woman: A Study of the Fortunes of Scholasticism and Medical Science in European Intellectual Life* (New York: Cambridge University Press, 1980), and *Her Immaculate Hand: Selected Works by and about the Women Humanists of Quattrocento Italy,* ed. Margaret L. King and Albert Rabil Jr. (Binghamton: Center for Medieval and Early Renaissance Studies, SUNY at Binghamton, 1981).

21. Barbara A. Hanawalt, ed., *Women and Work in Pre-Industrial Europe* (Bloomington: Indiana University Press, 1986); Daryl M. Hafter, ed., *European Women and Preindustrial Craft* (Bloomington: Indiana University Press, 1995). See also Ruth Mazo Karras, *Common Women: Prostitution and Sex in Medieval England* (New York: Oxford University Press, 1996), and, on France, Leah Lydia Otis, *Prostitution in Medieval Society* (Chicago: University of Chicago Press, 1985).

22. Natalie Zemon Davis has written a study of Glückel's life and memoirs in *Women on the Margins: Three Seventeenth-Century Lives* (Cambridge: Harvard University Press,

1995). Marvin Lowenthal's translation is available in paperback from Schocken Books. For context see *Jewish Women in Historical Perspective*, ed. Judith R. Baskin (Detroit: Wayne State University Press, 1991).

23. Heather Gregory, trans., *Selected Letters of Alessandra Strozzi* (Berkeley: University of California Press, 1997).

24. Norris J. Lacy, "Fabliau Women," *Romance Notes* 25 (Spring 1985): 318–27; Joan Young Gregg, *Devils, Women, and Jews: Reflections of the Other in Medieval Sermon Stories* (Albany: SUNY Press, 1997).

25. See, for example, Barbara J. Harris, "Marriage and Politics in Early Tudor England," *Historical Journal* 33 (1990): 259–81, and Sharon Kettering, "The Household Service of Early Modern French Noblewomen," *French Historical Studies* 21, no. 1 (1997): 55–85.

26. See, for example, Susan Frye, *Elizabeth I: The Competition for Representation* (New York: Oxford University Press, 1993), and Carole Levin *The Heart and Stomach of a King: Elizabeth I and the Politics of Sex and Power* (Philadelphia: University of Pennsylvania Press, 1994).

27. Lynne Lawner, *Lives of the Courtesans: Portraits of the Renaissance* (New York: Rizzoli, 1981).

28. Jane Bowers and Judith Tick, eds., *Women Making Music: The Western Art Tradition, 1150–1950* (Urbana: University of Illinois Press, 1986).

29. Christine de Pizan, *The Treasure of the City of Ladies or the Book of Three Virtues*, trans. Sarah Lawson. (New York: Penguin Books, 1985); John D. Lyons, ed. and trans., *The Princess of Clèves: Contemporary Reactions, Criticism / Marie-Madeleine de Lafayette* (New York: W. W. Norton, 1994).

30. Katharina M. Wilson and Frank J. Warnke, *Women Writers of the Seventeenth Century* (Athens: University of Georgia Press, 1989). For analysis of these and other early feminists see Erica Harth, *Cartesian Women: Versions and Subversions of Rational Discourse in the Old Regime* (Ithaca: Cornell University Press, 1996), and *Women Writers and the Early Modern British Political Tradition*, ed. Hilda L. Smith (New York: Cambridge University Press, 1998).

31. Many editions exist. The Cambridge Texts in the History of Political Thought groups it with her *Vindication of the Rights of Men*, ed. Sylvana Tomaselli (New York: Cambridge University Press, 1995).

32. Barbara Evans Clements, Barbara Alpern Engel, and Christine D. Worobec, eds., *Russia's Women: Accommodation, Resistance, Transformation* (Berkeley: University of California Press, 1991); Beatrice Farnsworth and Lynne Viola, eds., *Russian Peasant Women* (New York: Oxford University Press, 1992).

33. Olga Semyonova Tian-Shanskaia, *Village Life in Late Tsarist Russia*, ed. David L. Ransel (Bloomington: Indiana University Press, 1993).

34. James C. Scott, *Domination and the Arts of Resistance: Hidden Transcripts* (New Haven: Yale University Press, 1990). For a historical study of women's roles in popular disturbances see Cynthia A. Bouton, *The Flour War: Gender, Class, and the Community in Late Ancient Regime French Society* (University Park: Pennsylvania State University Press, 1993).

35. This course's structure parallels that used in Anderson and Zinsser, *A History of Their Own*, vol. 2. On the need to separate women into categories, see Denise Riley, *"Am I That Name?" Feminism and the Category of "Women" in History* (Minneapolis: University of Minnesota Press, 1988).

36. Ann Cornelisen, *Women of the Shadows*, 2d ed. (South Royalton, Vt.: Steerforth Press, 2001).

37. Lieselotte Steinbrügge, *The Moral Sex: Woman's Nature in the French Enlightenment*, trans. Pamela E. Selwyn (New York: Oxford University Press, 1995); Geneviève Fraisse, *Reason's Muse: Sexual Difference and the Birth of Democracy*, trans. Jane Marie Todd (Chicago: University of Chicago, 1994); Joan Landes, *Women and the Public Sphere in the Age of the French Revolution* (Ithaca: Cornell University Press, 1988).

38. Catherine Hall, *White, Male and Middle-Class: Explorations in Feminism and History* (New York: Routledge, 1992).

39. Leonore Davidoff and Catherine Hall, *Family Fortunes: Men and Women of the English Middle Class, 1780–1850* (Chicago: University of Chicago Press, 1987); Marion Kaplan, *The Making of the Jewish Middle Class: Women, Family, and Identity in Imperial Germany* (New York: Oxford University Press, 1991); Bonnie G. Smith, *Ladies of the Leisure Class: The Bourgeoises of Northern France in the Nineteenth Century* (Princeton: Princeton University Press, 1981). See also Barbara Corrado Pope, "Angels in the Devil's Workshop: Leisured and Charitable Women in Nineteenth-Century England and France," in *Becoming Visible: Women in European History*, ed. Renate Bridenthal and Claudia Koonz (Boston: Houghton Mifflin, 1977), 296–324.

40. Cited in Maurice J. Quinlan, *Victorian Prelude: A History of English Manners, 1700–1830* (New York: Columbia University Press, 1941), 1.

41. Some recent examples include Jo Burr Margadant, *Madame le Professeur: Women's Educations in the Third Republic* (Princeton: Princeton University Press, 1990); M. Jeanne Peterson, *Family, Love, and Work in the Lives of Victorian Gentlewomen* (Bloomington: University of Indiana Press, 1989); Mary Poovey, *Uneven Developments: The Ideological Work of Gender in Mid-Victorian England* (Chicago: University of Chicago Press, 1988); and Anne T. Quartararo, *Women Teachers and Popular Education in Nineteenth-Century France: Social Values and Corporate Identity at the Normal School Institution* (Newark: University of Delaware Press, 1995).

42. See, for example, Barbara Engel, *Between the Field and the City: Women, Work and Family in Russia, 1861–1914* (New York: Cambridge University Press, 1994), and Deborah Valenze, *The First Industrial Woman* (New York: Oxford University Press, 1995).

43. Rachel G. Fuchs, *Poor and Pregnant in Paris: Strategies for Survival in the Nineteenth Century* (New Brunswick: Rutgers University Press, 1992); Ellen Ross, *Love and Toil: Motherhood in Outcast London, 1870–1918* (New York: Oxford University Press, 1993).

44. Anna Clark, *The Struggle for the Breeches: Gender and the Making of the British Working Class* (Berkeley: University of California Press, 1995); Laura Lee Downs, *Manufacturing Inequality: Gender Division in the French and British Metalworking Industries, 1914–1919* (Ithaca: Cornell University Press, 1995); Barbara Franzoi, *At the Very Least She Pays the Rent: Women and German Industrialization, 1871–1914* (Westport: Greenwood Press, 1985).

45. Laurie Bernstein, *Sonia's Daughters: Prostitutes and Their Regulation in Imperial Russia* (Berkeley: University of California Press, 1995); Alain Corbin, *Women for Hire: Prostitution and Sexuality in France after 1850*, trans. Alan Sheridan (Cambridge: Harvard University Press, 1990); Judith Walkowitz, *Prostitution and Victorian Society: Women, Class, and the State* (New York: Cambridge University Press, 1980).

46. Gay L. Gullickson, *Unruly Women of Paris: Images of the Commune* (Ithaca: Cornell University Press, 1996); Sara E. Melzer and Leslie W. Rabine, eds., *Rebel Daughters: Women and the French Revolution* (New York: Oxford University Press, 1992); Marilyn Yalom, *Blood Sisters: The French Revolution in Women's Memory* (New York: Basic Books, 1993).

47. Gisela Bock and Pat Thane, eds., *Maternity and Gender Politics: Women and the Rise*

of the European Welfare State, 1880s to 1950 (London: Routledge, 1991); Seth Koven and Sonya Michel, eds., *Mothers of a New World: Maternalist Politics and the Origins of the Welfare States* (New York: Routledge, 1993).

48. For British women's wartime experiences see Gail Braybon and Penny Summerfield, *Out of the Cage: Women's Experiences in Two World Wars* (London: Routledge, 1987). For France see Mary Louise Roberts, *Civilization without Sexes: Reconstructing Gender in Postwar France, 1917–1927* (Chicago: University of Chicago Press, 1994). For a more transnational dimension, see *Lines of Fire: Women Writers of World War I*, ed. Margaret R. Higonnet (New York: Penguin, 1999).

49. Linda Edmondson, ed., *Women and Society in Russia and the Soviet Union* (New York: Cambridge University Press, 1992); Clements, Engel, and Worobec, eds., *Russia's Women*.

50. Martha A. Ackelsberg, *Free Women of Spain: Anarchism and the Struggle for Emancipation of Women* (Bloomington: Indiana University Press, 1991).

51. Victoria De Grazia, *How Fascism Ruled Women, Italy, 1922–1945* (Berkeley: University of California Press, 1992); Marion Kaplan, *From Dignity to Despair: Jewish Life in Nazi Germany* (New York: Oxford University Press, 1998); Alison Owings, *Frauen: German Women Recall the Third Reich* (New Brunswick: Rutgers University Press, 1993).

52. Barbara Taylor, *Eve and the New Jerusalem: Socialism and Feminism in the Nineteenth Century* (New York: Pantheon, 1983); Clare Goldberg Moses and Leslie Wahl Rabine, *Feminism, Socialism, and French Romanticism* (Bloomington: Indiana University Press, 1993). For a survey of the subject, see Karen Offen, *European Feminisms, 1700–1950* (Stanford: Stanford University Press, 2000).

53. Vicky Randall, *Women and Politics: An International Perspective* (Chicago: University of Chicago Press, 1987); Shirin M. Rai and Geraldine Lievesley, eds., *Women and the State: International Perspectives* (Bristol: Taylor and Frances, 1996); Alida Brill, ed., *A Rising Public Voice: Women in Politics Worldwide* (New York: Feminist Press, 1995).

54. Ida Blom, "Feminism and Nationalism in the Early Twentieth Century: A Cross-Cultural Perspective," *Journal of Women's History* 7 (Winter 1995): 82–94, published in the useful collection *Gendered Nations: Nationalism and Gender Order in the Long Nineteenth Century*, edited by Ida Blom, Karen Hagemann, and Catherine Hall (New York: Berg, 2000); Kumari Jayawardena, *Feminism and Nationalism in the Third World* (London: Zed Press, 1986); see also the series of articles on these issues in *Gender and History* 5 (Summer 1993).

55. Amy Swerdlow, "Engendering International Relations Theory: The Feminist Standpoint," *Journal of Women's History* 7 (Summer 1995): 160–63. For interesting comparisons, see also *Images of Women in Peace and War: Cross-Cultural and Historical Perspectives*, edited by Sharon MacDonald, Pat Holden, and Shirley Ardener (Madison: University of Wisconsin Press, 1987).

56. Moira Ferguson, *Subject to Others: British Women Writers and Colonial Slavery, 1670–1834* (New York: Routledge, 1992); Kathryn Kish Sklar, Susan Strasser, and Anja Schueler, eds., *Social Justice Feminists in the United States and Germany: A Dialogue in Documents, 1880–1933* (Ithaca: Cornell University Press, 1998); also see Ian Tyrell, *Woman's World, Woman's Empire: The Woman's Christian Temperance Union in International Perspective, 1880–1930* (Chapel Hill: University of North Carolina Press, 1991).

57. Bonnie S. Anderson, *Joyous Greetings: The First International Women's Movement, 1830–1860* (New York: Oxford University Press, 2000); Leila J. Rupp, *Worlds of Women: The Making of an International Women's Movement* (Princeton: Princeton University

Press, 1997); Carol Riegelman Lubin and Anne Winslow, *Social Justice for Women: The International Labor Organization and Women* (Durham: Duke University Press, 1990); Anne Winslow, ed., *Women, Politics and the United Nations* (Westport: Greenwood Press, 1995); Rebecca Cook, ed., *Human Rights of Women* (Philadelphia: University of Pennsylvania Press, 1994); Julie Peters and Andrea Wolper, eds., *Women's Rights, Human Rights: International Feminist Perspectives* (New York: Routledge, 1995). The complexities of the last decade are highlighted in *Gender Politics in Global Governance*, ed. Mary K. Meyer and Elisabeth Priigl (New York: Rowman and Littlefield, 1999). For an overview, see Deborah Stienstra, *Women's Movements and International Organizations* (New York: St. Martin's Press, 1994).

58. Marianne H. Marchand and Jane L. Papart, *Feminism/Postmodernism/Development* (New York: Routledge, 1995); Hilda Kahne and Janet Z. Giele, *Women's Work and Women's Lives: The Continuing Struggle Worldwide* (Boulder: Westview Press, 1992); Nahid Aslanbigui, Steven Pressman, and Gale Summerfeld, *Women in the Age of Economic Transformation: Gender Impact of Reforms in Postsocialist and Developing Countries* (London: Routledge, 1994). See also Patricia A. Roos, *Gender and Work: A Comparative Analysis of Industrial Societies* (Albany: SUNY Press, 1985) and Temma Kaplan, "The Disappearing Fathers under Global Capitalism," *Radical History Review* 71 (Spring 1998): 84–90. For statistics, see *The World's Women 2000: Trends and Statistics* (New York: United Nations, 2000).

59. Carol F. Karlsen, *The Devil in the Shape of a Woman: Witchcraft in Colonial New England* (New York: W. W. Norton, 1987). For a recent survey, see Robert W. Thurston, *Witch, Wicce, Mother Goose: The Rise and Fall of the Witch Hunts in Europe and North America* (New York: Longman, 2001); and Vern Bullough and Lili Sentz, eds., *Prostitution: A Guide to Sources, 1960–1990* (New York: Garland Publishing, 1992).

60. Jeffrey N. Wasserstrom, "Gender and Revolution in Europe and Asia, Part 2: Recent Works and Frameworks for Comparative Analysis," *Journal of Women's History* 6 (Spring 1994): 109–20; Louise Olga Fradenberg, ed., *Women and Sovereignty* (New York: Columbia University Press, 1993).

61. Renate Howe, "Gender and the Welfare State: Comparative Perspectives," *Gender and History* 8 (1996): 138–42; Seth Koven, "The Ambivalence of Agency: Women, Families, and Social Policy in France, Britain, and the United States," *Journal of Women's History* 9, no. 1 (1997): 164–73; Seth Koven and Sonya Michel, *Mothers of a New World: Maternalist Politics and the Origins of Welfare States* (New York: Routledge, 1993); Ulla Wikander, Alice Kessler-Harris, and Jane Lewis, eds., *Protecting Women: Labor Legislation in Europe, the United States, and Australia, 1880–1920* (Urbana: University of Illinois Press, 1995); Fay D. Ginsburg and Rayna Rapp, eds., *Conceiving the New World Order: The Global Politics of Reproduction* (Berkeley: University of California Press, 1995).

62. Karen Offen, Ruth Roach Pierson, and Jane Rendall, eds., *Writing Women's History: International Perspectives* (Bloomington: Indiana University Press, 1991); Caroline Daley and Melanie Nolan, eds., *Suffrage and Beyond: International Feminist Perspectives* (New York: New York University Press, 1994). For case studies from the nineteenth century to the late twentieth century, see *Women's Rights and Human Rights: International Historical Perspectives*, ed. Patricia Grimshaw, Katie Holmes, and Marilyn Lake (New York: Palgrave, 2001).

63. Amrita Basu, ed., *The Challenge of Local Feminisms: Women's Movements in Global Perspective* (Boulder: Westview Press, 1995); Chilla Bulbeck, *Reorienting Western Feminisms: Women's Diversity in a Postcolonial World* (New York: Cambridge University Press, 1998);

and Robin Morgan, ed., *Sisterhood Is Global: The International Women's Movement Anthology* (Garden City: Anchor Books, 1984). Mala Mathrani, "East-West Encounters and the Making of Feminists," *Journal of Women's History* 9 (Autumn 1997): 215–26, and Angela R. Miles, *Integrative Feminisms: Building Global Visions, 1960s-1990s* (New York: Routledge, 1996) also explore the evolution of new, less "Western" feminisms.

64. C. R. Boxer, *Women in Iberian Expansion Overseas, 1415–1815: Some Facts, Fancies and Personalities* (New York: Oxford University Press, 1975); Juan Francisco Maura, *Women in the Conquest of the Americas* (New York: P. Lang, 1997); Electa Arenal and Stacey Schlau, eds., *Untold Sisters: Hispanic Nuns in Their Own Words, Sixteenth–Eighteenth Centuries* (Albuquerque: University of New Mexico Press, 1989). Muriel Nazzari has written about Brazilian women during this early period. See, for example, "Relations between the Sexes in Spain and Its Empire," *Journal of Women's History* 4 (Spring 1992): 142–47.

65. Frances Karttunen, *Between Worlds: Interpreters, Guides, and Survivors* (New Brunswick: Rutgers University Press, 1994); Karen Anderson, *Chain Her by One Foot: The Subjugation of Women in Seventeenth-Century New France* (New York: Routledge, 1991); Natalie Zemon Davis, *Women on the Margins: Three Seventeenth-Century Lives* (Cambridge: Harvard University Press, 1995). For a more general collection of essays, see *"To Make America": European Emigration in the Early Modern Period*, ed. Ida Altman and James Horn (Berkeley: University of California Press, 1991). A number of Quaker women came to the British Atlantic and Caribbean colonies as preachers or became ministers in their new communities. Christine Levenduski has studied Elizabeth Ashbridge's eighteenth-century autobiography *Peculiar Power: A Quaker Woman Preacher in Eighteenth-Century America* (Washington: Smithsonian Institution Press, 1996).

66. Peter Hulme, "Out of England: Women, Travel and Empire," *Gender and History* 5 (Summer 1993): 284–89; Sara Mills, *Discourses of Difference: An Analysis of Women's Travel Writing and Colonialism* (New York: Routledge, 1991); JoAnn McNamara, *Sisters in Arms: Catholic Nuns through Two Millennia* (Cambridge: Harvard University Press, 1996); Fiona Bowie, Deborah Kirkwood, and Shirley Ardener, eds., *Women and Missions Past and Present: Anthropological and Historical Perceptions* (Providence: Berg, 1993).

67. "Women, Imperialism and Identity," *Women's Studies International Forum* 21 (May–June 1998); Nupur Chaudhuri and Margaret Strobel, eds., *Western Women and Imperialism: Complicity and Resistance* (Bloomington: Indiana University Press, 1992); Malia B. Formes, "Beyond Complicity versus Resistance: Recent Work on Gender and European Imperialism," *Journal of Social History* 28 (1994–95): 629–41; Thomas J. Prasch, "Orientalism's Other, Other Orientalisms: Women in the Scheme of Empire," *Journal of Women's History* 7 (Winter 1995): 174–88.

68. Vron Ware, *Beyond the Pale: White Women, Racism and History* (London: Verso Press, 1992); Antoinette Burton, *Burdens of History: British Feminists, Indian Women, and Imperial Culture, 1865–1915* (Chapel Hill: University of North Carolina Press, 1994); Kumari Jayawardena, *The White Woman's Other Burden: Western Women in South Asia during British Colonial Rule* (New York: Routledge, 1995); Billie Melman, *Women's Orients: English Women and the Middle East, 1718–1918* (Ann Arbor: University of Michigan Press, 1992); Julia Clancy-Smith and Frances Gouda, eds., *Domesticating the Empire: Race, Gender and Family Life in French and Dutch Colonialism* (Charlottesville: University Press of Virginia, 1998).

69. Dirk Hoerder and Leslie Page Moch, eds., *European Migrants: Global and Local Perspectives* (Boston: Northeastern University Press, 1996); Donna Gabaccia, *From the*

Other Side: Women, Gender, and Immigrant Life in the U.S., 1820–1900 (Bloomington: Indiana University Press, 1994); Christiane Harzig et al., eds., *Peasant Maids, City Women: From the European Countryside to Urban America* (Ithaca: Cornell University Press, 1997); Bruce M. Stave, John F. Sutherland, and Aldo Salerno, eds., *From the Old Country: An Oral History of the European Migration to America* (New York: Twayne, 1994); Eva Hoffman, *Lost in Translation: A Life in a New Language* (New York: E. P. Dutton, 1989).

70. Jane Kramer, *Unsettling Europe* (New York: Random House, 1980); Buchi Emecheta, *Second Class Citizen* (New York: Braziller, 1975); Ama Ata Aidoo, *Our Sister Killjoy; or, Reflections from a Black-eyed Squint* (London: Longman, 1977). Bonnie G. Smith first suggested Emecheta's writing as a resource for European history.

ADDITIONAL RESOURCES

The following journals have useful articles and reviews on women's history: *Feminist Studies, Gender and History, Journal of Women's History, Signs: Journal of Women in Culture and Society, Women's History Review,* and *Women's Studies International Forum.* See also the journals of the various area studies associations.

The following Web sites are also useful resources:

Diotima (materials for the study of women and gender in the ancient world):
http://www.stoa.org/diotima

Dutch Women's History (Vereniging voor Vrouwengeschiedenis, Amsterdam):
http://www.vrouwengeschiedenis.nl

Europa (official Web site for the European Community):
http://www.europa.eu.int

Gabriel (gateway to Europe's national libraries):
http://www.bl.uk./gabriel

Italian Women's History (Societa italiana delle storiche):
http://www.storiadelledonne.it/sis/index.html

Modern German Women's History:
http://www.kgw.tu-berlin.de/ZIFG (University of Berlin)
http://www.uni-bonn.de/Frauengeschichte/in (University of Bonn)

United Nations Web site for women:
http://www.un.org/works/women/womenl.html

ViVa (bibliography of articles in women's history from sixty journals from 1995 to the present):
http://www.iisg.nl/~womhistvivahome.html

Women and Gender in Early Modern Europe (access to H-Frauen-L, an Internet discussion site):
http://www.h-net.msu.edu/~frauen-1

Women's Writers Project at Brown University (texts of women's literary works from England, Scotland, Ireland, Wales, and the Colonies before 1830):
http://www.wwp.brown.edu

See also WISTAT, a CD-ROM of U.N. statistics on women.

4

Russia and the Soviet Union

BARBARA ENGEL

The revival of the women's movement in the late 1960s sparked a resurgence of interest in Russian and Soviet women, prompting historians to try to find women omitted from previous historical accounts. In 1978 Richard Stites published his monumental and pioneering study that surveyed subject matter other historians would later explore in greater detail and from different perspectives.[1] Some members of this cohort of scholars, myself among them, were personally and politically as well as intellectually motivated. Feminism encouraged women historians to seek "our" past, to tell "herstory." To correct the masculine bias of earlier accounts, we hunted through archives and published sources, looking for traces of women's experience, trying to hear women's hitherto silent voices. To the usual questions of historians, this feminist cohort added new ones, questions concerning the power that men exercised over women and its impact on women's ideas and experiences. We questioned the nature and sources of patriarchal power and asked how being female shaped a woman's choices and activities.

Much of this initial scholarship focused either on women of the intelligentsia or on the Bolsheviks' attempt to liberate women after 1917, in part because of the intrinsic importance of these topics and also because they left a relatively accessible paper trail. As the field matured and the focus broadened, the questions became more multifaceted and the methodologies more diverse. We now have studies of working-class and peasant women, of prostitution and the foundling trade, of religious and charitable women, and of the

various institutions that affected women's lives, including the family, education, and the law. The new focus on cultural history has further enriched
Russian women's history, as has the willingness of historians exploring other
topics to incorporate both gender and women. Much work remains to be
accomplished on women in the eighteenth century, in particular, and on the
nature and impact of Russian imperial policy toward the women of subject
nationalities, about which we know virtually nothing. Nevertheless, the new
scholarship has made it possible to provide a synthetic overview of the history of women in imperial, Soviet, and post-Soviet Russia and to assess some of
the ways that gender has shaped social and political developments. Such is the
purpose of this essay.

The Petrine Revolution

The history of imperial Russia begins with the reign of Peter the Great (1682–
1725). He brought about a revolution in aristocratic women's lives and initiated economic, social, and legal changes that touched women and men alike.
Taking the West as his model, Peter transformed the old system of governing,
built a standing army and navy, and attempted to create a new, Westernized
kind of man to administer them. A new kind of man required a new kind of
woman, likewise modeled along Western lines. As in so much else, the initiative came from the state. As Lindsay Hughes observes, "Upper-class Muscovite women were driven from the seclusion of the terem, or women's quarters, divested of their old-fashioned robes, squeezed into western corsets and
low-cut gowns and transformed into suitable companions for their 'decent
beardless' spouses."[2] Elite women were commanded to appear at social gath-
erings, to perform Western dances, to display the appropriate social skills, and
to converse with men in French. But even women lower in the social hierarchy became subject to the requirement that Russian women don European
dress. The law of 1701 mandating German clothes, hats, and footwear applied
to the wives and children of all ranks of the service nobility as well as of leading merchants, military personnel, and inhabitants of Moscow and other
towns; only clergy and peasants were exempted. Henceforward, women who
failed to wear German dresses, overskirts, petticoats, and shoes could be fined.[3]

Peter also attempted to reform marriage practices. Believing in marriage
by choice rather than by compulsion, he altered the Muscovite customs where-
in marriages were contracted by parents or, if they were dead, by close relatives. The bride and groom usually saw each other for the first time only after
the wedding ceremony. A law of 1702 required a six-week betrothal period
before the wedding, enabling the engaged couple to meet and get to know

one another. Should they decide against marriage, either party gained the right to terminate the engagement, the betrothed as well as their parents.[4]

The law very likely reflected Peter's own unhappy experience in a traditional marriage, arranged for him by his mother. Having placed his first wife, Evdokia, in a nunnery, Peter married for a second time in 1712 to Marfa, renamed Catherine I, a woman of common birth. The celebration was conducted in the spirit of the new era, featuring women who sat in the same rooms as men garbed in naval uniforms and wore low-cut gowns and elaborate French wigs. The event thus served as a kind of public spectacle in which new manners were acted out and the public instructed in the new ways. Despite the example of his own ceremony, Peter intended marital reform to affect everyone, regardless of social status. An edict of 1724 explicitly forbade forced marriages, including those arranged for "slaves" by their masters, and required both bride and groom to take an oath indicating that they consented freely to their union.

We know almost nothing about how the women of Peter's era experienced these changes; they left very few documents and composed no known autobiographies, memoirs, or diaries. Women of court circles seem to have embraced them, however, at least superficially. Peter's own sister, Natalia Alekseevna, converted completely to Western dress. A 1715 portrait shows her in an elaborately fashionable hairstyle and low-cut gown. Outside St. Petersburg, new customs caught on more slowly among the elite, and merchant women continued to dress in traditional ways.[5] Nevertheless, many men who shared Peter's ideals agreed with him that refined society required the participation of women. Fathers sought to bestow upon daughters the fruits of Western culture, hiring foreign governesses and tutors to instruct the girls. As a result, by the second half of the eighteenth century it was no longer unusual to meet cultivated Russian women, especially in the new Westernized capital, St. Petersburg.

Foreign literature, especially French, exerted an enormous influence on the educated elite and introduced new ideas concerning marriage and the family. Acting according to a companionate ideal of marriage, well-educated men often sought cultivated women as brides. When the nobleman Andrei Bolotov decided to marry in 1763, he sought a bride who would be "a comrade with whom I could share all my deepest feelings, joys, delights, cares and worries."[6] Conduct books and education manuals from abroad also brought a new conception of motherhood. Instead of the down-to-earth and practical understanding that had previously prevailed among the Russian nobility, these works celebrated motherhood's sanctity and instructed mothers to be the moral and spiritual guides of their children.[7] In the conviction that proper mothering would produce better citizens of the Fatherland, in 1764 Catherine the Great established the Society for the Training of Well-Born Girls (the "Smolnyi Institute"), a boarding school that admitted daughters of the upper ranks of the military and bureaucracy. New public schools admitted girls from more humble backgrounds.[8]

WOMEN'S ECONOMIC AND FAMILY ROLES

For noblewomen, education had practical significance as well. Military or civil service kept noblemen away from their rural estates for months or years on end. During a man's absence, his wife might manage the estate and oversee the farming operations. Literacy enabled her to keep accounts and maintain a correspondence on practical matters with the bailiff and her absent husband; it may also have assisted her to manage property of her own. Although patrimonial property laws continued to privilege male heirs, the law of 1731 that abolished the Petrine policy of single inheritance permitted nobles to bestow land on a widow or marriageable daughter and granted the woman the right to sell or mortgage that property and designate her own heirs. A decree of 1753 formalized married women's separate control of property. Thereafter, many noble families acted to secure their daughters' right to property in land, in the form of the dowry. In such cases the married daughter (rather than her husband), bore responsibility for collecting taxes, supplying serf recruits, and fulfilling other obligations connected with the ownership of land.[9] Consequently, many noblewomen played absolutely vital economic roles. According to Natalia Pushkareva, testimonials from the second half of the eighteenth century depict them "not only as capable housewives who knew the details of home economics but also as informed and prudent businesswomen who personally oversaw income and expenditure and understood the real-estate market."[10]

How can we reconcile this portrait of active and independent noblewomen with women's subordinate position according to law? Russian law defined family relations in terms of authority and duty and required wives to give unconditional obedience to husbands. By law, husbands enjoyed the power to control their wives' and children's activities and use corporal punishment if they failed to obey. Were noblewomen's enhanced property rights and economic role sufficient to mitigate the authoritarian and patriarchal relations dictated by law and custom? Court cases from the eighteenth century provide evidence of husbands who beat or tormented their wives to force them to mortgage or sell their dowry or who dissipated women's property without their knowledge. Court records, however, also show noblewomen taking action on their own behalf against husbands who dispossessed them and courts honoring a woman's claims. In some cases a woman's right to property brought her a measure of independence. One example is the noblewoman Aleksandra Krotkaia, who, after enduring years of abuse from her philandering husband, in 1768 petitioned Catherine the Great for the right to separate from him and live "a peaceful secure life" until the end of her days on the estate that her father had "deigned to grant" her.[11]

Evidence concerning the status of peasant women is equally ambiguous. There is no question that in the peasant household women's economic contribution was absolutely central. Peasants depended on the women in the family to weed and fertilize the fields and help bring in the harvest. Women performed all the household chores and all the spinning and weaving. Without a woman, a peasant household was not viable. Yet the very need for women's labor limited such choices as whether to marry or remain single. In a study of serfs belonging to wealthy landowners in Iaroslavl' and Moscow provinces, John Bushnell has found that in cases where peasant women were reluctant to marry, the demands of peasant men seeking wives led village communities (rather than noble landowners) to force the women to wed.[12]

Like noblewomen, peasant wives owed their husbands absolute obedience, and peasant husbands had the right to discipline wives physically. Yet according to Maria Minenko, a Russian ethnographer who studied the free peasantry of western Siberia, the significance of the peasant wife's labor won her status and respect. Minenko's archival sources yield evidence not only of severe male brutality and cruel treatment of wives but also of great mutual tenderness and concern between married couples. She quotes one literate peasant who wrote to his wife that he was "unable to bear the uncommon anguish of separation" from her. "Heat up the bathhouse for me, my wife, and let me toast myself there on your lap, like a little child, or rather like a great big child."[13]

Whatever their social estate, most women lived out their lives in a family setting. At least until the mid-nineteenth century the vast majority of Russians lived in the countryside, consuming products that they themselves had produced or, in the case of nobles, that their peasant serfs produced. Although there were very few ways for women to earn a living independently, the Petrine Revolution forced many to seek their own livelihood. During the eighteenth and early nineteenth centuries, hundreds of thousands of peasants and townsmen were recruited into the army to serve for twenty-five years or until disablement. Military recruitment created a new social category, the *soldatka* (soldier's wife). Unattached, an extra mouth to feed, and a potential threat to the other women of the household and the community, such women were often driven from the village. The cities to which they migrated offered them little in the way of respectable employment and large numbers of men prepared to pay for sexual companionship. Soldiers' wives acquired an unsavory reputation, and if they became pregnant they had nowhere to turn for help. As David Ransel observes, one consequence was that illegitimacy and infanticide became much more visible than in the earlier period—and perhaps more commonplace as well.[14]

In this period, a religious vocation offered one of the very few respectable alternatives to family life and might even exempt a peasant woman from the community's requirement that she marry. Religion also provided a model of pious and charitable female behavior that differed from the worldly Petrine ideal. An exemplar of this behavior was "Blessed Ksenia," who lived in St. Petersburg in the second half of the eighteenth century. Devastated by grief after the early death of her husband, a chorister in the imperial court, she gave all her possessions to the poor. She wandered about the city dressed in a ragged skirt and blouse, earning the veneration of the church and ordinary people because of her self-sacrifice and generosity toward the poor.

Other pious women similarly devoted their lives and fortunes to helping others. Catherine the Great's Church Reform of February 28, 1764, which confiscated church lands and substantially reduced the number of monasteries and convents, opened a door to private religious initiative. Thereafter, privileged women used their property rights to found *obshchiny* (unofficial women's religious communities), many of which were dedicated to service in charity or education. Women's religious communities cared for homeless, elderly, and widowed women and, later in the nineteenth century, established schools for girls.

Charitable activity of a more worldly sort became an outlet for wives and family members of leading public figures. Empresses and other female members of the imperial family began patronizing charities in the late eighteenth century, lending their names, as well as varying amounts of money and effort, to highly visible charitable endeavors.[15] Following this tradition, in 1812 the Empress Elizabeth, wife of Alexander I, joined with ladies of the aristocracy to establish one of the first Russian women's charitable organizations, the Women's Patriotic Society, which aided victims of the war against Napoleon. In subsequent decades it became almost routine for the wives of leading officials to found charitable associations.

THE CULTIVATED WOMAN

By the late eighteenth century, women's intellectual cultivation had become a distinctive characteristic of a sector of Russia's elite. Cultivated women—still a tiny minority, virtually all of them nobles—developed independent intellectual interests and enthusiastically pursued them. The erudition of a few of the women rivaled that of their European counterparts. One of the most well known was Catherine Dashkova, who in 1762 at age eighteen assisted Catherine the Great in seizing power. She was subsequently appointed the director of the Petersburg Academy of Sciences and became the founder and president of the Russian Academy (1783–94).[16] In the late eighteenth and early nineteenth centuries, dozens of elite women became published authors of poetry and prose. As salon hostesses, cultivated women also played a role in the development of Russia's nascent public sphere. Salons provided writers with meeting places and a critical link to their audience. They contributed to the refinement of the Russian language and the evolution of Russian thought. By entertaining Russia's emergent intelligentsia and shaping the atmosphere of her salon, a salon hostess helped to define "the values of both literature and public life in general."[17]

In the Decembrist uprising, the first open rebellion against autocracy, cultivated women also played a significant, if indirect, role. On December 14, 1825, noblemen and military officers staged an abortive coup with the aim of liberalizing Russia's social, economic, and political order and then paid for their rebellion with either death by hanging or a lifetime of penal servitude in Siberia. A number of their wives elected to follow them into exile, voluntarily abandoning all the comforts and privileges they had enjoyed as members of the elite and defying the government, which encouraged them to sever ties with the men. Providing a model of female heroism that combined wifely loyalty with saintly asceticism and self-sacrifice, these women, known as the Decembrist wives, exerted a powerful influence on women of subsequent generations.

In the period after the failed rebellion, male and female intellectuals developed the first critiques of women's customary roles. In the late 1830s such women writers as Elena Gan and Maria Zhukova published fiction that drew attention to the limitations of women's customary sphere and emphasized the plight of educated and able women whom society subordinated to men and denied an outlet outside their families. Tight censorship and a ubiquitous secret police made political activity both difficult and dangerous during the reign of Nicholas I, prompting men of the first generation of the intelligentsia to turn to personal life as an arena for change. Stimulated by the ideas of the German romantics and then by George Sand and the Utopian Socialists, the men examined their own lives and reevaluated and tried to alter their personal relationships with women. At first they exalted women and placed them on a pedestal: "Romantic culture assumed and required the presence of woman in the guise of beautiful lady, as bearer of the principle of the eternally feminine, and so forth."[18] Then, more successfully, they attempted to create equality between the sexes within their own circles. In the 1840s Natalie Herzen served as the "hostess, confidante, and at times guiding spirit" of her husband Alexander's circle, where the sexes mixed freely and formal-ism was completely absent.[19] Intellectuals discussed the legal and social status of women and the role women should play in transforming the family and regenerating Russian society.[20]

Reform and Reaction

Profound changes took place in the lives of vast numbers of Russia's women following the death of Tsar Nicholas II and the ascension of his son, Alexander II, while the "woman question" emerged as one of the central issues of the day. The emancipation of the serfs in 1861 proved a pivotal event that shook the economic and social foundations of Russia's traditional order by initiating the release of almost half the peasant population of Russia. The loss of serf labor deprived many nobles of easy living and forced their daughters to seek their own livelihood, but even in the absence of economic need the ethos embraced by progressive young women and men of the era encouraged women's economic independence. Rejecting the aristocratic culture and customs of their elders, they believed that no one had the right to live idly on the fruits of another's labor. Women should cease to be helpless and dependent. Whether married or single, a woman must never "hang on the neck of a man."[21]

In this turbulent era, as educated women and men attempted to extend the limits of permissible social and political action, intellectuals raised questions concerning the family order and women's roles more explicitly than ever before. The woman question was debated in university hallways (into which women briefly penetrated as auditors in the early 1860s), on the pages of progressive journals, in student apartments, and in the salons of the elite. One aspect of the woman question was the family, that "Realm of Darkness," according to the title of an article published in 1856 by the radical critic Nikolai Dobroliubov. Both as a substitute for the autocratic political order that it remained dangerous to challenge and as a source of oppression in itself, the patriarchal family became the subject of verbal and written critiques.

One of the most influential of these was Nikolai Chernyshevsky's novel *What Is to Be Done?* (1863), which provided an answer to the woman question and a blueprint for radical change.[22] Inspired by the experience of Russian women who had already begun to reshape their lives, and by the writings of the French utopian socialists, Chernyshevsky's formula for women's liberation consisted of a satisfying and egalitarian family life, organization of labor and life according to collective principles, and work for the social good. Radical thinkers of subsequent generations would also emphasize the importance of a public role for women and the connection between women's economic self-sufficiency and their personal happiness.

Chernyshevsky's novel inspired countless young women to rebel against "family despotism," as some termed it, and live as they chose. As a declaration of independence from conventionally feminine demeanor, daughters of nobles and government officials cropped their hair, dispensed with crinolines, and simplified their dress; they sought to advance their education and earn their own living. Young men encouraged and supported them, sometimes marrying the women solely to free them from the power of their parents. The fledgling women's movement, which emerged around the time of the serf emancipation, encouraged them as well. Three well-educated women of noble origin—Anna Filosofova, Nadezhda Stasova, and Maria Trubnikova—whose personal connections and social skills helped them overcome the government's limited tolerance for private initiative, led the movement. It was especially successful in the sphere of higher education. In this period, women gained the right to audit advanced lecture courses, known as the Alarchin Courses (1869); to attend courses that prepared women for secondary school teaching (1872); to earn a degree at courses for "Learned Midwives" and, after 1876, at medical courses exclusively for women; and to attend a women's university, the Bestuzhev Courses (1878). Many professions, such as the law and civil service, remained closed to women. Nevertheless, the new educational opportunities enabled thousands not only to advance their education but also to earn their own living, primarily as midwives, physicians, or teachers. Educational institutions also created social spaces where women could interact with each other without the constraints of family or the sometimes intimidating presence of men.

Education led some Russian women, as it did men, to critical thought and radical action. In the second half of the 1860s, women began to figure as active participants in Russia's revolutionary movement. Quite varied in their social origins, the majority of these female activists nevertheless came from noble or bureaucratic backgrounds, and virtually all had received some advanced education.[23] During the 1870s some tried to serve the peasants by working among them as teachers, midwives, and medical aides; others, disguising themselves as peasants, tried to rouse the peasantry to social revolution. Women figured prominently in populist organizations; a few, most notably Vera Figner and Sofia Perovskaia, assumed leadership roles. Perovskaia gave the signal for the assassination of Tsar Alexander II on March 1, 1881, becoming the first Russian woman to be hanged for a political crime. Profoundly unconventional in many respects, the experience of such women nevertheless suggests the ways that tradition can empower as well as debilitate. As a rationale for rebellion against the confining aspects of the established female role, women radicals and revolutionaries drew upon ideals of altruism and self-sacrifice that were rooted in religious tradition—just as the Decembrist wives had done half a century before.

The political reaction that followed Alexander II's assassination and the ascension of Tsar Alexander III (1881–94) directly affected elite and educated women. Because the tsar believed that higher education bred radicalism, educational opportunities for women became narrowly circumscribed. The Women's Medical Courses ceased to admit students in 1881 and were shut down in 1886; women's higher courses were closed in Moscow and provincial university towns. The Bestuzhev Courses survived, but in 1889 their enrollment was drastically cut and, to discourage poorer women from attending, fees were raised. A quota, aimed mainly against Jews, limited non-Christian enrollment to 3 percent. The government became suspicious even of charitable work, which in the immediate postemancipation period had provided a significant outlet for women who sought a wider sphere than the family but felt no commitment to radical social or political change.

PEASANT AND WORKING-CLASS WOMEN

Living in peasant villages, the vast majority of Russia's women remained unaffected by these limitations. In the decades following the emancipation of the serfs, change occurred slowly in the countryside, if at all. Cathy Frierson has drawn attention to the contradictory images of peasant women that circulated in this period, expressing the hopes and fears of their educated contemporaries.[24] Historians also disagree about the character of peasant women's lives. Some have stressed the abject subordination of peasant women as a result of patriarchal peasant family organization and peasant men's sole access to land and to representation in the *skhod*—the organ of peasant self-administration.[25] Others have drawn attention to the informal power that women enjoyed as a result of their role in social reproduction as well as their centrality to the peasant economy. Christine Worobec points out that adult women maintained and perpetuated many of the rituals that ensured the community's cohesion. They arranged marriages and presided at childbirths and christenings, central events in village life. "Control over the domestic hearth, the ability to affect social relationships, the functions of matchmaker, mother, mother-in-law, midwife and herbalist provided women with power bases extending beyond the household," she contends.[26] Female kin might join together to rebuff attempts to encroach upon their sphere, as they did, for example, when physicians attempted to modernize peasant child-care practices toward the end of the nineteenth century. Networks of village women also engaged in acts of collective opposition to outside authorities who threatened the subsistence of the household or the community. Women large with child or holding babies to their breast might articulate the community's collective rights or confront the authorities with hunger in the village. Such women found a source of resistance in their family roles as wives and mothers.[27]

Education provided a source of change in the countryside. According to the census of 1897, a mere 9.8 percent of peasant women were literate, but even that figure represented an advance over earlier times. During the reign of Alexander III the numbers of both primary schools and students attending them increased more than threefold, and a growing minority of the students were girls. The teaching profession itself became increasingly feminized in rural areas; the proportion of female rural teachers rose from 20 to 36.4 percent between 1880 and 1894. Peasants were often overtly hostile to these women teachers. Yet, as Ben Eklof inquires, "Who can measure the impact that such 'ladies' had on young village girls," exposing them to conduct and values quite different from those that prevailed in their villages?[28]

Industrialization and the growth of a cash economy provided another source of change in villages. When peasant men went off to work elsewhere, women often shouldered men's responsibilities. This pattern was especially prevalent in the northern provinces, where the need for cash was greatest and the land least productive. The new demands for cash affected women's work in other ways as well. In the vicinity of Moscow, peasant women took in foundlings for cash paid by foundling homes and turned motherhood itself into a trade. Other peasant women earned money by producing such items as cloth, lace, and knitwear at home for the growing national market. Working in their huts and depending upon a middleman (more rarely, woman) to market their goods, these women became connected to the market by virtue of their income-producing activities while remaining within the traditional, patriarchal household.[29]

The vast majority of peasant women never left home. Nevertheless, as the nineteenth century drew to a close, a growing minority also began to seek wages elsewhere. Unmarried women and widows, whose ties to the village were the most tenuous, were the most likely to leave, but marriageable girls and even married women increasingly departed as well. The majority worked as domestic servants, but more and more found employment in factories. By the early twentieth century women constituted a significant minority of the migrant peasant population of both St. Petersburg and Moscow, and the proportion of women in the burgeoning factory labor force had grown since 1885 from about one in every five workers to about one in every three.

The move from village to city or factory dramatically altered these women's lives, although very few sought change for its own sake. Most peasant women left home because of the pressing need to feed themselves and, if possible, to contribute to their family economy. Those who worked in factories experienced demoralizing working and living conditions. Before factory legislation mandated a work day of 11.5 hours in 1897, women workers often labored fourteen or more hours a day, six days a week. They lived in factory dormitories where dozens were crowded together in a single large room, or they rented a corner just big enough for their bed. Factory women may have dreamed of a room of their own, but on their meager earnings it was an unattainable luxury. The working and living conditions of domestic servants were even more austere. In overcrowded urban apartments, many lacked even the modest refuge available to their servant sisters to the West. Instead, they spent the night behind a screen in the passageway, or in the kitchen, or even by the bed of their employer. The servant's wage was low, her position often insecure, and her work never-ending.

Historians disagree about the impact of migration and industrial work on women. Did industrial labor leave the woman worker isolated and oppressed, so poorly paid that she was barred from the entertainments her male counterparts enjoyed, as Rose Glickman has contended? Were domestic servants merely "white slaves," forced to do the most degrading and undesirable of women's work and so deprived of a private life that they became easy prey for sexual exploitation? David Ransel notes that domestic servants were disproportionately represented among women who abandoned their illegitimate children to foundling homes. Or did migration offer a new kind of independence and freedom from patriarchal control? There is evidence that some women workers took advantage of the opportunities offered by city life and a wage of their own, however modest, to extend their horizons and forge a new identity. Such women might spend their money on urban-style fashions, enjoy cheap urban amusements, attend evening classes and Sunday schools, or participate in amateur factory theatrical performances. Urbanization eroded social boundaries and made social estate increasingly irrelevant.[30]

It was the freedom rather than its limitations that most struck tsarist officials. The growth of prostitution served as the most visible and troubling symbol. Suspecting all women of the underclass and on their own of "trading in vice," the state attempted to substitute its own patriarchal power for absent husbands and fathers. In 1844 it had introduced a network of laws to regulate prostitution and control venereal disease, laws that affected all women who were poor and thronged to Russia's cities in the latter part of the century. Even those who plied the trade casually and intermittently—or perhaps not at all—risked encountering the police and becoming registered as "professional" prostitutes, receiving a "yellow ticket" that clearly identified their trade and subjected them to police surveillance and medical supervision. The regulation system seriously reduced the women's autonomy and freedom of movement. In the words of Laurie Bernstein, "Whether or not women registered with the police as prostitutes, they were still living with regulation."[31]

POLITICS AND THE WOMAN QUESTION

Intellectuals also responded to the growing visibility of peasant and working-class women in urban Russia. As increasing numbers of women penetrated public and previously male space, the woman question took on new life. Laura Engelstein has demonstrated the complex ways in which women's bodies became part of the terrain over which educated society struggled for power in the final decades of the nineteenth century. Even as the basis for women's dependent status began to erode—a result of women's migration and participation in waged labor—jurists revised laws treating sexual crime and prostitution, denying women's capacity for independent action and ensuring that individual autonomy remained a male preserve. When they discussed abortion and infanticide, the only forms of birth control accessible to women who had no money, male physicians and jurists expressed anxieties about uncontrolled women and sought to substitute their own authority for the power of the patriarchal state. When they opposed state regulation of prostitution, for example, male physicians rarely argued for complete abolition of the system of surveillance and registration; instead, they wanted the system amended and medical authority over the women to replace the power of the police.

As a civil society gradually took shape, women, too, claimed expanded and more autonomous public roles. In some cases they simply extended their customary sphere. In *zhenskie obshchiny* (women's religious communities), for example, women broke free of the limitations of traditional monastic life and moved from contemplation to action, in the form of charity for the poor and education of the young. Despite the suspicion toward charitable activity that followed the ascension of Alexander III, women's communities that operated in rural areas remained relatively free of government interference.[32]

During the reign of Nicholas II (1894–1917), charitable activity grew easier and experienced a major revival, the result of growing numbers of women, particularly privileged women who sought an opportunity to serve others without violating accepted ideas concerning women's place. New educational and professional opportunities became available to women, too. In 1897 a Women's Medical Institute was opened in St. Petersburg, which granted women equality with men in medical practice, and higher courses for women, the Guerrier Courses, reopened in Moscow in 1900. In 1901 graduates of the Bestuzhev Courses gained the right to teach in the upper grades of girls' *gymnasia*. When the feminist movement reemerged in the early years of the twentieth century, educated women, many of them professionals, filled its ranks.

In 1905 long-suppressed discontents finally exploded in revolution. Industrial workers, students, professionals, and even nobles and industrialists became caught up in the wave of resistance that swept Russia in the wake of Bloody Sunday (January 9, 1905), when tsarist troops fired on a peaceful demonstration of working-class women and men, killing more than a hundred people and wounding many more. During the ensuing period of upheaval, female industrial workers, clerical workers, pharmacists, professionals, and even domestic servants joined unions and walked off their jobs to attend mass meetings and demonstrations calling for an end to autocracy and some kind of representative form of government. The intense politicization and pervasive use of a language of rights stimulated some women to speak on their own behalf and claim a place in the expanding public sphere. Working-class women were among the first to raise their voices. At the end of January 1905 they objected in print when the government called for the convening of a commission to study the reasons for worker discontent and permitted women to vote for representatives to the commission but only male workers to be elected to it. The women protested their lost opportunity to "loudly proclaim . . . the oppression and humiliation that no male worker can possibly understand."[33]

Women workers also participated actively in the burgeoning strike movement. In the textile industry, where they constituted about half of the workforce, strike demands clearly reflected their presence. Workers in one textile mill after another raised demands for day care, maternity leave, nursing breaks, and protection of women workers—reflecting not only the preponderance of women but also the influence of the Marxist Social Democratic Labor Party and of liberals, both of which had long supported maternity-related benefits. Even as they claimed for women significant rights in the workplace, however, such demands also reinforced gender differences and a gender division of labor. As Rose Glickman has emphasized, virtually all demands that applied to women touched on their role as mothers, not on their actual working conditions. Almost never did workers claim that a woman should be paid as much as a man for performing identical work. Nevertheless, vast numbers of working-class women were swept up in the events of 1905 and came to embrace the working-class movement as their own. This became clear in December during a last, desperate confrontation with the authorities, when working-class women and men took to the barricades. Alongside men, women labored tirelessly, chopping wood, breaking up telegraph poles, and disassembling tram cars to construct barricades against government troops, who nevertheless crushed the working-class movement.

During the revolution of 1905 women of the educated classes took political action of a different sort. The feminist movement, or, more precisely, feminist movements, reemerged on a much more substantial scale and embraced far larger numbers than before. The primary goal was woman suffrage, which became an issue as soon as men claimed a political voice. The largest and most visible feminist group and the only one to play a significant role in 1905 was the All-Russian Union for Women's Equality, a national women's political organization established by thirty female liberals a month after Bloody Sunday. By the time of their first congress, held in Moscow from May 7 to 10, twenty-six chapters had formed.

Feminist activists derived primarily from the emergent middle classes. Such independent professional women as journalists, physicians, and teachers (those whom Soviet historians used to call the laboring intelligentsia) were, however, far more numerous than they appear to have been in the feminist parties of Western Europe or the United States. The Union for Women's Equality cast its lot with the broader liberation movement, embracing the idea that women's liberation was inseparable from the liberation of society as a whole. In addition to its call for specifically women's rights such as equality of the sexes before the law, equal rights to the land for peasant women, laws to protect women workers, and coeducation at all levels of schooling, the platform the union adopted in May 1905 repeated the demands of the liberation movement. Their common ground of opposition to autocracy led the women of the Union for Women's Equality to collaborate with liberal and leftist men far more extensively than feminists did elsewhere in Europe or the United States.

Feminist support for the liberation movement, so generously given, was rather less generously returned, however, as Linda Edmondson has demonstrated. The October manifesto enfranchised only men, leaving women dependent on the loyalty of their former male allies. The liberal Kadet Party, which dominated the first Duma, was divided over the issue of woman suffrage. Parties to the left, although staunch advocates of women's rights, because of their working-class orientation were with one notable exception suspicious of and reluctant to support "bourgeois feminism." Moreover, social divisions among women divided their ranks. Working-class and peasant women felt more affinity with the men of their class than they did with middle-class feminists, whom they tended to view as "bourgeois." Thus, the social divisions that weakened opposition to autocracy divided the women's movement as well.

More decisive than male ambivalence or social divisions was the fact that the revolution had ended and the tsar had begun retracting his concessions. When the first Duma was dissolved after three months, its members were preparing to consider the fruit of feminist lobbying, a draft law on women's equality. The erosion of civil liberties and the "coup" of June 3, 1907, which gave still greater electoral weight to the propertied sectors of society, brought political demoralization. Membership in the women's movement sharply declined, as it did in radical political parties in general. Despite the lack of concrete achievements, the experience of 1905, in particular participation in acts of protest and the use of a language of rights, left an ineradicable trace on the consciousness of thousands of women and men at all levels of society, from the most privileged to the most deprived.

After 1905 sexual issues preoccupied the educated. The failure of the revolution to bring fundamental political change served to politicize the "sexual question," while eased censorship enabled the press to discuss sensitive issues more freely. Only a few published works, however, explored female, rather than male, sexuality. One was the immensely popular boulevard novel *The Keys to Happiness* (1910–13) by Anastasia Verbitskaia. In six volumes and 1,400 pages the author explored the life of a sexually self-assertive modern heroine, Mania, who takes several lovers and struggles to retain her independence and artistic ambitions in the face of intense passion.[34]

A few feminists also addressed issues relating to female sexuality. The most visible was Maria Pokrovskaia, a physician and editor of a feminist journal, who fought unceasingly against regulated prostitution and denounced Russia's punitive abortion laws as unwarranted restrictions on female autonomy. Invoking the concept of voluntary motherhood, she called for full decriminalization of abortion, claiming that only women were in a position to know their own needs. But like most of her Russian feminist colleagues, Pokrovskaia swam against the sexual tides of the early twentieth century. Even as she denounced the double standard she urged that men adopt the female example of chastity, not that women emulate the sexually adventurous behavior of men. By contrast, the socialist—subsequently Bolshevik—feminist Alexandra Kollontai was in advance of her time. In her lengthy essay "The New Woman," first published in 1913, Kollontai claimed for women the right of sexual choice and tried to theorize the link between personal emancipation and social change.[35] Kollontai also insisted upon her right to follow her own sexual yearnings even as she fought for social revolution, thereby challenging a radical political culture that for decades had celebrated women's capacity for self-sacrifice and self-abnegation. Kollontai's efforts to incorporate intimate aspects of women's experience into the Marxist worldview won few converts among her comrades, and her romantic liaisons would be used to discredit her during the intraparty political struggles of the 1920s.

War and Revolution

The outbreak of World War I mobilized Russian women at unprecedented levels as new jobs opened in factories that men abandoned for the front. By 1917 the proportion of women in Russian industry as a whole rose to 43.2 percent, although, as before, most remained concentrated in trades that required little skill and paid low wages. Still, the number of women (and children) working in weapons factories grew dramatically. In Petrograd (prewar St. Petersburg), the heart of Russia's elite metalworking industry, women constituted 20 percent of metalworkers on the eve of the revolution. In the absence of men, peasant women shouldered all responsibility for fieldwork or left home in search of employment. Several thousand female volunteers had even joined special units of the armed forces by the end of August 1917.[36] World War I thus helped prepare the way for the more profound transformations the Bolsheviks would undertake after 1917. The war blurred gender boundaries and for the first time drew out to work hundreds of thousands, perhaps millions, of women.

The war years also markedly increased political discontent by creating severe economic dislocation. Consumer prices rose sharply, and items of primary necessity like bread and sugar became scarce. Within a year after the outbreak of war the strike movement had resumed, with thousands of workers, women as well as men, going out on strike every day. The increasing difficulty of buying food in the marketplace prompted working-class and peasant women to be more assertive in their family roles. By the spring of 1915 subsistence riots had begun to erupt in Russia's cities and towns. The participants, primarily women of the underclass, attacked and destroyed the shops of merchants suspected of speculation or broke into shops and appropriated goods for themselves at prices they believed to be just, resisting the efforts of police and cossack detachments to stop them. Women's behavior reflected the growing alienation of Russia's laboring people. Equally unnerving for the authorities, women's protests in the marketplace sometimes spilled over onto the factory floor. In the wake of subsistence riots, thousands of male and female workers might walk off the job, demanding higher wages or lower prices.[37]

The situation reached a critical point on International Woman's Day, February 23, 1917 (March 8, new style). In Petrograd, angry working-class women, both housewives and factory workers, ignored the pleas of labor leaders to stay home and staged a demonstration calling for bread and peace. The working-class response was decisive. Over the next few days hundreds of thousands of workers joined the demonstrators, while soldiers refused orders to fire upon them. The women's protest quickly turned into a full-scale revolution, forcing Tsar Nicholas II to abdicate the throne on March 2.

The provisional government that succeeded him soon acquiesced to many feminist demands. Women received the right to vote, the right to serve as attorneys and act as jurors, and equal rights within the civil service (of particular value to teachers). Many privileged women supported the provisional government's policies, including the continued war effort, because the war had offered them unprecedented opportunities to participate in public life as nurses or collectors of clothing and medical supplies for troops, for example. By contrast with privileged women, many working-class women opposed the provisional government, especially after it became evident that the new regime would provide neither the bread nor the peace that the women had demanded in February. The socialist-led labor movement for the first time exerted significant influence over women workers, some of whom struck with impressive tenacity and self-discipline. Even hitherto quiescent groups, such as laundresses and soldiers' wives, participated in strikes and demonstrations during the eight months the provisional government remained in power.[38]

THE BOLSHEVIK REVOLUTION AND WOMEN

After the Bolsheviks seized power on October 23 and 24, 1917 (November 7 and 8), they attempted to implement a vision of social transformation that included the emancipation of women. Although prerevolutionary feminism disappeared as an independent political and intellectual current, a Bolshevik variety of feminism became part of the official discourse. The new regime proposed to equalize the relations between the sexes by entrusting household tasks to paid workers, thus freeing women to become full and equal participants in wage labor. Bolshevik feminists called for the emancipation of women from all social constraints save those that women chose for themselves. The party leader, Vladimir I. Lenin, was particularly emphatic about the need to relieve women of household chores so they could participate in socially useful production. "Petty housework crushes, strangles, stultifies and degrades" a woman, Lenin wrote, chaining her to the kitchen and the nursery and wasting her labor.[39] Once free of the need to exchange their domestic and sexual services for men's financial support, women would engage in relationships with men as equals. Eventually the family itself would wither away, and women and men would unite their lives solely for love. In 1918 the government promulgated a family code that was extraordinarily advanced for its time. The code equalized women's status with men's, removed marriage from the hands of the church, allowed a marrying couple to choose either the husband's or the wife's surname, and, for the first time in Russia, granted illegitimate children the same legal rights as legitimate ones. Divorce, hedged with obstacles in the tsarist period, became easily obtainable at the request of either spouse. In 1920 abortion became legal if performed by a physician.

The revolution also brought new opportunities for working-class and peasant women to join together and speak for themselves. In November 1918 an All-Russian Conference of Working Women attracted 1,147 women, far more than the three hundred whom organizers had anticipated. In August 1919 the Central Committee of the Communist Party granted permission for the formation of the Zhenotdel (Women's Bureau) to coordinate the party's work among women. Inessa Armand became its first leader, and after Armand's death from typhus in 1920, Alexandra Kollontai led the organization until she fell from favor in 1922.[40] Their successors were Sofia Smidovich, Klavdiia Nikolaeva, and Aleksandra Artiukhina. The party conceived of the Zhenotdel as an agency to mobilize women to support its objectives and inform women of their new rights. It was to be a transmission belt from the top downward. Because the Zhenotdel's leaders had their own vision, however, it quickly became far more. Despite a perpetual shortage of funds, the Zhenotdel did its best to keep the question of restructuring everyday life on the agenda of the leadership and establish a basis for women's liberation by setting up child-care centers, communal dining halls, and other services. In addition, the Zhenotdel sought to mobilize women by training factory workers, who would temporarily leave the workplace to gain the political preparation that would enable them to become more active on the local level. Thus, the Zhenotdel broadened the horizons of millions of women and encouraged them to participate in political life.[41]

Zhenotdel activists also played a key role in implementing Soviet efforts to emancipate the Muslim women of Central Asia (Kazakstan, Kyrgyzstan, Tadzhikistan, Turkmenistan, and Uzbekistan). To the Communist Party these women constituted a "surrogate proletariat" (in the words of Gregory Massell) whose mobilization on behalf of social and religious change would undermine the authority of traditional, anticommunist elites and compensate for the absence of an indigenous working class. At the same time, Muslim women appeared to party leaders to be little better than slaves. According to Islamic law, the minimum age of marriage for women was nine; polygamy was widely practiced, and the groom paid a substantial bride-price. In some regions, Uzbekistan in particular, women and girls appeared on the streets in cloak-like garments that hid the contours of the body and wore waist-length, horse-hair veils that concealed their faces and hair. Veils served as a powerful symbol of women's oppression.[42]

The Soviet government undertook to change all this. Between 1921 and 1923 it banned practices such as polygamy and bride-price and raised the minimum age of marriage for girls to sixteen. Zhenotdel activists worked hard to publicize these new laws and held meetings and rallies during which they explained the new rights to Muslim women. They also encouraged Central Asian women to play an active role in the legal process, training a few in legal procedures and offering practical support to many more. Perhaps most important, Zhenotdel activists became involved in consciousness-raising activities among local women. Organizing women-only social clubs that offered a range of medical, legal, and educational services, activists created a secluded environment in which local women could feel at ease. The first activists were almost all Russian communists, but during the second half of the 1920s a few Central Asian women joined their ranks.

Communist achievements proved compelling to women outside the Soviet Union and won new converts to communist parties. Some French feminist newspapers enthusiastically backed the Soviet cause. Advocates of women's rights, such as Madeline Pelletier of France, journeyed to Russia and returned impressed. In Britain, Sylvia Pankhurst, the militant suffragist, helped found the British Communist Party. Such women supported the Soviet-dominated Third Communist International in the belief that the Russian Revolution heralded the victory elsewhere of the feminist and socialist revolution for which they had struggled for so long.[43]

The material conditions that followed the revolution, however, were not propitious for anyone's emancipation. When the food situation became catastrophic during the civil war, the Bolsheviks attempted to feed the urban population collectively in public dining halls and canteens; to care for homeless and abandoned children, they established shelters and children's homes. These state-sponsored efforts to assume domestic functions were miserable affairs, crippled by the terrible material scarcity of those years as well as by their ad hoc nature. Instead of serving as shining examples of the socialist future, they left a negative impression on the people who used them. Hardship and hunger took their toll as well. Epidemic diseases killed millions, typhus alone took the lives of 1.5 million people between 1918 and 1919. Thus, in the short run at least, the revolution worsened most women's and children's lots. The deaths of millions of men during World War I and the civil war deprived wives of husbands and children of fathers and destroyed fragile family economies. Millions of homeless children wandered the streets, their parents dead or unable to care for them.

Women's lives grew no easier after the civil war ended, as Wendy Goldman has convincingly demonstrated. Demobilization returned soldiers to their workplaces, where men resumed their previous positions. Women lost their jobs and had difficulty finding new ones. The New Economic Policy, proclaimed in March 1921 with the aim of restarting the ruined economy and winning the loyalty of the alienated peasantry, affected most working women negatively. State spending was sharply curtailed, reducing the number of public day-care centers and other institutions for children and leaving their largely female staffs without work. Now required to account for their costs, factory and plant managers preferred hiring men over women because women might require costly maternity leave and creches for their infants. Despite decrees that forbade it, managers dismissed pregnant and nursing women; they used laws banning nightwork for women as an excuse to lay them off.

Unemployment escalated in the 1920s, and one-third to one-half of the hundreds of thousands of workers who lost their jobs were female. Official figures on female unemployment did not include women seeking jobs for the first time. With no other recourse, thousands of women turned to prostitution to support themselves and their families.

Family instability compounded women's economic problems. In the period after the revolution, millions of Russians took advantage of the new right to divorce easily; 14 percent of Soviet marriages ended in divorce in the early 1920s, twice as many as in Germany and almost three times as many as in France, which had the next highest levels. When a couple with children divorced, the courts determined the amount of child support. What kind of settlement could a court award when a man was seeking to end his fourth or fifth marriage? Reports circulated of men marrying and divorcing as many as fifteen times, leaving ex-wives and their children to fend for themselves. Unregistered sexual unions had also become commonplace, but if the woman bore a child the law provided no means to obtain support from the father.

Peasant villages, where families were much more stable, presented even more formidable obstacles to women's emancipation. Peasant men fiercely resisted efforts to liberate peasant women. Moreover, the lack of economic alternatives to the patriarchal family made it exceedingly difficult for a woman to live on her own in the village, especially after the disappearance of the noble households that had once hired peasant women as servants. And how could a peasant household provide child support to the divorced wife of one of its members when household property was collective and consisted mainly of land and a cow or sheep? To the many women more victimized than liberated by social change, promises of sexual equality rang hollow.

The leadership's commitment to women's emancipation was insufficient to overcome such obstacles; indeed, people in high positions were often part of the problem. Party bureaucrats tended to make work among women a very low priority or to dismiss it altogether. Many Bolshevik cadres resisted women's emancipation and barely concealed their contempt for the Zhenotdel. Men resented working under women's direction, and they opposed their wives' taking responsibilities that might deprive the men of domestic comforts. Trade union leaders often disliked cooperating with the Zhenotdel or providing facilities for its meetings. Even paid female trade union organizers tended to regard the mass of women workers as hopelessly backward, "a stagnant swamp, impossible to budge."[44] Their male co-workers routinely sabotaged women's effort to upgrade their work status by acquiring advanced skills—"skill" itself being considered a male attribute. Diane Koenker has demonstrated that in such trades as printing, which men had dominated before the revolution, shopfloor culture remained overtly and aggressively masculine.

Women who ventured into this terrain were subjected to verbal, physical, and sexual harassment.

Recent research on the 1920s has also shown the myriad ways that the Bolshevik Revolution reconfigured rather than abolished gender hierarchies, providing men with privileged access to public space. From the first, the hero of the new era—the proletarian—was construed as generically male. In the decade following the revolution, poster artists manifested a distinct preference for the male form when they depicted the new proletarian hero who personified the Bolshevik regime. When artists did portray women, the women figured as helpers of men unless the poster was specifically designed for a female audience. Health-care and sex education campaigns relied upon comparably gendered imagery, appealing to a male audience and coding sexual illness as female. Postrevolutionary culture in general glorified the lifestyle of the revolutionary male worker, privileging public life and the point of production while downgrading private life and the family—the spheres identified with women.

Research on the Komsomol (League of Young Communists) has revealed some of the consequences for women of the privileging of public life. Despite its declared goal of liberating women, the Komsomol proved actively hostile to "women's issues." Idealizing exuberant, unencumbered, and communal forms of behavior best befitting an adolescent male, the Komsomol considered all women "backward" and even dangerous because of their association with the private sphere. As a result, the organization had little to offer women, especially those burdened by family responsibilities. Concludes Anne Gorsuch, "In this environment, all that it took to marginalize young women was their very sex, which was constructed by male Komsomoltsy to mean everything other than what these young men wanted to be."[45] Women-oriented activists and their ideas became marginalized in the international movement, too. Finding the Comintern authoritarian and insufficiently attentive to women's needs, early enthusiasts such as Madeline Pelletier and Sylvia Pankhurst soon severed connections with it.

The Central Asian experience offers an apparent contrast. There, the leadership continued to regard women's emancipation as absolutely key to overturning traditional hierarchies and undermining resistance to Bolshevism. In autumn 1926 Moscow decreed an intensification of the emancipation campaign in the form of the mass unveiling of Uzbek Asian women. The first large-scale display took place on International Woman's Day—March 8, 1927—and others followed. Administrative measures were adopted to further the campaign. Women who discarded the veil received special privileges, and husbands of women who failed to do so could be penalized. Some jobs required that a female employee relinquish her veil. Indoctrination in all available media accompanied the campaign.

For Uzbeks, mass unveiling constituted an assault on their most fundamental social institutions—gender and family relations and the division between public and private space. It provoked violent resistance. Families frequently rejected women who removed their veils; more than a thousand were murdered, often by members of their own families. Hundreds of activists lost their lives as well. Only the terror of the 1930s put an end to this opposition. But by then, the goal of the campaign had been achieved. It had become rare to see a fully veiled woman in the cities of Central Asia.

THE SECOND REVOLUTION

The wave of change that broke over the Soviet Union in the late 1920s left virtually no woman's life untouched. New factories, mines, and plants that provided work for millions ended the burden of unemployment disproportionately borne by women. Propaganda encouraged working-class and peasant women to become economically self-sufficient producers. So did a wage policy that set most wages so low that families required at least two wage-earners in order to survive. Scores of women entered such traditionally male industries as metalworking. Institutions of technical and higher education welcomed women as students; working-class and peasant women became the first in their families to receive professional training. Writes Barbara Clements, "Nowhere else in the European world were there so many female lawyers, professors, scientists, and artists, as well as judges and party secretaries" as in the Soviet Union during the 1930s.[46]

Yet much of the population experienced the decade as a time of hardship rather than opportunity. Often with women in the lead, peasants resisted collectivization as an assault on their traditional way of life. Manipulating official perceptions of peasant women as backward and ignorant, the women engaged in *bab'i bunty* (women's riots), which proved instrumental in changing party policy and brought a temporary halt to forced collectivization, permanently ending the socialization of domestic livestock and gaining peasants the right to maintain a private plot.[47]

Industrialization also had a negative impact on workers in less favored sectors of industry, and they, too, resisted. The industrialization drive shifted investment from the female-dominated light and consumer industries to the heavy industries in which most workers were men. In 1932 the resulting intensification of labor, decline in earnings, and reduction of rations led more than sixteen thousand workers, the majority female, to go out on strike in the Ivanovo industrial region. The strike compelled the regime to shift resources to light industry and raise wages; it also, however, precipitated a crackdown on worker resistance and indiscipline.[48] In Central Asia, women's workforce participation often meant labor in the cotton-growing industry, where the majority worked on a seasonal basis, performing the backbreaking job of harvesting cotton by hand.

Then, starting in 1934 and gaining momentum between 1936 and 1938, the government launched a campaign of repression against alleged "enemies of the people." Millions, mostly men, were arrested, imprisoned, and sentenced to forced labor or execution. The terror of the second half of the 1930s more often affected women as relatives of the repressed than as victims. Women have penned some of the most moving testimonies describing the sufferings that people endured during these years.[49]

The industrialization drive rearranged rather than displaced gendered hierarchies. Male workers continued to resist the idea of women fulfilling the roles of men. Because male workers refused to work alongside them, for example, women in some Moscow factories were forced to create special female brigades.[50] Sexual harassment remained common in the workplace. Moreover, just as hundreds of thousands of women were entering the workforce, the leadership abandoned efforts to assist them to advance on the job or transform everyday life. In December 1928 all women's organizers within trade unions were eliminated, thereby halting efforts to train, promote, and defend women workers on the shopfloor. In 1930 the Zhenotdel itself was abolished, ending advocacy within party circles on behalf of women and women's issues. In the aftermath, "[w]omen's work was dissolved in 'general' work and women's issues subsumed under the larger, and more important, campaigns for industrialization and collectivization."[51]

State policy ensured that throughout the Soviet Union the labor force remained sexually segregated, with the majority of women in the lowest-paid positions despite the highly acclaimed breakthroughs of a relative minority. Medicine became a predominately female profession, as did teaching. Except for the highest supervisory positions, which men usually occupied, both physicians and teachers were poorly paid. Men dominated the party, the military, and the state hierarchies, while the wives of such men were instructed to make husband and family their first priority—expectations reminiscent of the traditional bourgeois ideal. For the first time since the revolution, full-time housewives economically dependent on their husbands were treated with respect and invited to join in the creation of a new society by consuming in a "cultured" way and contributing their unpaid labor to hostels, canteens, nurseries, kindergartens, and the like—institutions traditionally associated with the women's sphere and neglected by the economic planners.[52]

For the majority of married women, the abandonment of efforts to transform everyday life brought a double burden, all the heavier because the Five-Year Plan gave such short shrift to the consumption needs of families. Collectivization of agriculture severely disrupted food production. In the absence of sufficient housing, the flood of peasants into cities led to terrible overcrowding. It became almost impossible to find clothing or basic household items. Day-care centers, communal laundries, and other facilities that were supposed to socialize domestic labor remained scarce. How did married women meet the often conflicting demands on them as wives, workers, and mothers under these difficult circumstances? Many turned to their own mothers or to servants for help. Servants were women too old or girls too young to take advantage of new work opportunities or peasant women in desperate flight from the village. The 1930s witnessed the continuation of the prerevolutionary pattern of young peasant girls migrating to the city to become domestic servants. There were fifty thousand domestic servants registered in Moscow in the early 1930s, according to urban censuses that undoubtedly underestimated their numbers.[53] Even workers' families employed them in the 1930s and 1940s.

The multiple demands on them, the overcrowded conditions, and a lack of social support made it imperative for women to limit their number of children. Yet in 1936 the government adopted an explicitly pro-natalist position, defining motherhood as a responsibility to society that must not be avoided and attributing to all women "natural" maternal instincts. Abortion was outlawed and, in an effort to stabilize the family, the government made divorce both complicated and expensive. Illegitimate children were identified with a blank space on their birth certificates in the place where the father's name would have been.[54] The government began to trumpet the virtues of the socialist family and to grow less tolerant of casual liaisons. Yet despite the pronatalist policies of the government and an absence of reliable contraception or trustworthy sources of information about controlling fertility, family size did not increase in the 1930s. It rose only briefly after the abolition of abortion and then continued to decline. To control their childbearing after abortion became illegal, women resorted to back-alley abortions.[55] Although there is no way of knowing how many took this desperate step, or how often, the relatively stable birthrate among the Russian population suggests that substantial numbers resisted the coercive power of the state in the realm of reproduction.

In Central Asia, by contrast, the birthrate continued to be high. Despite rising literacy rates and increased participation in the workforce, despite the introduction of Western-style medical services and the reduction of infant mortality, despite increased female visibility in public life, family patterns remained remarkably resistant to change. Indeed, Shirin Akiner argues that it was the very intensity and pace of change in this region that prompted women (and men) to embrace more firmly than ever the prerevolutionary domestic order.[56] As a result, marriage remained patrilocal, the extended family predominated, and the birthrate continued to be high because even working mothers could rely on other women to help with child care and domestic chores. Thus, while Central Asian women adapted to new public roles they colluded in the preservation of traditional arrangements in private life instead of rebelling against them, as the Soviet regime had intended.

WORLD WAR II AND ITS AFTERMATH

The outbreak of World War II dramatically slowed repression and forged new unity in a divided society and also wreaked extraordinary destruction, divided families, and left women once again to fend for themselves. Hundreds of thousands of women volunteered for service at the front. About two hundred thousand women served in the air defense forces, and tens of thousands were rank-and-file soldiers, machine gunners, snipers, sappers, or driver-mechanics in tank units. By 1943 women constituted about 8 percent of military personnel. Women also occupied nonmilitary positions that put them in the direct line of attack—in medical battalions, as telegraph operators, and as laundresses for fighting units, for example. Behind the lines, they kept the economy going, bearing the burden of work in collective farms and on factory floors.[57]

Despite the central role women played in the war effort, war did not transform the unequal relations between the sexes. Wartime propaganda drew on gender distinctions and reinforced them, representing women as the embodiments of home and family for which men risked their lives. Even women who served as soldiers were depicted as girlish by contrast with brave and manly men. In the military and medical hierarchies, men usually remained superior to women. Men who survived the terrible toll of war were almost ensured of upward mobility, especially if they joined the Communist Party, while with some exceptions women usually were not. After the war, women who had served at the front were expected to forget the experience, take off their uniforms and boots, put on dresses and high heels, marry, and have children.[58] Many concealed their wartime experience in the hopes of finding a husband, although the devastating Soviet losses made the odds against that high. Approximately twenty-seven million people were killed in the war; in 1946 women outnumbered men by almost twenty-six million. The cult of motherhood intensified. The state encouraged women to reproduce by increasing maternity leaves and introducing benefits for childbearing that grew according to the number of children. It also tried still harder to "stabilize" the family. The new family code introduced in 1944 raised the cost of divorce and no longer permitted women to bring paternity suits. A tax was levied on the income of people with fewer than three children.[59]

AFTER STALIN

Stalin's death in March 1953 eased political controls and brought gradual improvements in material life. Abortion was officially restored in 1955; the laws governing divorce were eased in 1968. Economic planners began to pay more attention to human needs. Most Soviet women, however, continued to carry a heavy "double burden." The vast majority worked eight or more hours a day outside the home and bore the full burden of housework and child care.[60] The still-backward economy made housework exceedingly time-consuming even in urban areas, requiring women to stand in multiple lines in shops every day, to accompany their children long distances to school or day care in overcrowded transport, to prepare meals in communal kitchens, and to wash clothes at the bathroom sink. In rural areas, where women continued to perform the bulk of arduous physical labor, they also bore almost sole responsibility for the home and child care. Although most rural homes were supplied with electricity and gas, the vast majority were (and many still are) without running water, indoor plumbing, or central heating. Most villages lacked properly stocked shops or adequate consumer services. As a result, rural women enjoyed even less free time than their overburdened urban counterparts. Everywhere, contraceptives were hard to obtain and rarely reliable, so abortion remained the principle form of birth control. Women used it extensively because their own fertility was one of the few aspects of private life over which they were able to exercise control. Everywhere but in Central Asia the birthrate continued to decline, dropping to about eighteen births per thousand people in the late 1970s compared to 31.2 in the year before the outbreak of World War II.[61]

Concern over the decline in the birthrate and in industrial productivity prompted renewed attention to women's social roles. The woman question, declared "resolved" in the 1930s, was officially acknowledged to be "unsolved," opening the way for a lively debate that began in the late 1960s and continued through the early 1980s. Sociologists, economists, demographers, lawyers, and journalists offered a wide variety of views concerning women. Some were explicitly essentialist, defining gender differences as biologically based and immutable, with motherhood and childrearing among women's "natural" roles. But others called upon the state to deliver on the original socialist promise of equality for women and take responsibility for advancing women at the workplace and easing their lot at home by increasing the supply of kindergartens, creches, and public dining rooms. A few even broached the subject of men's responsibility for housework.[62]

There nevertheless remained limits to the permissible range of debate in the state-controlled press. When, in the fall of 1979, a group of Leningrad women launched a *samizdat* (underground) magazine entitled *Woman and Russia: An Almanac,* the KGB summoned the editors and demanded that they cease publication. The women refused. After two more issues appeared the four leaders were deprived of their Soviet citizenship and deported.[63]

Gorbachev and After

In March 1985 Mikhail Gorbachev assumed leadership of the Communist Party and initiated a policy of glasnost that by the end of the decade permitted unprecedentedly frank discussion of social problems such as prostitution and domestic violence and articulation of explicitly feminist ideas.[64] Glasnost, however, also permitted an explosion of pornography, hitherto banned, and exposed a powerful gender backlash that drew on the most conservative elements of Soviet discourse. The backlash intensified after the fall of Gorbachev and the collapse of the Soviet Union. Conservatives accused the communists of destroying the family and undermining women's "natural role" as wife and mother and guardian of the family hearth. They argued that it had become imperative to stop "driving" women into the labor force, to enable them to return to their proper sphere, the home.[65] The reaction was even stronger in some of the newly independent states of the former Soviet Union, where many saw "emancipation" of women as an artificial construct, the byproduct of their colonized status during the Soviet era. In Central Asia, an Islamic resurgence led some women voluntarily to don the Muslim headscarf or even veil and ankle-length clothes; in a few areas (Tadzhikistan, for example) it was men who set the standard for female modesty. As pre-Soviet practices reemerged in Central Asia, both polygamy and bride-price, never fully eradicated, were increasingly viewed in a positive light.

Everywhere, the number of women in positions of authority declined after the fall of the Soviet Union and the end of the quota system that mandated a proportion of women in elected posts. Once free access to higher education ended, financially strapped parents—the majority—often had to choose which of their children to educate. Almost invariably they favored the boys. Everywhere, too, economic restructuring brought wholesale firing of women. Although there is disagreement concerning the actual percentage of female unemployment, most estimates placed the proportion of women among the unemployed at around 70 percent by the mid-1990s.

By the end of the decade, a far greater number of women and families faced economic hardship than was the case during the late Soviet era. Women were rarely in a position to take advantage of privatization or of new business opportunities, whereas wealthy "new Russians" often insisted that their wives remain at home. Job advertisements for private firms frequently required physical attractiveness from female applicants as well as readiness to perform sexual services. Domestic violence increased, and pornography continued to flourish. For the first time since the revolution, advertising became obsessed with women's bodies.

The changes also had a positive dimension, however, at least for some. Birth control devices and a range of commodities became available to women with money. Often supported with funds from abroad, new feminist initiatives flourished in Russia and the former Soviet states with ties to Western Europe, such as Latvia and Lithuania. Feminist-oriented conferences for women became relatively commonplace. Gender centers in major cities generated woman-oriented scholarships and offered women various forms of self-help.[66] By 1997 a few universities began offering women's studies courses, and feminist scholars began to discuss the development of a women's studies degree.

Equally important to the topic of this essay, the writing of history has begun to free itself from the restrictions imposed by the Soviet state, and young historians have started to explore the hitherto neglected area of women's history. Although at present few of their works are available in English, their scholarship has already brought fresh perspectives to the issues I have discussed. In that sense, at least, the changes that occurred in the late 1990s are encouraging.

Conclusion

Attempts of nationalists and conservatives to redefine women's roles represent the recurrence of a long-standing Russian practice, according to which others define women's individual well-being in terms of their own goals. Since the days of Peter the Great, the state has played a substantial role in shaping the public and private lives of Russia's women. Recognizing the importance of gender in structuring social relations, Russia's rulers often treated women either as agents of modernization or as sources of social stability. The state's opponents did so as well. The state's readiness to manipulate gender relations and reconfigure gender hierarchies as a means of fostering social change or consolidation encouraged a comparable concern with gender relations among those who contested the state's power.

The woman question that engaged intellectuals during the late tsarist era has resurfaced since the collapse of the Soviet Union, although it is no longer referred to by that old-fashioned name. The current discussion is at least as wide-ranging as in prerevolutionary times and, as before, it is distinguished by the presence of educated and articulate women who struggle to define and pursue a woman-oriented politics (although not necessarily a feminist politics in the Western sense). Now, however, the numbers are larger and the backgrounds far more varied than was the case in the imperial period, thanks in large part to the policies of the Soviet era. It remains to be seen how contemporary female activists will deal with the powerful tradition of female self-sacrifice for the common good.

Notes

1. Richard Stites, *The Women's Liberation Movement in Russia: Feminism, Nihilism, and Bolshevism, 1860–1930* (Princeton: Princeton University Press, 1978).

2. Lindsay Hughes, "Peter the Great's Two Weddings: Changing Images of Women in a Transitional Age," in *Women in Russia and the Ukraine*, ed. Rosalind Marsh (New York: Cambridge University Press, 1996), 31.

3. The decree is translated in *Major Problems in the History of Imperial Russia*, ed. James Cracraft (Lexington: D. C. Heath, 1994), 110–11.

4. The law was rescinded in 1775.

5. Lindsay Hughes, "Between Two Worlds: Tsarevna Natal'ia Alekseevna and the 'Emancipation' of Petrine Women," in *A Window on Russia: Papers from the V International Conference of the Study Group on Eighteenth-Century Russia, Gargnano, 1994*, ed. Maria Di Salvo and Lindsay Hughes (Rome: La Fenice, 1996), 29–36; Lindsay Hughes, "From Caftans into Corsets: The Sartorial Transformation of Women during the Reign of Peter the Great," in *Gender and Sexuality in Russian Civilization*, ed. P. I. Barta (London: Routledge, 2001), 17–32.

6. Quoted in Natalia Pushkareva, *Women in Russian History* (Armonk: M. E. Sharpe, 1996), 165.

7. Catriona Kelly, *Refining Russia: Advice Literature, Polite Culture, and Gender from Catherine to Yeltsin* (New York: Oxford University Press, 2001), 28.

8. J. L. Black, "Educating Women in Eighteenth-Century Russia: Myths and Realities," *Canadian Slavonic Papers* 20, no. 1 (1978): 23–43; Carol Nash, "Educating New Mothers: Women and the Enlightenment in Russia," *History of Education Quarterly* 21 (Fall 1981): 301–16.

9. Michelle Lamarche Marrese, "The Enigma of Married Women's Control of Property in Eighteenth-Century Russia," *Russian Review* 58 (July 1999): 380–95.

10. Pushkareva, *Women in Russian History*, 174–75.

11. Gregory Freeze, ed., *From Supplication to Revolution: A Documentary Social History of Imperial Russia* (New York: Oxford University Press, 1988), 98–99; Lee Farrow, "Peter the Great's Law of Single Inheritance: State Imperatives and Noble Resistance," *Russian Review* 55 (July 1996): 430–47. For a semifictional account of such abuse and of both authoritarian and egalitarian styles of noble family life in the late eighteenth century, see Sergei Aksakov, *The Family Chronicle* (New York: E. P. Dutton, 1961). William Wagner argues that the disadvantaged legal status of women prevented them from exercising their right to property. Michelle Marrese disagrees. Her meticulous study provides substantial evidence of women who actively engaged in management of their own as well as a spouse's estates. Michelle Lamarche Marrese, *A Woman's Kingdom:*

Noblewomen and the Control of Property in Russia, 1700–1861 (Ithaca: Cornell University Press, 2002).

12. John Bushnell, "Did Serf Owners Control Serf Marriage? Orlov Serfs and Their Neighbors, 1773–1861," *Slavic Review* 52 (Fall 1993): 419–45.

13. Quoted in Pushkareva, *Women in Russian History*, 166–67.

14. David Ransel, *Mothers of Misery: Child Abandonment in Russia* (Princeton: Princeton University Press, 1988), 21–22.

15. Adele Lindenmeyr, "Public Life, Private Virtues: Women in Russian Charity, 1762–1914," *Signs* 18, no. 3 (1993): 564, 569; Brenda Meehan-Waters, "Popular Piety, Local Initiative and the Founding of Women's Religious Communities in Russia, 1764–1907," *St. Vladimir's Theological Quarterly* 30 (1986): 137.

16. Dashkova's memoirs have been reprinted, with an excellent introduction by Jehanne M. Gheithm, as *The Memoirs of Princess Dashkova* (Durham: Duke University Press, 1995).

17. Lina Bernstein, "Women on the Verge of a New Language: Russian Salon Hostesses in the First Half of the Nineteenth Century," in *Russia-Women-Culture*, ed. Beth Holmgren and Helena Goscilo (Bloomington: Indiana University Press, 1996), 209–12. On women writers in this period see Judith Vowles, "The 'Feminization' of Russian Literature: Women, Language, and Literature in Eighteenth Century Russia," in *Women Writers in Russian Literature*, ed. Toby W. Clyman and Diana Greene (Westport: Greenwood Press, 1994), 35–60, and *Dictionary of Russian Women Writers*, ed. Marina Ledkovsky, Charlotte Rosenthal, and Mary Zirin (Westport: Greenwood Press, 1994).

18. Lydia Ginzburg, *On Psychological Prose*, trans. and ed. Judson Rosengrant (Princeton: Princeton University Press, 1991), 44.

19. Judith E. Zimmerman, "Natalie Herzen and the Early Intelligentsia," *Russian Review* 41 (July 1982): 264.

20. Stites, *The Women's Liberation Movement;* Barbara Alpern Engel, *Mothers and Daughters: Women of the Intelligentsia in Nineteenth-Century Russia* (New York: Cambridge University Press, 1983); Grigorii A. Tishkin, "The Women's Question and Legal Thought in Russia during the 1850s and 1860s," *Russian Studies in History* 33 (Fall 1994): 6–62.

21. Quoted in Engel, *Mothers and Daughters*, 80.

22. For an excellent, annotated English translation of the book, see Nikolai Chernyshevsky, *What Is to Be Done?*, trans. Michael Katz and annotated by William Wagner (Ithaca: Cornell University Press, 1989).

23. Five of them tell their stories in *Five Sisters: Women against the Tsar*, ed. Barbara A. Engel and Clifford Rosenthal (New York: Routledge, 1995). See also Vera Figner, *Memoirs of a Revolutionist* (DeKalb: Northern Illinois University Press, 1991).

24. Cathy Frierson, *Peasant Icons: Representations of Rural People in Late Nineteenth-Century Russia* (New York: Oxford University Press, 1993), 161–80.

25. Rose Glickman, "Women and the Peasant Commune," in *Land Commune and Peasant Community in Russia: Communal Forms in Imperial and Early Soviet Society*, ed. Roger Bartlett (New York: St. Martin's Press, 1990), 321–38.

26. Christine Worobec, "Peasant Women and Patriarchy," in *Peasant Economy, Culture and Politics of European Russia, 1800–1921*, ed. Esther Kingston-Mann and Timothy Mixter (Princeton: Princeton University Press, 1991), 181. Research on the informal power of peasant women has thus far concentrated on the postemancipation period. Given, however, the other continuities in peasant life across the divide of emancipation, it seems reasonable to read back such patterns into the earlier period.

27. Women's family-based resistance is discussed in Nancy Frieden, "Child Care: Medical Reform in a Traditionalist Culture," in *The Family in Imperial Russia: New Lines of Historical Research*, ed. David Ransel (Urbana: University of Illinois Press, 1978), 236–59; and Barbara Alpern Engel, "Women, Men, and the Languages of Peasant Resistance, 1870–1907," in *Cultures in Flux: Lower-Class Values, Practices, and Resistance in Late Imperial Russia*, ed. Stephen P. Frank and Mark D. Steinberg (Princeton: Princeton University Press, 1994), 34–53.

28. See the discussion in Ben Eklof, *Russian Peasant Schools: Officialdom, Village Culture, and Popular Pedagogy, 1861–1914* (Berkeley: University of California Press, 1986), 186–89, 287–88. Most of the schools that opened in this period were church parish schools.

29. Barbara Alpern Engel, "The Woman's Side: Male Out-Migration and the Family Economy in Kostroma Province," *Slavic Review* 45 (Summer 1986): 257–71; David Ransel, "Abandonment and Fosterage of Unwanted Children: The Women of the Foundling System," in *The Family in Imperial Russia: New Lines of Historical Research*, ed. David Ransel (Urbana: University of Illinois Press, 1978), 189–217; Judith Pallot, "Women's Domestic Industries in Moscow Province, 1880–1900," in *Russia's Women: Accommodation, Resistance, Transformation*, ed. Barbara Clements, Barbara Engel, and Christine Worobec (Berkeley: University of California Press, 1991), 163–85.

30. The leveling tendencies of urbanization and commercialization are explored by Louise McReynolds, "'The Incomparable' Anastasia Vial'tseva and the Culture of Personality," in *Russia-Women-Culture*, ed. Beth Holmgren and Helena Goscilo (Bloomington: Indiana University Press, 1996), 273–94, and Christine Ruane, "Clothes Make the Comrade: A History of the Russian Fashion Industry," *Russian History* 23, nos. 1–4 (1996): 311–43.

31. Laurie Bernstein, *Sonia's Daughters: Prostitutes and Their Regulation in Imperial Russia* (Berkeley: University of California Press, 1995), 41.

32. More than eighty of the women's religious communities ran some sort of school for girls. Brenda Meehan-Waters, "From Contemplative Practice to Charitable Activity: Russian Women's Religious Communities and the Development of Charitable Work, 1861–1917," in *Lady Bountiful Revisited: Women, Philanthropy and Power*, ed. Kathleen McCarthy (New Brunswick: Rutgers University Press, 1990), 142–56.

33. Quoted in Rose Glickman, *Russian Factory Women: Workplace and Society, 1880–1914* (Berkeley: University of California/Princeton University Press, 1984), 190.

34. An abridged version, edited and translated by Beth Holmgren and Helena Goscilo, has been published: Anastasya Verbitskaya, *Keys to Happiness: A Novel* (Bloomington: Indiana University Press, 1999).

35. A translation of this essay can be found in Alexandra Kollontai, *The Autobiography of a Sexually Emancipated Communist Woman* (New York: Herder and Herder, 1971). Other writings by Kollontai are available in *The Selected Writings of Alexandra Kollontai*, translated and with an introduction by Alix Holt (Westport: Greenwood Press, 1978). Kollontai is one of the few female leaders of this period to have received sustained biographical treatment. Barbara Evans Clements, *Bolshevik Feminist: The Life of Alexandra Kollontai* (Bloomington: Indiana University Press, 1979); Beatrice Farnsworth, *Alexandra Kollontai: Socialism, Feminism and the Bolshevik Revolution* (Stanford: Stanford University Press, 1980).

36. Melissa K. Stockdale, "'My Death for the Motherland Is Happiness': Women, Patriotism, and Soldiering in Russia's Great War, 1914–1917," *American Historical Review* 109 (Feb. 2004): 78–116.

37. Barbara Alpern Engel, "Not by Bread Alone: Subsistence Riots in Russia during World War I," *Journal of Modern History* 69 (Dec. 1997): 696–721.

38. Steve Smith, "Class and Gender: Women's Strikes in St. Petersburg, 1895–1917, and in Shanghai, 1895–1927," *Social History* 19 (May 1994): 159–68; M. Donald, "Bolshevik Activity amongst the Working Women of Petrograd in 1917," *International Journal of Social History* 27 (1982): 129–60.

39. *The Woman Question: Selections from the Writings of Karl Marx, Frederick Engels, V. I. Lenin, Joseph Stalin* (New York: International Publishers, 1951), 56.

40. On Armand, see R. C. Elwood, *Inessa Armand: Revolutionary and Feminist* (New York: Cambridge University Press, 1992).

41. Carol Hayden, "The Zhenotdel and the Bolshevik Party," *Russian History* 3, pt. 2 (1976): 150–73; Wendy Goldman, "Industrial Politics, Peasant Rebellion and the Death of the Proletarian Women's Movement in the USSR," *Slavic Review* 55 (Spring 1996): 46–77.

42. Dress codes were less severe in nomadic and seminomadic communities. Material on Central Asian women is drawn from Shirin Akiner, "Between Tradition and Modernity: The Dilemma Facing Contemporary Central Asian Women," in *Post-Soviet Women: From the Baltic to Central Asia*, ed. Mary Buckley (New York: Cambridge University Press, 1997), 261–304; Gregory Massell, *The Surrogate Proletariat: Moslem Women and Revolutionary Strategies in Soviet Central Asia: 1919–1929* (Princeton: Princeton University Press, 1974); and especially Douglas Northrup, *Veiled Empire: Gender and Power in Stalinist Central Asia* (Ithaca: Cornell University Press, 2004).

43. Elizabeth Waters, "In the Shadow of the Comintern: The Communist Women's Movement, 1920–1943," in *Promissory Notes: Women in the Transition to Socialism*, ed. Sonia Kruks, Rayna Rapp, and Marilyn Young (New York: Monthly Review Press, 1989), 29–56.

44. Diane Koenker, "Men against Women on the Shop Floor in Early Soviet Russia," *American Historical Review* 100 (Dec. 1995): 1,443; see also Elizabeth Wood, "Class and Gender at Loggerheads in the Early Soviet State: Who Should Organize the Female Proletariat and How?" in *Gender and Class in Modern Europe*, ed. Laura Frader and Sonya Rose (Ithaca: Cornell University Press, 1996), 294–310.

45. Anne Gorsuch, "'A Woman Is Not a Man': The Culture of Gender and Generation in Soviet Russia, 1921–1928," *Slavic Review* 55 (Fall 1996): 660; Frances Bernstein, "Envisioning Health in Revolutionary Russia: The Politics of Gender in Sexual-Enlightenment Posters of the 1920s," *Russian Review* 57 (April 1998): 191–217; Lynn Mally, "Performing the New Woman: The Komsomolka as Actress and Image in Soviet Youth Theatre," *Journal of Social History* 30 (Fall 1996): 79–95; Isabel A. Tirado, "The Komsomol and the Krest'ianka: The Political Mobilization of Young Women in the Russian Village, 1921–1927," *Russian History* 23, nos. 1–4 (1996): 345–66.

46. Barbara Evans Clements, *Bolshevik Women* (New York: Cambridge University Press, 1997), 250.

47. Lynn Viola, "Bab'i bunty and Peasant Women's Protest During Collectivization," in *Russian Peasant Women*, ed. Beatrice Farnsworth and Lynn Viola (New York: Oxford University Press, 1992), 189–205. Images of peasant women during this period are discussed in Victoria E. Bonnell, "The Peasant Woman in Stalinist Political Art of the 1930s," *American Historical Review* 98 (Feb. 1993): 55–82.

48. Jeffrey J. Rossman, "The Teikovo Cotton Workers' Strike of April 1932: Class, Gender and Identity Politics in Stalin's Russia," *Russian Review* 56 (Jan. 1997): 44–69.

49. Among those available in English are Anna Akhmatova, *Requiem*, trans. D. M.

Thomas (Athens: Ohio University Press, 1976); Lydia Chukovskaya, *Sofia Petrovna* (Evanston: Northwestern University Press, 1988); Eugenia Semyonovna Ginzburg, *Journey into the Whirlwind* (New York: Harcourt Jovanovich, 1967); Anna Larina, *This I Cannot Forget: The Memoirs of Nikolai Bukharin's Widow* (New York: W. W. Norton, 1993); and Nadezhda Mandelstam, *Hope against Hope* (New York: Atheneum, 1970). On women writers as conservators of culture and memory, see Beth Holmgren, *Women's Works in Stalin's Time: On Lidiia Chukovskaia and Nadezhda Mandelstam* (Bloomington: Indiana University Press, 1993).

50. David L. Hoffman, *Peasant Metropolis: Social Identities in Moscow, 1929–1941* (Ithaca: Cornell University Press, 1994), 119–22.

51. Goldman, "Industrial Politics," 63.

52. Mary Buckley, "The Untold Story of the Obshchestvennitsa in the 1930s," *Europe-Asia Studies* 48, no. 4 (1996): 569–86; Sheila Fitzpatrick, "'Middle-class Values' and Soviet Life in the 1930s," in *Soviet Society and Culture: Essays in Honor of Vera S. Dunham*, ed. Terry L. Thompson and Richard Sheldon (Boulder: Westview Press, 1988), 20–38; Rebecca Balmas Neary, "Mothering Socialist Society: The Wife-Activists' Movement and the Soviet Culture of Daily Life," *Russian Review* 58 (July 1999): 396–412; Susan E. Reid, "All Stalin's Women: Gender and Power in Soviet Art of the 1930s," *Slavic Review* 57 (Spring 1998): 133–73.

53. Hoffman, *Peasant Metropolis*, 118.

54. An English translation of this legislation can be found in *The Family in the USSR: Documents and Readings*, ed. Rudolf Schlesinger (London: Routledge and Kegan Paul, 1949).

55. Underground abortion is discussed by several of the narrators in *A Revolution of Their Own: Voices of Women in Soviet History*, ed. Barbara Alpern Engel and Anastasia Posadskaya-Vanderbeck (Boulder: Westview Press, 1998).

56. Akiner, "Between Tradition and Modernity," 276. A discussion of the role of Soviet medical policy in changing the lives of Central Asian women can be found in Paula A. Michaels, "Medical Traditions, Kazak Women, and Soviet Medical Politics to 1941," *Nationalities Papers* 26, no. 3 (1998): 493–509.

57. K. Jean Cottam, "Soviet Women in Combat in World War II: The Ground Forces and the Navy," *International Journal of Women's Studies* 3 (July–Aug. 1980): 345–55; John Erickson, "Soviet Women at War," in *World War II and the Soviet People: Selected Papers from the Fourth World Congress for Soviet and East European Studies, Harrogate, 1990*, ed. John Garrard and Carol Garrard (New York: St. Martin's Press, 1993), 53–76.

58. Barbara Alpern Engel, "The Womanly Face of War: Soviet Women Remember World War II," in *Enlisted With or Without Consent: Women and War in the Twentieth Century*, ed. Nicole Dombrowski (Westport: Garland Publishing, 1997), 138–61; Richard Stites, *Russian Popular Culture: Entertainment and Society since 1900* (New York: Cambridge University Press, 1992), 100, 111–12, 115.

59. The 1944 code is reproduced in *The Family in the USSR*, ed. Schlesinger.

60. The 1970 census reported that 86 percent of able-bodied women were employed full time. Jo Peers, "Workers by Hand and Womb—Soviet Women and the Demographic Crisis," in *Soviet Sisterhood*, ed. Barbara Holland (Bloomington: Indiana University Press, 1985), 118.

61. Peers, "Workers by Hand and Womb," 127. Wages in Central Asia were so low that the additional benefits deriving from sizeable families (five to six or more children) could comprise a substantial part of the household budget.

62. On essentialism, see Lynn Attwood, "The New Soviet Man and Woman—Soviet Views on Psychological Differences," in *Soviet Sisterhood*, ed. Barbara Holland (Bloomington: Indiana University Press, 1985), 54–77. The evolution of the woman question is discussed in Mary Buckley, *Women and Ideology in the Soviet Union* (Ann Arbor: University of Michigan Press, 1989). A selection of Soviet writings on women's roles can be found in *Women, Work and Family in the Soviet Union*, ed. Gail Warshofsky Lapidus (Armonk: M. E. Sharpe, 1982).

63. Selections from the publications are available in English in *Woman and Russia, the First Feminist Samizdat*, trans. Woman and Eastern Europe Group (London: Sheba Feminist Publishers, 1980) and *Women and Russia: Feminist Writings from the Soviet Union*, ed. Tatyana Mamonova (Boston: Beacon Press, 1984).

64. On prostitution, see Elizabeth Waters, "Restructuring the Woman Question: Prostitution and Perestroika," *Feminist Review* 33 (Autumn 1989): 3–19.

65. Larissa Lissyutkina, "Soviet Women at the Crossroads of Perestroika" in *Gender Politics and Post-Communism: Reflections from Eastern Europe and the Former Soviet Union*, ed. Nanette Funk and Magda Mueller (New York: Routledge, 1993), 274–86.

66. Elizabeth Waters, "Finding a Voice: The Emergence of a Women's Movement," in *Gender Politics and Post-Communism: Reflections from Eastern Europe and the Former Soviet Union*, ed. Nanette Funk and Magda Mueller (New York: Routledge, 1993), 287–302. The First Independent Women's Forum is discussed in Cynthia Cockburn, "Democracy without Women Is No Democracy," *Feminist Review* 39 (1991): 140–48. Materials from the Second Independent Women's Forum have been published in Russian and in English: *From Problems to Strategy: Second Independent Women's Forum, Dubna, Russia, 1992* (Moscow: Center for Gender Studies, 1993; Hilversum, Netherland: Foundation Women's Activities Promotions, 1993). The Ariadne Europe Fund, P.O. Box 1564, 1200 BN Hilversum, Netherlands, supported the publication of this volume. See also *Feminist Theory and Practice: East-West: Papers Presented of [sic] International Conference. St. Petersburg, Repino. June 9–12, 1995* (St. Petersburg: Petersburg Center for Gender Issues, 1995). Two valuable collections of Russian-authored articles that deal primarily with contemporary issues are *Women in Russia: A New Era in Russian Feminism*, ed. Anastasia Posadskaya (New York: Verso Press, 1994), and *Women in Contemporary Russia*, ed. Vitalina Koval (Providence, R.I.: Berghahn Books, 1995). More recent developments are described in Sue Bridger, Rebecca Kay, and Kathryn Pinnick, *No More Heroines? Russia, Women, and the Market* (New York: Routledge, 1996).

5

Latin American Women's History: The National Period

ASUNCIÓN LAVRIN

In Latin America, a number of nations exist independently, have their own histories, and view each other as neighbors. Geographical, economic, racial, ethnic, and language diversity characterize the area, which is not the sum of its parts but rather a complex set of countries that interact among themselves and with the rest of the world. In addition to the original indigenous stock, Europeans and Africans have lived and mingled throughout centuries and give the continent a unique character, with layers of cultures actively influencing each other in a dynamic imbrication leavened by concepts of class inherited from the past and difficult to eradicate owing to different degrees of economic development.

Disparities exist among nations. Some continue to struggle with unyielding economies and difficult political systems, whereas others have thriving financial and industrial centers. Three official languages are spoken in nations of "Latin" or Mediterranean cultural extraction, although the hundreds of native languages still spoken in certain areas of Central and South America are barely represented in the academic output on the feminine condition or history. In this essay I will only include countries that shared a Spanish or Portuguese colonial past.

After independence from Spain and Portugal, the former colonies divided into nations that developed along different political and economic lines but still shared key cultural elements. Brazil, a former Portuguese colony, became independent in 1824 and adopted a monarchic system of government, remaining an empire until 1889. Cuba and Puerto Rico remained possessions of Spain until 1898. In 1902 Cuba became an independent country, and Puerto Rico passed into a protectorate of the United States, later to be recognized as a "commonwealth." The rest of the nations in Latin America have been independent since roughly the third decade of the nineteenth century, making comparisons with other colonized areas of the world difficult.

During the past two centuries the process of nation-building has entailed a search for political identity and stability, social and economic justice, and economic development. Unforgiving global market pressures have obliged many to remain providers of raw materials and sources of migration to the United States rather than fully industrialized nations. Large populations live in capital cities, the sites of centralized governments and industrial and technological resources. Rural areas lag behind the advanced facilities of cities.

Despite social and economic disparities, Latin America as a whole is a dynamic continent where accoutrements of "the West" have deep historical roots and commingle with indigenous non-Western traditions and imported African cultural traits. Tensions between colonial understructures and the modern postindustrial world played themselves out throughout the nineteenth and the twentieth centuries, endowing the region with tantalizing contrasts of modernity and traditionalism. The role of women in this complex process has only recently become a subject of academic historical interest. There are no comprehensive surveys of women's history in all Latin America during the national period, either in English or in Spanish. As such, women's history is best reviewed using overarching themes extracted from monographs and primary printed sources.

A brief overview of important historical moments in the history of women in Latin America in the early and mid-national period (roughly between 1820 and 1910) should evaluate the effects of the transition from colonialism to full nationhood. The definition of gender relations and family law, gleaned from legislation and the civil codes, provides the framework to the ideological debates of women's social and economic roles after independence. Church and state had important confrontations that were to define legal rights and either challenged or reinforced values guiding gender relations. Liberalism, positivism, and conservatism were more than philosophical stands as statesmen shaped and reshaped the contours of politics and legislation during the process of nation-building.

One of the great ideological battles of the mid- and late nineteenth century was over civil marriage, which most countries adopted before the end of the century. Divorce, however, was more difficult to attain, and the struggle to incorporate it into law was carried well into the mid-twentieth century.

The assumption of public education by the state in the nineteenth century profoundly affected women because education provided opportunity to become teachers, write and read, and assimilate the basic concepts of civil life. Primary public education systems centers began to develop during the 1860s, secondary education began between the 1870s and 1880s, and university education became available to a few daring women by the end of the nineteenth century even though it was not significant to many until the mid-1930s. Female literacy increased, and women in cities began to write, gaining their own voices in the representation of their interests. By the early 1930s women teachers had become the backbone of elementary education in all nations. The contribution of formal education to the legitimation of women's lives and work outside the home and their emergence into the public arena is largely the result of this rather complex and not well-researched aspect of history.

The incorporation of women into the urban industrial labor market was also a significant trend of the period. Previously, women in cities had few choices in paid occupations. Only domestic work was open to women who were poor and of the urban underclass. Those in the countryside labored in many occupations in homes and fields as key elements of the domestic economic unit. Slavery still survived in some countries through the second half of the nineteenth century, and female slaves labored on plantations as well as in urban households. Typically, neither nation-builders nor later historians took much notice of female labor before the introduction of factories in the cities.

Although textile factories operated in some countries since the late eighteenth century, urbanization and demographic growth at the end of the nineteenth century created a demand for female and child labor in most capital cities. As nations began to industrialize and/or vie for international markets, credit, and the paraphernalia of technology, women began to join the labor force, changing the economy of households. Their participation in the labor market strengthened the arguments of socialists, feminists, and social reformers on behalf of women's political and legal equality in the early twentieth century.

Between the mid-1920s and the late 1990s, education, blue-collar labor, and professional occupations enhanced women's civil and political rights and kindled active participation in civic and revolutionary movements, the arts, and literature. Women's activism during the 1920s and 1930s was critical in developing self-consciousness about their rights and potential participation in their nations' destinies. Aided by the first feminist organizations, urban women first sought to gain more personal freedom as well as control over their children through the reform of family law, as defined in the civil codes. From there they moved on to accessing the political rights leading to full citizenship. The first country to grant the vote was Ecuador, in 1929; the last was Paraguay in 1961. The push for woman suffrage contributed considerably to fostering the ideal of democracy in Latin America while many countries struggled under military or civil dictatorships. More politically conscious women fully participated in movements that brought down regimes of the right and the left.

Women by the late twentieth century had become a factor to be reckoned with in national polities. Photographs show only men at the political meetings of the 1920s, but by the late 1980s women's faces are everywhere. The same can be said for female participation in a labor market sustained by an enormous growth in the population. When economists turned to developmentalism in the 1960s it was assumed that the labor market would include women in all sectors, as it did. The unfortunate aspect of that assumption was that women in general were supporting national growth while they were either non-wage-earning family members or underpaid workers. These themes will be developed throughout this essay under several key sections.

The discipline of history by itself does not provide all the materials desirable to discuss or teach women's history for the national period. Political activities, development, and labor issues have been favored over others. In most cases, history has assumed a more interdisciplinary approach, using questions and materials developed by sociologists, anthropologists, and political scientists. Historians of women and gender in Latin America also face the problem of a scarcity of personal, family, and private institutions' papers. Even women who "made" history paid little attention to keeping diaries and systematic records of their activities, nor did they write memoirs. Yet national and governmental records and a rich press are strong pillars sustaining the development of the history of women after independence.

It was not until the 1960s that the history of women began to follow new and more rigorous paths. Biographical collections on "notable" women are still printed in Latin America, but they now represent popular historical literature rather than academic endeavor. Since the 1980s, systematic studies have begun to delve into social, economic, and cultural issues; gender relations; and the daily lives and family histories of women. Monographs and edited volumes have also begun to develop national histories of women from the sixteenth century to the present.

The burgeoning North American academic interest in Latin American women and gender issues has produced an increasing number of studies that cross disciplines and are available in English. Even so, publications in Spanish are still the most important source of information because they are independently produced in each nation. My analysis here is framed by those circumstances and based on English, Spanish, and Portuguese sources, even though most citations in the bibliography are of titles in English.

Several themes drive the field by the sheer weight of numbers and scholarly attention: history of social issues such as labor and development, sexuality and gender relations, and social and political movements. Interwoven into those themes are the experiences of women as testimonials of agency. They give historians opportunity to assess and contrast the personal and social experience of women of different racial, ethnic, and social classes in various national locations.

The Lives of Women: The Common and the Notable

Women began to become their own historical subjects in the late nineteenth century when they joined male literary figures and journalists in the process of building a national self-identity. A balance between the "exceptional" and the "common" female experience is hard to achieve. Among historians, the latter marks the prevailing trend; among literary historians, the former predominates. There is pedagogical value in exploring the ways in which some exceptional women represent common paradigms. Biographical materials are very useful in introducing the topic to beginners or general readers and serve well the interdisciplinary purposes of women's studies courses.

The national saga of independence produced the first cohort of female heroines. National historiographies have not treated them as "republican mothers" but rather as exceptional women who had no lasting influence. Independence gave women the opportunity to recast themselves in temporary heroic roles that showed more about their personal capability to rise to the challenge of a political upheaval as supporters of freedom than about their ability to change their own or their nation's social and political circumstances.

Ironically, mothering and nurturing remained desirable choices after independence, a prototype also favored by men who desired no changes or challenges to their patriarchal roles. That pattern prevailed in the lives of real women as well as in the construction of women's history and remained entrenched in historical literature throughout the first half of the twentieth century. Women such as Juana Azurduy de Padilla of Bolivia and Policarpa Salavarrieta of Colombia have become typical sacrificial archetypes of independence. Azurduy fought with her husband in the war against Spain in what is today Bolivia. Salavarrieta conspired with the patriots in what is today Colombia and was put to death for treason by the Spanish authorities.

The numbers of politically heroic female figures had decreased by the mid-nineteenth century, overwhelmed by the many difficulties of early nationhood. The exceptions were Cuban women, who participated in several wars of independence (1868–78 and 1895–98), and women in Paraguay, a country involved in a war with some of its neighbors (1865–70). In the Paraguayan case, women played a key economic role after the war, although that nation's men did not consider giving women broader social rights or improving their lives in other ways.[1]

Everywhere in Latin America scores of women continued to live and struggle as members but not citizens of new nations, adjusting to or contesting the many cultural and legal restrictions that framed their lives. Their history is just beginning to be written by historians interested in gender relations and the role of the state and the judiciary in shaping them. Some studies of working women do exist, however, and more recently, histories of family life and domestic relations. A history of daily domestic life and gender relations of Costa Rica during the first half of the nineteenth century, for example, shows that social attitudes on marriage, domestic violence, marital separation, and female honor remained traditional among people of different social extraction.[2] Nuances in behavior among the rich as well as the poor were still overruled by a conservative respect for family ties and patriarchal values. Continuities rather than change characterized marriage, family life, and gender relations.

During the second half of the nineteenth century women writers used their pens to construct a national literature as well as their own histories. Their writing, which appeared in newspapers and magazines, covers all genres. Juana Manuela Gorriti, Clorinda Matto de Turner, Soledad Acosta de Samper, and Mercedes Cabello de Carbonera are among those women, most of whom were upper-middle-class, who reflected on the anxieties and expectations of an emerging cultural elite born into tradition but hoped for a change that would enable them to gain greater social freedom for their sex.

To the extent that their writing helps illuminate the process of state-building and gender redefinition throughout time, their work is useful to all students of women's history. A unique diary kept by a young Brazilian woman, Helena Morley, whose English grandmother encouraged her to write, remains as an exceptional testimonial that late-nineteenth-century Brazil was still torn by overt racism and sexism. Historians have also resorted to the writing of many women travelers who visited Latin American countries. The observations of Fanny Calderón de la Barca, the Spanish wife of the English ambassador to Mexico in mid-century, for example, are considered a classic source of information for details of daily life that escaped other historians. Although the travelers' sources contain biases and misrepresentations, they provide females' views of other women and portray both the observers and the observed, which helps readers discover meaningful nuances in the women's universe.

The reconstruction of women's history in the second half of the nineteenth century is still rather tentative. Silvia Arrom's broad picture of women up to the mid-nineteenth century in Mexico City includes legislation and family law issues as well as information on labor and divorce cases. Probing suits for divorce confirms that the nature of gender relations and the attitude of church and state had changed little from the colonial past. Recent studies on marriage and the family use them to test the validity of the patriarchal system that national political and religious leaders upheld at the time. The study of divorce cases and ecclesiastic and judicial records of the period yields important data on how the law, as enacted by men of the ruling elite, reaffirmed patriarchal domination while women of all social strata made efforts to redefine themselves and their roles in society.[3] The disappearance of a colonial institution in Brazil, the dowry, has been seen as a reinterpretation of marriage and gender relations whereby men became more independent in business or had career options that did not necessitate reliance on their brides' dowries.[4] A different interpretation of the lessening of value and numbers of dowries in nineteenth-century Lima argues that they were still meaningful for women of the lesser social classes as a legal means to build arguments for economic entitlement and protection.[5] But while opportunities for self-assertion were opening for women, a male backlash took place, consisting in higher demands for virtuous behavior in women. Nonetheless, for the majority of women the dowry was a dead institution by the beginning of the twentieth century. What remained was the patriarchal domination of females through a complex legal system embodied in judiciary codes.

All nineteenth-century Latin American civil codes constructed a family law whereby the man became economically and socially responsible for the family, demanding in exchange the submission of wife and children despite the fact that for a majority of women opportunities were opening for self-assertion through education and work. The protection afforded by legal mechanisms did not apply to the many couples who lived in consensual arrangements. Nonetheless, women who were poor found ways to challenge ideological assumptions in civil courts and claimed (but did not necessarily obtain) with their own independent behavior a more equitable position with men in their families. They also began to use the concept of citizenship as a basis for their standing.

Law and custom in the second half of the nineteenth century reflected the desire of the founders of the new nations to preserve patriarchal values inherited from the past. Many nations saw the need to break ties with the church and place family law under state control by adopting civil marriages and birth registries. In reality, the state replacement of the church as the arbiter of gender relations did not mean a modernization of patriarchal values. Other factors began pushing changes in that direction. The contradiction created by the incorporation of thousands of women into the labor market and their "legal" limitations did not escape the growing number of social reformers, among whom were the first cohort of women graduated from secondary schools and the universities between the 1880s and 1910. By the end of the first decade of the twentieth century, pressure to reform the Civil Codes was in full swing, and the discussion of the possibility of divorce had appeared in the public forum.

Divorce was accepted in the 1888 Civil Code of Costa Rica in 1907 in Uruguay and in 1917 in Mexico, but these nations' decisions came from above and not as the result of a sustained popular campaign. Until the second half of the century, other nations remained unwilling to break with the church and with the traditional view of the family in which the matrimonial bond guaranteed social order despite changes in other sectors of the national life.

Unquestionably, the period between 1880 and 1920 was a complex one. Models of "Victorian" motherhood and propriety were accepted by the burgeoning middle and upper class. Education for young women of the middle class and aspiring working class began to create a body of primary and eventually secondary school teachers who were neither elite nor "working class" proper. These women were highly regarded as the epitome of female virtue, an element capable of making a difference in the strengthening of the family, the training of male citizenry, and the "advancement" of women in society. Teaching captivated the minds of nation-builders of the early twentieth century and created a core of women who accepted the task of "modernizing" their nations without really eroding the traditional structures of family and gender relations. This generation was savvy about its own role and supported reforms that would give women more faculties in the public space. In Costa Rica, Cuba, Chile, Argentina, and Brazil, teachers and writers supported suffrage and the reform of family law and helped women to assume a more vigorous role in society.[6] As a largely urban group, they cared for the problems specific to cities but had little impact on rural women and could not do much to change policies at the national level.

Travelers from abroad did not fail to notice the disparities between the Europeanized upper classes and the mottled crowds of women who toiled as servants and peddled their wares in town markets or on the streets of large urban areas. The reconstruction of the lives of poor women of all races is still taking place. Those who worked as petty traders, in small domestic artisan shops, and in the cultivation of certain crops have been a permanent feature of Latin American urban and rural areas. Their labor took place either under slavery, as in Brazil, or in freedom, as in the case of indigenous and poor white women in the markets of urban areas.

In Brazil, freed and slave women could be found together in city streets as well as in the fields. Their tasks ranged from household service to helping in the production of cash crops. The availability of manumission granting all rights of freedom offered possibilities of social mobility not found in North America. Whether servants in Rio de Janeiro or rural workers in Goais, freedom and race were was the most important features that separated women in nineteenth-century Brazil, although social and biological mingling created nuances of social intercourse. The lives of female slaves in Rio de Janeiro's Afro-Brazilian population were harsh, but manumission and eventual freedom after 1888 created pockets of economic and personal opportunities that were used creatively.

Lima's slaves in the first half of the nineteenth century did not live in an individualistic universe but in a female and family universe where freedom was a goal inspiring individual effort. Freedom created pockets of economic and personal opportunities that women used creatively.[7] In Mexico, indigenous women formed the bulk of the working and servant population, lacking education and remaining on the lower rungs of society. Yet Mexican society was not sharply divided into Indian and white. Rather, centuries of race-mingling had created an increasingly mestizo nation in which education, entrepreneurship, and internal migration could change opportunities.[8] If those factors were missing, race and class reinforced the division among servants, market women, and the elite women they served. The employer's and servant's worlds were separated by class-consciousness, creating wedges between women that increased industrialization and the availability of other forms of employment would not obliterate. The class gap remained difficult to bridge, as noted by sociological studies of twentieth-century servants in Peru.[9]

The development of testimonials, a recent genre, permits us to recapture the lives of the urban and rural poor in Latin America. The testimonials deal with women's experiences across class and race and provide, with intimacy and directness, firsthand accounts of the opinions and experiences of women of the "popular" classes. As such, testimonials are excellent texts for unveiling and discussing the multiplicity of socioeconomic and cultural factors affecting women on the lower rungs of society, their agency, and their political activism. Often, testimonials involve women who have joined social movements or political pressure groups at the local and national levels. Some testimonials date to the mid-1970s, suggesting that concern over poor women's issues has a respectable academic and intellectual pedigree in Latin America, where the genre of testimonial is popular because of a solid feminist belief that each woman's experience deserves respect and generates authority.

Because they are neither biographies nor autobiographies, the methodology used to record data poses the problem of determining the influence of mediation. The recorder's persona, whether foreign or national, becomes a filter affecting the character of the original voice and creates concern for the possibility of conscious or unconscious direction. Also, just as in autobiographies, a subject chooses her memories and her own scenario. As the debate on the verifiability of events narrated by Rigoberta Menchú demonstrates, there is no testimonial exempt of weakness. Yet they help establish patterns of non-elite personal worldviews, gender relations, lifecycles, family bondings, and self- and social esteem. Among the best-known testimonials in English are those of Domitila Barrios, a Bolivian; Maria Teresa Tula from Salvador; and Elvia Alvarado of Nicaragua. Others record lesser-known lives, such as Thomas Tirado's account of a Mexican midwife, and amplify the availability of women's experiences.

Testimonials also cover groups of women. Interviews with women of several economic classes and races are very popular in Latin America itself. They allow a sampling of experiences as well as opinions on marriage, sex, work, family, and gender relations. The variety of experiences recorded in these works defies classification. Some women challenge traditional gender roles; others illuminate their personal struggles or involvement in political and social movements. Testimonial and group portraits present worlds that are not exactly alike yet bear the mark of a similarity conferred by gender, regardless of class, race, or education. The experience of maquiladoras (sweatshop workers) along the Mexico-U.S. border, as portrayed in *Beautiful Flowers of the Maquiladora,* and the working women of Cuernavaca in Sarah LeVine and Clara Sunderland Correa's *Dolor y Alegría* remain unrivaled in their ability to convey the daily struggles, hopes, disappointments, and sustaining ideals of working women.

In a class of their own are the several diaries and works on Maria Carolina de Jesus, a black trash collector who lived in the favelas of São Paulo, Brazil. The original diary published in translation in 1962, her second diary, her autobiography, and other writing by her and her daughter, in addition to a biographical work by Robert Levine, have created a corpus of readings on this humble woman. Her dignity in the midst of despair and her boundless hope are what continue to evoke interest. Although she never placed her race above all other signifiers in life, Carolina de Jesus was still a poor black woman struggling against all odds. Her recollections of early life, her savvy and ironic view of politicians, and her remarkable street wisdom are examples of the potential hidden within many poor women. Just as exceptional is the rich tapestry of Brazil's urban and rural society, which unfold subtly between the lines of the narrative. The work centering on Maria Carolina de Jesus is a challenging source of information that stretches between the biographical and the social and provides exciting reading for any class.

In contrast to the experience of working and/or poor women, biographies of exceptional women of the twentieth century should provide opportunity to assess the circumstances under which they could exercise either power or influence—rare commodities in Latin America, as exemplified by the case of Princess Isabel, heiress to the Brazilian throne. Biographies about Latin American women are scarce; books on Eva Perón of Argentina dominate the field.

To date, few women have become presidents or key political figures in any country. Those who do reach such positions are likely to stand out. They have largely achieved power through a traditional method—the use of a male relative as leverage. Perón, the first woman to advance politically in a large Latin American country, was no exception. As a member of the populist regime headed by her husband, Juan Perón her power was extraordinary, and her popularity among working people unrivaled. Eva Perón's origins in the underclass gave her cause to emphasize her position with respect to the national elite, which included the rich as well as middle-class independent intellectuals who disliked her husband's brand of politics.

Embodying one woman's welfare service to the working class that supported her husband's government, Eva Perón also became a relentless enemy of his enemies, wielding enough power to become a paradigm of a female caudillo. Her biographers either admire or scorn her. Contemporary studies such as those of Marissa Navarro and Nicholas Fraser and Alicia Dujovne, however, search beyond the glamour, gossip, mythification, and vilification of Eva Perón to analyze how she rose to power and manipulated friends and enemies. Dujovne highlights psychological aspects of her life and delves into the roots of her ambition. Although Perón was not educated enough to write an autobiography, the ghostwritten account of her life (*My Mission in Life*) as well as what are presumed to be her final writings provide challenging resources for analyzing her feelings. As propaganda tools they are an excellent means of studying the self-representation of a woman in power at mid-century, when men, neither in Argentina nor any other nation, were not ready to accept women in politics.

The spectrum of exceptional female life experiences broadens with the inclusion of the biographies of female artists and writers, women who achieved national or international recognition and expressed personal aspirations and frustrations through their work. The status of Frida Kahlo, a Mexican and perhaps the archetypal female painter, changed as she went from being Diego Rivera's wife to the subject of her own story as a person, an artist, and a politically committed woman.

Eva Perón and Frida Kahlo have elicited enough attention to generate documentaries and films that make the exploration of these multifaceted women a fuller intellectual exercise unrivaled by work on any other Latin American female personality. Women such as Gabriela Mistral, a Chilean;

Rosario Castellanos of Mexico; and, more recently, Gioconda Bello of Nicaragua and Luisa Valenzuela and Christine Lispector, from Argentina and Brazil, respectively, have gained enough intercontinental prestige that exploring the meaning in their writing (beyond the purely artistic, as representations of women's experience and sensibility) is a valid enterprise. Further, today's women writers are politically engaged. Their writing reflects the political climate of their countries as well as their own involvement in the pursuit of freedom, social justice, and equality, and attests to their discontent with the dominant patriarchy.

Collective Experiences in the Twentieth Century: The World of Female Labor

The narrative of personal experience is strongly tied to the history of the female labor force. Mapping women's participation in the labor market, and their impact on the national or regional economy, is a new phenomenon in the study of Latin American women. Rescuing women's work from oblivion was a response to theories of development and dependence, the rapid decline of Marxist theories, a return to economic neoliberalism, and establishment of a global economy in which women played key roles in manufacturing plants worldwide. Latin American social scientists rather than historians have produced a copious literature that maps the main features of the female labor market and women's role in the economic development of their nations during the second half of the twentieth century.

Urban industrial work has received the most attention, although strong concern with the informal sector of the economy is also evident. Transnational enterprises, especially in the garment industry, are of special interest, given their growth since the 1970s, whereas analyses of professional occupations, including primary school teaching and work in agriculture, remain neglected. Current studies of women in the labor market reflect the theoretical and political philosophies of their authors as intently as they purport to provide factual information on numbers and dissect the structural, behavioral, and ideological features of the female labor market, primarily that since the 1960s. They provide a useful template that historians may use to answer questions for earlier periods.

For the earlier parts of the twentieth century, and for South America in particular, urban female labor incorporated between one-quarter and one-third of all adult women into the wage labor market.[10] Those figures did not change much throughout the century. Female labor was first concentrated in the textile, garment, and food-processing industries as well as in domestic service. By the middle of the twentieth century, however, women's opportunities, supported by increasing female literacy, were no longer restricted to those narrow confines. Women had taken over most jobs in primary and secondary education, had become essential in running state and business bureaucracies, and were employed in technical occupations demanding professional training. The percentage of those in the domestic-service sector had declined, although the population of women in pink-collar jobs had grown, maintaining a constant demand for servants from poor urban and rural sectors. The increasing number of women in the so-called informal sector (street vendors) reflects unstable economies, pervasive poverty, and inequality in the division of wealth. Most women in these occupations are of Indian or African descent. The class and race gap that was evident in the nineteenth century has narrowed but not been bridged.

Did women's work create a different gender culture in society and the family? Their industrial and clerical labor provoked mixed feelings among many, including male workers who saw female labor as either competition or a further example of capitalist exploitation. Still infused with patriarchal views of home, the goal of well-meaning leaders was to relieve wives and female relatives of the burden of labor and imitate the model of a middle-class wife, totally dedicated to her home. It was not until after the 1920s that solidarity with female workers, not just sympathy for their predicament, took root in male unions. Instability in national economies and the spiraling costs of living put the working class in difficult economic strictures, and men began to appreciate women's contributions to the family budget. Even so, in times of economic depression women had to bear the brunt of male backlash in the form of job cuts.

Although women also became aware of their value in the household, at a personal level the preeminence of male roles within the family and society was not overturned. Historians see no weakening of the patriarchal stronghold in Latin America despite women's economic input to the family budget. The female presence in northern mining camps in Chile repeated traditional forms of sexual behavior—prostitution, promiscuity, and physical abuse.[11] To counter those problems, companies promoted the value of women homemakers and formalized domestic relationships. The agrarian reform promoted by presidents Eduardo Frei and Salvadore Allende validated the role of men as heads of households and their social and sexual authority over women despite recognizing women's vital roles at home and in the community. As corroborated by Farnsworth-Alvear, the powerful textile industries in Colombia advocated and supported traditional values.[12]

In labor politics, women have acted largely, although not exclusively, as supporters, whereas decision-making remained in the hands of men. Female participation in labor movements and the leadership of labor organizations began to increase only during the second half of the century. By the end of the twentieth century female labor activism was directly correlated to the nature of the occupation, the collaboration of male co-workers, and the support of the women's families. Populist regimes and unions have paid more attention to the potential political power of female workers, but, in general, working women do not play a key role in labor politics, even though in some instances their positions within unions have been strengthened, as appears to be the case with some Brazilian industrial workers and in the Argentine meatpacking industry.[13] Unionized Mexican teachers were still being represented by men in the 1980s because the majority of women teachers were reluctant to adopt leadership positions and encountered strong resistance from established union leaders if they showed interest.

Supportive welfare legislation has been granting women such benefits as paid pre- and postpartum rest and child care since the mid-1930s, but the enforceability of those benefits depended on the solvency and stability of each country. Similarly, women's working conditions have improved in countries where there are strong labor unions and a history of populism. The gap between male and female wages and incomes remains, however, and working conditions varied considerably at the end of the twentieth century.

Regardless of how women engaged in wage labor, cultural understanding of gender roles determined almost all aspects of performance and potential achievement, from hiring to retirement. Domestic ties to home and motherhood followed working women at all levels of professionalization, limiting their ability to assess and assert their interests as workers. Gender "typing" in manual and intellectual labor, and the feminization of certain sectors of the labor market, have been difficult to overcome. Born of the seeming desirability of certain occupations for women, the result has been an abnormal predominance of women in some work categories in the public and private sectors, which reinforces such work as being low-paying while managerial positions remain in male hands.

Although women have been mobilized in active support of the national economy, their male relatives may not necessarily approve of that labor, even in "revolutionary" regimes that have mobilized women to remap or save the national economy. Higher levels of education, however, have created a segment of women who work to fulfill their abilities or for economic independence rather than for sheer need.

Labor has not created a strong bond of common interests among women. The diversity of female occupations and class barriers hinder that process, and working women's consciousness of themselves as being part of a working-class movement is limited. Domestics, for example, have little in common with women employed in clerical and professional work.

As development studies have pointed out, the "feminization" of labor is connected to the feminization of poverty, whereby women carry a significant part of the burden of coping with increasing poverty. They relieve their families from the worst consequences of draconian state policies for balancing budgets or broadening markets. Since the 1960s the massive intrusion of women in the labor market has been largely the response to the globalization of labor to supply cheaper goods to the wealthier nations. Globalization has resulted in the establishment of numerous maquilas, the best-known of which are on the Mexico-U.S. border although they also flourish in Nicaragua, Guatemala, the Dominican Republic, and Colombia. Maquila is also putting-out work carried out at home, dating back to the turn of the twentieth century. State policies take an ambiguous line between "development" and labor protection legislation and allow the growth of maquilas because they provide much-needed employment. In that sense Latin America does not seem to be very different from other parts of the less-developed world.

Yet it has been argued that in some newly developed economic sectors there are women who earn more than some men and that it is necessary to analyze further local labor markets and move away from stereotyped interpretations. In the Argentine labor market between 1980 and 1993, Rosalía Cortés argues, the educational level of women may have favored them in activities that prefer women to men. She cites an increase of well-paid educated women in urban private enterprises and even some specialized state organizations such as public administration and social services and opposes blanket statements on the "marginalization" of women in the labor market. Heleith I. B. Saffioti, a Brazilian sociologist, is of the opinion that women in the technical world of the future may surpass men, given their adaptability to new forms of labor and behavior.

Although there are more dimensions to rural women than labor, most of the attention they have received has focused on the analyses of the 1970s and 1980s, which privileged their role in the labor market. Departing from the assumption that rural poor women were never taken into consideration in formulating national and international policies, these studies were often microregional in nature, underlining the value of women's labor in commercial agriculture as well as the complexity of gender relations in rural homes and communities. Female poverty, lack of state attention to issues specifically affecting women, the domination of men in very traditional forms of rural patriarchies, and the need for migration to urban areas as a means of improving economic and educational conditions are common to all rural regions in Latin America. Ethnicity and class are important in these studies because most rural women, like poor urban women, are indigenous, black, or of mixed blood; lacking in formal education; and often silenced by cultural assumptions of the preeminence of the male in the family and society.[14]

By translating female labor output into statistical data and connecting that data to policymaking institutions, development studies have addressed issues of what have been called the "practical needs" of women and children: housing, health care, safe water sources, sewage, and child care. Based on working women, the development literature "democratized" women's, sociological, and economic studies and opened the door to reinterpretations in academic analysis as well as policymaking. Development studies have not focused exclusively on economic issues but have tried to encompass the whole female universe of law, history, education, political activities, and gender relations to diagnose women's condition and propose remedies to bring all women to the highest standard of rights and protection. A mixture of Marxist and gender role theories with a utilitarian objective, development studies have energized the field of women's studies since the 1970s.

Women Politics and Feminism

Interest in the political activities of Latin American women from the 1970s onward emerged from the dramatic roles women played in resistance, whether underground or above-ground, to dictatorial regimes in Nicaragua, Brazil, Paraguay, Uruguay, Argentina, and Chile. Politics, however, is more than resistance to dictators, elections, and suffrage. Politics, understood as pressure and negotiation of issues through channels other than suffrage, is a concept historians have developed as a successful alternative for understanding the meaning of movements and their difference from the traditional struggles for national power. Whether in encounters between townspeople and local authorities or in the organization of the first trade unions or workers' welfare associations, women's ability to discern common interests through various forms of association is evidence of their political acumen.

For most of the nineteenth century, most men and women lacked access to national politics because, in constitutional systems, qualifications of literacy or property deprived them of suffrage. Even after the adoption of male universal suffrage, voting and traditional politics were meaningless in countries dominated by dictators. Not until the late 1970s did women participate openly and widely in social and political movements, and they did so because the more open, inclusive political culture of the late twentieth century permitted and encouraged them.

One arena in which women of the early twentieth century experienced political ideologies was that of labor. Working women at the turn of the century were courted by ideologies of the left such as socialism, anarchism, and even communism. The right, mostly represented by the church, ran an effective set of unions or mutualist societies. The interaction of labor, the left, and revolutionary political ideologies has been better studied than right-wing or conservative movements. Yet the right carried a great deal of political weight (and still does) and often has been effective in mobilizing women around themes of home and family throughout the twentieth century.[15] At several points during the process of debating woman suffrage, divorce, or equal rights, the power of traditional or conservative ideologies and the church created either fear in the left or hope for the right. It is only in the very recent past that the idiosyncrasies of political activities among women and the potential strengths of women acting as a unit have begun to be appreciated.

Does women's political behavior have distinctive features? At the outset of national political activism during the 1920s, women, supported by men, resorted to themes and behavior that stressed their feminine and maternal aspects. Feminist groups developed political strategies to lobby male politicians and intellectuals and earn the support of other women.[16] Unofficial women's "parties" were founded to train women in political discussion, and sometimes they ventured beyond national issues and involved themselves in antiwar and pacifist campaigns.

Between 1929 and 1961 female suffrage became a reality in all countries. In some, it was the result of one man's presidential decision; in others, lively debates took place, with women leaders taking a vigorous part. The hope of early-twentieth-century feminists that female suffrage would change the nature of politics and give women a larger voice in framing policies energized many early activists. Although those hopes never crystalized, women began to define agendas of their own and act upon them, independent of men.[17]

Cultural traditions and inhibitions have conspired against the emergence of strong female leaders in Latin America. National politics remain under the control of men and are heavily infused by masculine values. In most countries women have yet to enter the political arena as candidates in numbers large enough to form effective and lasting gender-based interest groups capable of sustaining political pressure for long periods. In her overarching study of women and politics, Nikki Craske makes it clear that one must consider the connections among labor, unions, literacy, effectiveness of social movements and professional organizations, and revolutionary agendas. Given the many nuances of politics in Latin America it is difficult to identify with precision any model for female political behavior, but political identities have changed over time. Women's groups are capable of putting political pressure on the government and design special objectives under special circumstances. Such efforts, however, seem to peak and then ebb.

How women have developed political personae, under what circumstances, and with what results remain key unresolved questions for historians. Despite a scarcity of historical studies on those subjects, a broad definition of politics as involvement in the search for social justice has enabled Francesca Miller to describe a panorama of women's political activities in Latin America under the assumption that women have invested their political acumen in pursuit of social and individual equality. A basic ideology of maternalism—issues that affect women as mothers—and social concern for freedom and social justice have given women authority that has been used as a base for a variety of objectives such as social and legal reform, mass mobilization, and even revolutionary activities. Although there are other possibilities, monographic studies confirm the importance of maternalism in defining political issues throughout the twentieth century.

In countries where elections have been possible, women's political activities (beyond vote casting) have been slow to develop. Only in exceptional cases, as in the massive support of such populist male figures as Juan D. Perón in Argentina or Getulio Vargas in Brazil, have women been enthusiastic supporters. They have, however, bolstered opposition to some regimes, which affects the outcome of political crises, as was the case with João Goulart and Salvador Allende in Brazil and Chile, respectively. In Mexico, women have been caught up within the system of a one-party political dominance and have been more voters than activists, a situation that appeared to be changing after the 2000 defeat of the Institutional Revolutionary Party after seventy years of rule.

In the past, the appointment of women to lesser cabinet positions or as ambassadors to small countries was an easy and popular form of seeking political correctness. This situation is changing slowly. The number of women elected to legislative posts has never been above 6 to 8 percent of the total membership of congressional chambers. During the late 1980s, women legislators began to form political caucuses to gain strength, and during the 1990s, under pressure from women's groups, several countries adopted the concept of female quotas. Under that system women must be included on candidate lists as a means of expanding the possibility of true political representation. Some see this as a positive gain, but critics point out that the women's names usually appear at the bottom of the lists, making election difficult.

Those who receive political appointments are often channeled into "feminized" areas of politics such as tourism or health, although that appears to be changing. The phenomenon of a woman being elected president and finishing her term, as did Violeta Chamorro in Nicaragua (1990–96), does not guarantee immediate change in presidential politics. Yet the election of a woman president in Panamá in 1999 suggests that exceptional as such events may be, the door for female leadership may be more than just ajar. In fact, some women candidates are rapidly moving into new terms of full political engagement. In 2002 Colombia had a female presidential candidate who campaigned into guerrilla-infested territory and was kidnapped. The example of Eva Perón, who had great power yet operated in her husband's shadow, is unlikely to be repeated. Women are no longer seeking political participation under those conditions.

At the bottom of most political analyses is the issue of the effectiveness of women's activities, which is the source of discontent among them throughout the continent. Haydée Birgin of Argentina, a critic of the political goals of women's groups and nongovernmental organizations (NGOs) in her country, argues that the mere presence of women in political posts, especially those associated with traditional female activities, does not guarantee a transformation of the culture of politics.[18] She argues that if women and their organizations continue to encourage policies that stereotype them as "victims" or worthy of "special" attention they will never become true equals of men. Some women in politics adopt this position as a matter of pragmatism to achieve their goals and have demonstrated the capacity to engage in the political process. Owing to deeply embedded inhibitions and strong social pressure, however, advances are slow-paced.

The political panorama of the second half of the twentieth century offered another important path for the mass political mobilization of women: revolution. Chronologically, the Mexican Revolution was the first to involve women in many dramatic ways, but they raised no specific demands and gained no unity through that upheaval. Changes in the legal status of women were shaped by men. It was not until the 1930s that women fully engaged in different forms of labor, educational, and intellectual activism.

In other countries experiencing deep social changes—Bolivia, for example—women attempted to involve themselves in the process. It may be argued that with the success of the National Revolutionary Movement in Bolivia in 1952 they assumed coherent forms of socially conscious activism. Indigenous and urban working-class women supported that movement on nationalist and class grounds. Leadership emerged among those who had never before expressed themselves politically and continued to be politically aware after the movement had crumbled and been replaced by military authoritarianism. Domitila Barrios, who was married to a miner, paved the way for active groups such as the Bartolina Sisas, which was formed by indigenous women deeply involved in support groups for miners' political issues. Domitila Barrios's work, the first successful personal testimonial available in English, remains a useful tool for understanding the formation of political consciousness among indigenous women under conditions of extreme duress.

Cuba represents a more dramatic case of female revolutionary mobilization. In planning and initial stages the government lacked a specific plan for female participation in forms other than traditional supportive activities. As the nation came under U.S. pressure, however, nationalistic consciousness paved the way for female inclusion. The organization of a Federation of Cuban Women in 1962 under strict government control helped define gender-oriented goals.

The revolution did not encourage organization of women under the banner of feminism; mass education and the ethics of national service helped incorporate them into the revolution. The Federation of Cuban Women formulated the country's agenda pertaining to women, and that agenda's needs and objectives were to serve the political purposes of the Cuban Communist Party and its leader, Fidel Castro. The control the state exercised over the women's agenda precluded alternatives. Along with their families, those who differed with the government left Cuba in massive numbers and went into political exile. Revolution-oriented women were effectively mobilized into supporting the revolution's economic policies and political stand. Their level of education rose significantly because they were encouraged to move into higher education and serve the needs of the nation. Child and health care were provided by the state.

Although women gained a great deal of authority as a result of engagement in the nation's political pursuits, by the mid-1990s they played no key role in the country's political leadership. Men still dominated the public and private spheres. Women's authority had been enhanced, but their power had not. Some old problems such as prostitution aimed at the tourist industry reappeared during the 1990s as a result of economic need, and cabaret shows for tourists continued to exploit the stereotype of sexy mulatta women. At the end of the century there was no indication that any of the traditional general features of gender relations had changed radically.

The Nicaraguan Revolution, which had much less time than Cuba's to put a program of change in gender relations into effect, had strong female support during its period of struggle. Once in power, however, the male directorship (Sandinistas) was subjected to internal pressure from feminist revolutionaries to depart from traditional ways of dealing with women politically. Under economic and political siege, the short duration of this political regime offers an example of the limitations imposed by underdevelopment and international pressure to any attempt at radical changes in the political as well as gender relations systems. Ideology alone seems unable to sustain social and economic changes. Recent studies of the Nicaraguan and Cuban revolutions argue that revolutions do not guarantee societal and familial change in cultural patterns of male dominance.[19]

Revolutionary regimes seem to aim at providing welfare services and education to remedy the needs of the majority of women and guarantee their continued political support. The mystique of social service to a national cause helps mobilize women in politics, whether revolutionary or not, but does not lead to a predictable pattern of change in personal and social attitudes or in political opportunities.

Resistance to dictatorial military regimes provided another political choice for women in the 1970s and 1980s. Patricia Chuchryk, Sonia Alvarez, and Jane Jaquette have studied the dynamics of women's protest in the process of return to democracy after years of military dictatorship and popularized the concepts of redemocratization and "engendering" democracy. A useful synthesis of many authors' views is contained in Jane Jaquette's edited work, which features historians, sociologists, and political scientists studying seven countries and the mobilization of women to challenge military rule.[20]

Women's participation in resistance superseded previous assumptions of their acting in supportive roles. As active members of the opposition they became, for the first time in twentieth-century history, open targets of political violence. In some instances, as in the Brazilian and Chilean cases, there was a feminist aspect of the resistance to dictatorship. Women opponents to repression also desired gender equality in issues concerning family, law, labor, and politics. Ironically, the military regimes' oppression of the citizenry created the opportunity to criticize and oppose all forms of authoritarianism, including that of men over women. By the late 1980s activists and academics of several countries reinforced this position and exposed the personal aspects of women's subjection to androcentric political values.

Unfortunately, hopes for rapid incorporation into politics and civic life in restored democratic regimes were not fulfilled. At the end of the twentieth century activist women were still struggling in a variety of organizations (state-supported as well as private) to make a greater impact on politics. Given the turn to political and economic conservatism of most constitutional governments, it was the consensus that the political feminist agenda has lost impetus, although that does not apply to less ideologically committed women's groups working for more practical goals.

In the late 1970s and early 1980s the Madres de la Plaza de Mayo, and more recently the *abuelas* (grandmothers) of the same affiliation, gained worldwide attention with "passive" demonstrations against the military regime in Argentina. Purporting to seek the truth about their children who had been arrested and "disappeared," either victims of murder or jailed for political reasons, the women became an emblem of resistance embodied in a most respectful form of motherhood, raising consciousness among a terrorized population.[21] After the fall of the Argentine military regime in 1984 and 1985 the mothers continued to demand explanations (which were not forthcoming) for the deaths and disappearances. Some have remained visible as aging grandmothers, still without full answers to their questions.

Also in the 1970s, Chilean women organized resistance groups, in some instances protected by the church, that eventually became public and vociferous once the regime of Augusto Pinochet began to show some signs of weakness. When a referendum was put to the nation in 1988 to either retain or reject his regime, women on both sides of the political spectrum participated intensely in the national campaign. These two examples underline the need to study women's ability to define goals and mobilize in the pursuit of discrete political objectives that are pragmatically attainable. We must also be aware that conservative ideologies have political appeal among women and that the right wing has proved to be effective in mobilizing women.[22]

As in the early part of the century, the ideological foundation of women's groups or organizations pursuing social and political reforms varies considerably. Some are middle class and intellectually aware of feminist concepts; others are more focused on obtaining benefits of a more immediate nature such as housing, electricity, medical services, and potable water. Maxine Molineux has defined the latter as focusing on practical gender interests, whereas the former are "strategic" goals involving such personal rights as sexual and reproductive freedom and the elimination of violence. Many poor women's organizations in Latin America are keener on practical gender pursuits, close to what we know as grass-roots organizations and composed of women of all social and ethnic backgrounds, rural and urban. They are flexible in order to accommodate to political contingencies. Despite attempts to present these organizations as popular forms of feminism, most analysts agree that their activities are independent of feminist ideology although they may have connections with feminists and be cognizant of feminist "strategic" goals. Nongovernmental organizations have proliferated in Latin America to address myriads of social problems. In all cases such mobilization suggests that the pursuit of practical gender interests gives women of all social classes a political "expertise" that is widening to include questioning traditional political identities and encouraging female agency.

Feminism has a respectable pedigree in Latin America, although its history has remained largely ignored and unknown until recently. It had many nuances and appeared at different stages of the nations' histories between the early 1900s and the late 1930s. Political instability or outright militarism delayed feminism's appearance and development in some countries, but before World War II all nations had feminist organizations and supporters as well as opponents of feminism. When between 1890 and 1920 women began to write of their concerns about education, family legislation, economic issues, and roles in society, they also began to discuss the meaning of feminism and follow its advance in other countries.

Largely using the concept that motherhood conferred authority, and arguing that the labor of women earned them the right to become full citizens, those who declared themselves as feminists adopted a variety of political strategies, leaning toward either socialist or liberal feminism. Protection for women and children rather than individual feminism or suffrage was the preferred goal of early-twentieth-century feminists. Equality with men before the law, greater control over children, less subjection to the rigidity of pater familias laws, and recognition of female intellectual equality were the key objectives. Feminists assumed that revision of civil codes would open the gates for other reforms, such as regulation of female and child labor, protection of working mothers and motherhood in general, and a reverse of the double standards of morality.

Early-twentieth-century feminism propitiated the emergence of recognized national women leaders such as Amanda Labarca in Chile, Alicia Moreau de Justo in Argentina, Paulina Luisi in Uruguay, and Bertha Lutz in Brazil. While Lutz focused on suffrage, Luisi and Moreau de Justo wrote widely on economic and educational policies and national politics, rising to the challenge of addressing national and international issues. Their activities and writing are not well known beyond their own countries.

The responses of male politicians and leaders to calls for full citizenship for women varied before 1940 from fear, denial, and delays to full support. Women in some countries (Ecuador, Dominican Republic, Uruguay, Brazil, and Cuba) achieved suffrage before 1945, but the exercise of the vote was not a political success and had to wait until the 1960s to become meaningful reality in most. Woman suffrage became ideologically inevitable after 1945 because the world battle for democracy made it incongruous to continue to withhold it. The aims of early feminists seemed to have been achieved during the 1960s, when full citizenship, growing opportunities for paid work, a loosening of the legal controls of fathers and husbands over women, and state-sponsored social welfare became realities.

The neofeminism that began to develop in Western nations during the 1970s created new questions about issues that remained unresolved or had become relevant under the new political circumstances. The most pressing concerned further refinement of family law and labor and effective enforcement of labor regulation given the expansion of the industrial and service sectors. Other concerns also became paramount, such as reproductive rights, protection from domestic violence, an end to stereotypes of male domination and female subordination, and real political access for women.

Although there was no unity in feminist groups of the 1980s and 1990s, their message transcended the confines of their organizations and reached national audiences through the media. Also important was the creation of international channels of communication that kept these groups in close touch, whether among themselves or with global trends in feminism. The organization of more than a half-dozen inter-American and international feminist encounters, and at least an equal number of national meetings, helped bring together women from different nations to discuss the variety of circumstances that affected their lives and colored their views of women's liberation.

Not all women interested in women's issues call themselves feminists. The term seems to provoke antagonistic reactions among many. Yet feminist organizations and individuals with a firm conviction maintain a network of contacts and information. In many subtle ways feminism has permeated many layers of society and changed many forms of behavior, especially as they pertain to a personal choice rather than to state-dependent policy decisions.

Theoretical Approaches to the Study of Women

One obstacle that feminism faced was its opponents' accusation that it was a foreign ideology alien to Latin American culture and tradition. Although that was obviously inaccurate, it became desirable to think in terms of theoretical approaches that would give the study of women a respectable base using the historical and cultural roots of Latin America. Evelyn Stevens and Elsa Chaney coined the terms *marianismo* and *supermadre* to explain gender relations and spheres of female power in the family and society, and since the mid-1970s they have become points of departure and debate.

Stevens proposed the existence of a special form of female behavior known as marianismo (from the assumed nature of the Virgin Mary) as the counterpoint of machismo, or extolment of male values in social and political issues. Marianismo celebrates the values of patience, stoicism, mediation, and nurturing that are presumed to be the qualities of Mary as preached by the Roman Catholic Church and apply to all women as desirable forms of personal behavior. It also implies the existence of a special female space—the home and the indoors—where women exercise power supported by the specific ethical values ascribed to womanhood and motherhood. The domain of men is the public space, politics, and public affairs. Stevens argued that men respect and value the role of women as mothers, but when women venture beyond their assigned space they may be risking their security.

According to Chaney, marianismo has a role beyond the home. In her study of the political behavior of women in Peru and Chile, she put forward the concept of the supremadre, a politicization of marianismo. The key to political success for women is to bring into the public realm the values of motherhood for the benefit of the community and the home.

The concepts of marianismo, machismo, and supermadre have been used extensively to analyze gender relations, but they have also been subjected to close scrutiny, especially since the early 1980s when the cultural concept of patriarchy began to be regarded as a more useful, precise, and universal tool of analysis. Nonetheless, they are still useful points of departure in discussing certain features of Latin American political and gender cultures. Historians have not fully tested the cultural meaning of these terms, but their strong polarization is no longer accepted as a satisfactory explanation of gender behavior. Equally, the interpretation of separate public and private spaces to describe engendered domains of power needs corrective reinterpretation.

The interplay of male and female values with other factors such as class, ethnicity or race, educational level, and economic leverage produces a more subtle picture of masculine and feminine values engaged in "contestation" or political give-and-take. Among the educated middle class there are fewer assumptions of the existence of a machismo-marianismo dyad than among the provincial or strongly religious and poorly educated members of society. Even among the latter, gender values are not necessarily unchallenged. Further, students of indigenous societies allege that the complementary understanding of the roles of the sexes in indigenous communities leaves little room for gendered polarities. One may also argue that as women gain more educational and economic power the features of this dyad become less well defined. In real life, female and male behavior may also follow deeply rooted cultural values of engendered propriety, as Ann Farnsworth-Alvear suggests in her study of Medellin's textile factories in the mid-twentieth century.

Maternalism—a concept devoid of the religious content of marianismo and connecting motherhood more emphatically and assertively to plans for social reform, social legislation, and political activism—has slowly replaced the use of marianismo. Maternalism also explains early feminist ideas as well as the political message of women who live under repressive regimes. A case in point is that of the women in Chile who lost male and female relatives during the military regime of the 1970s and 1980s. They recorded their frustrations and their stand against the military in a very feminine and traditional manner—by embroidering their stories onto cloth squares like those used in the AIDS quilt in the United States and mounting a campaign of quiet resistance that helped others strengthen their own convictions.

The madres' activities in Argentina highlight the problems of interpreting women's activities. They pitted maternalism against feminism. Feminists have argued that the madres were unable to go beyond a carefully delineated personal agenda. Women active in Argentine politics in the 1990s were certainly not the heirs of the madres, whose narrowly focused interest in their families they regard as ineffective in raising more general issues of social and gender justice and change in the balance of power between genders.

No doubt those who have analyzed the discourse of men and women during the national period have plenty of evidence that maternalism since the nineteenth century has been a successful tool in the pursuit of important changes in legislation affecting the family, labor, the educational promotion of women, and public health. Yet caution should be exercised before giving this cultural factor the strength of a "total" explanation.

The use of maternalism (or even marianism) as an analytical tool of women's activities in Latin American societies can become a reductionist interpretation obscuring the agency of women in political and social activities inspired by needs other than the fulfillment of maternal values. The ability of women to think beyond maternal triggering mechanisms is evident in the earliest forms of female organizations and writing. Women thought of economic needs—of politics in terms of gaining the powers of self-expression, self-authorization, and decision making—without constantly resorting to maternalist arguments. If and when they used maternal metaphors, they were consciously using a tool they knew would work. There was political savvy in that decision, not a complete surrender to its premises.

Maternalist policies can be double-edged, and repressive regimes can also use motherhood by fostering maternal values and reinforcing the traditional attitudes of passivity, respect for the male hierarchy, and patriotism understood as order without opposition.

The struggle against dictatorial regimes in Brazil, Chile, Argentina, Uruguay and Paraguay, Nicaragua, and El Salvador during the 1970s fostered deeper awareness of the issue of human rights. Resistance was illegal and dangerous. Nonetheless, it triggered intense empowerment and protagonism in many women, enabling them to articulate their political views, especially after their countries returned to normality. Women who joined the struggle against dictatorships cannot be assumed to have been consciously feminist. Their exposure to violence made them aware of the fragility of the legal systems and liberal concepts of justice as well as of the power of human rights as a venue of freedom and empowerment that could be applied to women.

The use of human rights as a means of understanding the basic concepts of oppression, whether individual, social, or political, has gained considerable purchase. Repression taught women how to relate to other women anywhere, because the loss of freedom is understood beyond national borders. After long years of underground struggle, human rights began to emerge as a main concern for national and international agencies as they apply to *both genders*.

The revitalization of the demand for women's rights, human rights, and the emergence of women's studies in the 1980s are not chance phenomena. They were the result of women's service to the cause of political democratization and the realization that democracy is not an issue valid only for political crises but also implies equality and respect to women on a long-term basis and in the privacy of the family.

Ironically, the consideration of human rights as part of the text of social and gender justice is the result of recognizing women's participation in political movements as agents and also victims of torture, murder, disappearance, and exile. The gruesome report issued by the Argentine Commission on Disappeared People and similar reports of violence from Paraguay, for example, have emphasized that violence recognizes no gender in civil wars and women's history is not confined to issues of family and motherhood. These are the premises under which a large number of works in Spanish and English have recorded the experience of women during the 1970s and 1980s. They include literature such as Alicia Partnoy's powerful *The Little School* and Marjorie Agosin's multiple publications as well as personal exposés of women's experiences, openly ideological in outlook but certainly material for history now and in the future. Alda Facio, a Costa Rican, has made a case for seeing human rights as a venue for understanding and enhancing feminism and women's special needs and political concerns. She argues that human rights is a concept capable of embracing and contesting all forms of discrimination, regardless of gender. Latin American historians and political scientists are contributing significantly to the world dialog on this topic.

Two Latin American feminist theoreticians not well known in the United States sought answers to gender relations based on national or regional experiences. One, Julieta Kirkwood from Chile, died of cancer in the mid-1980s. Living under the military regime of Augusto Pinochet, Kirkwood organized a seminar on the study of women and connected history with an analysis of Chilean society in her time. She asked trenchant questions about women's condition, the meaning of politics for women, and how women could gain political leverage and participate in policymaking. Women, she argued, are silent because they do not perceive themselves as subjects of their own liberations. She proposed *protagonismo* (protagonism), or the conscious decision to act and prevent being absorbed by movements in which her gender was not recognized as a signifier. She advanced a feminism without division between activist leaders and base organizations. All participants should pursue the same goals: learning how to recognize oppression, its reasons and effects, and what actions were necessary to eliminate it.

Marcela Lagarde, from Mexico, is an anthropologist who has become a new popular icon of Latin American feminism since the publication of her book. A thick tome of anthropological theory, it revolves around the many forms of women's captivities within the patriarchal system. Lagarde pursues a historical context for her theories and has thoroughly searched for historical material, Mexican and universal, to support her theories. She argues that appropriating female sexuality to make it an issue of service for others deprives women of a choice in their lives and excludes them from decision making. Women's subjectivity is constructed in relation to others. Dependency and submissiveness become attributes of femininity, equated with happiness represented as loyalty, abnegation, giving oneself to noble causes, caring, and love. As women live their own objectification they help construct their oppression. Lagarde, following a very Latin American tradition, does not seek a struggle with men. Her wish is to construct gender identities free from any antagonistic, exclusionary positions between men and women, a position that historically fits well into Latin American societies.

Neither Lagarde nor Kirkwood are the sum of all thinking that has taken place in Latin America on the subject of women and gender relations. They are in good company in a field of female activists and thinkers who have been writing since the mid-1970s, searching for the Latin American core within the universality of gender themes and issues. In Peru, Virginia Vargas has been an advocate of a socially conscious feminism, and Esther Andrada and Ana María Portugal give women of all social classes the freedom of their voices in *Ser mujer en el Perú*.[23] Portugal was also the coordinator of one of the first feminist movements in Peru in 1973.

Argentina's Gloria Bonder, María del Carmen Feijóo, and Elizabeth Jelin, among many others, are key figures in contemporary feminist writing. Throughout Latin America, centers for the study of women are actively engaged in redefining the terms of women's status and contributing to rewriting their future. In Lima, the women's center Flora Tristán has the double task of carrying out social work and feminist consciousness awareness. In Mexico, the Interdisciplinary Program for the Study of Women (PIEM) in El Colegio de Mexico has seen its activities emulated by a key number of academic institutions. *Fem*, an outstanding feminist journal, is more than seventeen years old.

Sexuality

Sociologists and historians have been at the cutting edge of studies of gender representation and sexuality. Sexuality is not a new topic of discussion in Latin America. Early-twentieth-century anarchists, feminists, social reformers, and physicians seeking "social prophylaxis" were the first to look into and discuss sexuality. Late-nineteenth and early-twentieth-century republican censuses unveiled significant numbers of consensual unions, children born out of wedlock, and amazing rates of child mortality. Although such facts were hardly new, they triggered passionate debates and ushered in a new era of more open talk about sexual behavior.

As Lavrin and Guy have discussed for the Southern Cone nations and James Green and Katherine Bliss corroborate for Brazil and Mexico, physicians looked for remedies in science whereas socialist and political radicals saw the root in the ills of capitalism, the social hypocrisy of the church, and the subjection of women to antiquated social norms. Feminists seeking equal responsibilities in sexual behavior condemned double standards of morality. Sex education, eugenics, premarriage certificates of sexual health, abortion, and contraceptives were widely discussed in Argentina, Uruguay, Brazil, and Mexico.[24]

Those early-twentieth-century commentators discovered that the "traditional family" was a social construction of the upper classes, carefully nurtured by the triad of state, church, and pater familias—thus, the shock created by increasing rates of prostitution and venereal disease. But that shock indicated the need to redraft a more nuanced definition of gender relations. The introduction of new sensibilities about eroticism and sexuality challenged conservative and traditional sectors of society. Films and new dances, fashions, and sports eroded the inhibitions and restrictions of "public" and private behavior, at least in the growing urban centers. There is ample evidence that the conservative and Catholic ethos did not yield ground easily. Catholic Action and similar organizations agitated among workers and the middle class to uphold traditional patterns of morality that could be inculcated in schools and places of work.[25] Even in the 1980s young women were subjected to pregnancy inspections in some Mexico-U.S. border maquilas.

As in other parts of the world, prostitution increased significantly during the last decades of the nineteenth century, possibly as a result of important structural changes in the economy that forced the growth of cities, inflation, and exploitation of service and industrial work. Women migrating to the cities and lacking skills resorted to prostitution as a means of making a living. As the numbers of practitioners increased, physicians' concerns about the consequences of sexually transmitted diseases for public health triggered strong responses from the state to control female prostitutes and all female sexuality. Historians have begun to explore some of the themes of this early period, most of them concentrating on the politics and manipulation of prostitution and its uses in redefining gender roles, social policies, and the construction of models of desirable womanhood. Equally important are the analyses of female social and state control through legislation and judicial interpretation.

Donna Guy's groundbreaking work on prostitution in Buenos Aires has led to a consideration of prostitution as a way to study how a nation builds a proper model of family, female virtue, and national social order. Margaret Rago, focusing on Brazil, and on Mexico and Guatemala, William French, Katherine Bliss, and David MacCreary, also underline the social and political constraints on commercial sex and its role in counter-defining models of female propriety at a national level in the first half of the century.

In Latin America, centralized states have overarching power to define and control sexual behavior. In view of the economic burdens posed by rapid population growth, some nations have undertaken policies for population control discreetly covered by terms such as "family planning." The Mexican state carried out a successful campaign for smaller families during the 1970s. In that same period Argentina (1974) forbade the over-the-counter sale of contraceptives, forcing the state's view of sexuality on its population. Prolific motherhood became less desirable in one case while in others it was used to substantiate politics of nationalism under patriarchal control and the porosity of the concept of motherhood.

Early-twentieth-century feminists were the first to call attention to issues of sexuality, but by the middle of the century feminist groups had shifted toward issues of political participation. Sexuality did not resurface until the late 1970s. In the 1980s and 1990s feminists and women's groups primarily addressed the issue of control over their own bodies and reproductive rights. They struggled against the still-popular views of women as being reproductive vessels, objects of desire, or embodiments of seduction and deceit. Close attention was paid to the issue of abortion, given the constraints of poverty and guilt created by the cultural and religious worship of motherhood, the high cost of contraception, and the very limited incomes of a majority of the population.

Feminist groups have struggled over the decriminalization of abortion without much success. The contemporary examination of sexuality omits nothing. Rape, marital abuse, prostitution, adolescent pregnancy, lesbian and gay issues, and crimes of passion are all on the table for discussion. As an issue of solidarity, feminist groups have shown a sympathetic although not strident support of lesbianism. The topic, however, is found largely in magazines and newspapers rather than in academic works, most of which are in progress.

Despite the reputation of machismo as something typically Latin American, research on masculinity is in its initial stages. Most of it is in the hands of social scientists, whose observations on current patterns of behavior are the backbone of the literature. Historical studies have established that the military service provided a means of social mobility for men and reinforced male values and have begun to make inroads into the study of male bonding in public life.[26]

State-builders must appear to be virile because masculinity is a yardstick for public as well as private behavior. The self-assurance of men in positions of authority demands a female counterpart in gracious submission. Studies based on crime records of the early twentieth century point to a male subculture of bonding through stereotypical images of masculinity as the power to make another (male or female) submit. Sociological studies, urban and rural, have analyzed popular concepts of masculinity as expressed in everyday language, in sports, or in the representation of local politicians.

Machismo should not be confused with masculinity, as Rafael Ramírez, a Puerto Rican, argues. Masculinity is a complex set of values that begin to be inculcated during childhood; they are culturally specific and not always or exclusively oriented toward women. Latin American ideals of masculinity should not be stereotyped as being simply machista because that term includes positive values of responsibility and is influenced by class and even ethnicity. National or regional variations can be expected, as can changes over time. In his study of contemporary gender culture in a poor neighborhood of Mexico City, Matthew C. Gutmann describes male and female self-perceptions of masculinity and femininity, fathering, mothering, and sex. His findings raise doubts about stereotypes long held as truisms by uncritical writers. Machismo, Gutmann argues, is a recent cultural construct, partly of foreign origin, and has been transformed from an hegemonic into an ideological position undermined by constant challenges from within. Historical research needs to corroborate this interpretation.

One of those challenges is the interest in gay and lesbian studies, which, like those of masculinity, are still in their infancy. Traditionally homophobic and strongly influenced by religious beliefs on this subject, Latin American culture has rejected homosexuality as a sin, an unnatural act, a social perversion, source of embarrassment, and regrettable "deviation" from the natural norm. Controlled prostitution has, at times, been held as "desirable" against the threat of homosexuality, reflecting fears of the subversion of masculinity. Buttressed by the strict ethics of the Catholic Church, straight sexuality could become the symbol of patriotism and nationalism. Homosexuality has also acquired a political meaning as an undesirable expression of weakness that may hurt a state's defense mechanisms and representation through straight virility. The feminization of the other, whether an antagonist in a football game, a political adversary, or even a threatening foreign investor, has revealed the deep roots of "straight" sexual representation in most nations.

Literary and sensationalist exploitation depicting lesbians and gays as associated with the night, drug addiction, and prostitution have perpetuated images of anomaly. Of special interest are studies of the homophobic stance of the Cuban Revolution that expose the magnitude of traditional attitudes.

Cuba's authorities have shown little intention of changing their negative attitude about lesbians and gays, who are considered as deviants or sick. Revolutionary iconography of the 1960s projected images of virile men, guns in hand and ready to die for their values. The presence of women engaged in subversive and military activities did not change the imagery, which has supported the view that heterosexuality is at the root of clean family life and good communist values. The only historically grounded study of homosexuality available today is James N. Green's *Beyond Carnival: Male Homosexuality in Twentieth Century Brazil*, a thorough study of gays in that country from the 1890s to the 1980s. Carefully researched, the work traces the complex history of homosexual behavior and the reactions it engendered in Brazilian society. Covering social attitudes, self-perception, medical views, testimonials, lifestyles, and analysis of carnival as a public space for gay behavior, Green's book is an example of serious historical research.

Conclusion

One may argue that negotiation of economic, social, and cultural factors in the totality of female experiences and their strong connection to state-based and state-controlled mechanisms has been a characteristic of Latin American women's history since 1825. The degree to which gender may unite women behind an objective (be it political or social) is conditioned by the depth of the perceived harm to the general concept of womanhood. A woman of high class and education, such as Victoria Ocampo of Argentina, could, in 1936, make a statement of solidarity with Chilean working women who had been threatened by a bill to subject female government employees to "quotas." Ocampo could do so because she could empathize with an undisguised threat to all womankind. Equally, the Mothers of the Plaza de Mayo and the Salvadorean Comadres could evoke solidarity among other women because they appealed to a universal concern toward children and a basic demand for respect to all human life.

Yet gender itself does not guarantee the permanence of solidarity, which tends to be rather fragile and constantly threatened by other factors such as class, education, race, and religiosity. Tension between individual self-perception and a feeling of belonging to a group or category will be a constant challenge to "definitive" conclusions about women in Latin America. It stands to reason that the complexity of Latin America is more than nominal and at the bottom of the continent's historical experiences. Women inhabit many worlds at many levels. The challenge lies in understanding the nature of that variety and approaching their history with an open mind.

What seems to be distinctive of the studies so far developed in Latin America is that they investigate non-elite subjects, partaking of that general desire to remain socially conscious and developing a body of works on *campesinas* (peasant women), indigenous women, *pobladoras* (dwellers) of new urban dwellings, and members of the urban informal sector in an attempt to remove them from the margins of attention. These women are the protagonists of a new drive intended to give them a voice in the national dialogue. The role played by "testimonial" literature in this process cannot be ignored because it translates the experience of being female for posterity, thus creating a historical memory for activists and being a source of information and thought for academics.

The fact that these researchers, most of whom are urban professionals, are now conscious of the realities of the women's lives should be stressed. As a historian, I am aware of how since the 1930s recognition of the alterity of women has been a task undertaken and carried out by women themselves. The mediation of educated women as midwives to the birth of a new female consciousness is itself a phenomenon that will likely be an object of study in the future. Here, I wish to call attention to it and suggest that we begin thinking on the terms of such mediation and of any negotiation thereof among women of different classes and ethnicity, as well as the way they relate that experience to men who still retain the main levers of power in Latin America.

Recent studies on the history and status of women celebrate the "condition" of being women. Questioning and challenging will certainly continue, and the answers will be as varied as demanded by the complexity and diversity of Latin America. A comparative study of the condition of women in several nations in Latin America could be a commendable exercise insofar as the diversity of economic and political situations, education, class, race, and ethnicity creates a mini cosmos where similarities and differences interact in unexpected ways. Equally feasible is a comparison of certain trends and ideologies that help in understanding the ultimate universality of many problems affecting women as well as some of the ways to cope with them. A comparison between Latin American feminism and feminism elsewhere in the world would also be extremely fruitful.

The ideological foundation for patriarchal domination in the newly created republics in the nineteenth century has much in common with similar systems elsewhere and offers an interesting contrast with the situations of newly emerging nations of the twentieth century. Participation in the labor market, migration from rural to urban areas, representation of women in the cinema and popular culture, treatment of women and children in the welfare systems developed after World War I, the shifting situation of women in national politics, and the plight of human rights groups are among many of the topics that are potentially useful to study, not only for Latin Americans but also for the wider world.

Notes

1. Potthast-Jutkeit, *Paraíso de Mahoma o País de las mujeres¿* passim.
2. Rodríguez, *Hijas, novias v esposas*, passim; see also Dore, *Gender Politics*, and Dore and Molineux, *Hidden Histories*, passim.
3. Díaz, *Female Citizens*, passim.
4. Nazzari, *Disappearance of the Dowry*, passim.
5. Hunefeldt, *Liberalism in the Bedroom*, passim.
6. Palmer and Chaves, "Educating Señoritas," passim; Hahner, *Emancipating the Female Sex*, passim; Besse, *Restructuring Patriarchy*, passim.
7. Karasch, *Slave Life in Rio de Janeiro*, passim; Karasch, "Slave Women in the Brazilian Frontier in the Nineteenth Century," passim; Hunefeldt, *Paying the Price of Freedom*, passim.
8. Arrom, *The Women of Mexico City, 1790–1857*, passim.
9. Chaney and Garcia Castro, eds., *Muchachas No More*, passim.
10. French and James, eds., *The Gendered Worlds of Latin American Workers*, passim; Hahner, *Emancipating the Female Sex*, passim; Lavrin, *Women, Feminism and Social Change*, passim.
11. Klubock, *Contested Communities*.
12. Tinsman, *Partners in Conflict*, passim; Farnsworth-Alvear, *Dulcinea in the Factory*, passim.
13. James, *Doña Maria's Story*.
14. León and Deere, eds., *La mujer y la política agraria*, passim; Deere, *Rural Women and State Policy*, passim; Bourque and Warren, *Women of the Andes*, passim; Salamini and Vaughn, eds., *Women of the Mexican Countryside*, passim.
15. McGee Deutsch, "The Visible and Invisible," passim; McGee Deutsch, "The Catholic Church, Work and Womanhood"; McGee Deutsch, *The Extreme Right in Argentina, Brazil and Chile*, passim.
16. Macías, *Against All Odds*, passim; Hahner, *Emancipating the Female Sex*, passim; Stoner, *Latinas of the Americas*, passim; Lavrin, *Women, Feminism and Social Change*, passim.
17. Rosemblatt, *Gendered Compromises*, passim; Enriqueta Tuñon, *¡Por fin . . . y a podemas*, passim.
18. Birgin, "Acción publica y ciudadania," passim.
19. Molineux, "Mobilization without Emancipation?" passim; Smith and Padula, *Sex and Revolution*, passim.
20. Jaquette, ed., *The Women's Movement in Latin America*, passim.
21. Guzmán Bouvard, *Revolutionizing Motherhood*, passim.
22. Power, *Right-Wing Women*, passim.
23. Andrada and Portugal, *Ser mujer en el Perú*, passim.
24. Bliss, *Compromised Positions*, passim; Abreu Esteres, *Meninas Perdidas*, passim; Rago, *Os prazeres*, passim.
25. McGee Deutsch, "The Catholic Church, Work and Womanhood," passim.
26. Beattie, *The Tribute of Blood*, passim; Kirkendall, *Class Mates*, passim.

Bibliography

Abreu Esteres, Martha de. *Meninas Perdidas: Os populares e o cotidiano do amor no Rio de Janeiro da belle époque.* Rio de Janeiro: Paz e Terra, 1989.

Abshagen Leitinger, Ilse, ed. *The Costa Rican Women's Movement: A Reader.* Pittsburgh: University of Pittsburgh Press, 1997.

Acosta-Belén, Edna, and Christine E. Bose, eds. *Researching Women in Latin America and the Caribbean.* Boulder: Westview Press, 1993.

Agosín, Marjorie. *Circle of Madness: Mothers of the Plaza de Mayo.* New York: Pine Press, 1992.

Alberi Manzanares, Pilar. "'Donde quiera que me paro, soy yo': Mujeres indígenas desde una perspectiva de género." *Anuario de Estudios Americanos* 51, no. 1 (1994): 287–301.

Alegría, Claribel. *They Won't Take Me Alive: Salvadorean Women in Struggle for National Liberation.* London: Women's Press, 1987.

Allpanchis (Cuzco), 21:25 (1985). Issue devoted to Andean rural women.

Alvarez, Sonia E. *Engendering Democracy in Brazil: Women's Movements in Transition Politics.* Princeton: Princeton University Press, 1990.

Andrada, Ester, and Ana María Portugal. *Ser mujer en el Perú.* Lima: Ediciones Mujer y Autonomía, 1978.

Arrom, Sylvia M. *The Women of Mexico City, 1790–1857.* Stanford: Stanford University Press, 1985.

Azize Vargas, Yamile. *La mujer en Puerto Rico: Ensayos de investigación.* Rio Piedras: Ediciones Huracán, 1987.

Babb, Florence. *Between Field and Cooking Pot: The Political Economy of Market Women in Peru.* Austin: University of Texas Press, 1989.

Balderston, Daniel, and Donna Guy, eds. *Sex and Sexuality in Latin America.* New York: NYU Press, 1997.

Barman, Roderick J. *Princess Isabel of Brazil: Gender and Power in the Nineteenth Century.* Wilmington: Scholarly Resources, 2002.

Barnes, John. *Evita: First Lady: A Biography of Eva Perón.* New York: Grove Press, 1978.

Barrig, Maruja. *Las obreras.* Lima: Mosca Azul, Editores, 1986.

Barrios de Chungara, Domitilia, with Noema Viezzer. *Let Me Speak: Testimony of Domitila, a Woman of the Bolivian Mines.* New York: Monthly Review Press, 1978.

Beattie, Peter. *The Tribute of Blood: Army, Honor, Race and Nation in Brazil, 1864–1945.* Durham: Duke University Press, 2001.

Benería, Lourdes, and Marta Roldán, *The Crossroads of Class and Gender: Industrial Homework, Subcontracting, and Household Dynamics in Mexico City.* Chicago: University of Chicago Press, 1987.

Benjamin, Medea. *Benedita da Silva: An Afro-Brazilian Woman's Story of Politics and Love.* 1997.

———. *Don't Be Afraid Gringo: A Honduran Woman Speaks from the Heart.* New York: Harper and Row, 1987.

Bergmann, Emilie et al. *Women, Culture, and Politics in Latin America.* Berkeley: University of California Press, 1990.

Besse, Susan K. *Restructuring Patriarchy: The Modernization of Gender Inequality in Brazil, 1914–1940.* Chapel Hill: University of North Carolina Press, 1996.

Birgin, Haydée. "Acción pública y ciudadanía: ¿políticas públicas para las mujeres o derechos ciudadanos?" In *Acción pública y sociedad: Las mujeres en el cambio estructural,* compiled by Haydée Birgin, 13–36. Buenos Aires: CEADEL and Feminario Editora, 1995.

Bliss, Katherine. *Compromised Positions: Prostitution, Public Health, and Gender Politics in Revolutionary Mexico City.* University Park: Pennsylvania State University, 2001.

Bonder, Gloria. "The Study of Politics from the Standpoint of Women." *International Social Science Journal* 35 (1983): 569–83.

Bose, Christine E., and Edna Acosta-Belen, eds. *Women in the Latin American Development Process.* Philadelphia: Temple University Press, 1995.

Bourque, Susan, and Kay B Warren. *Women of the Andes: Patriarchy and Social Change in Two Peruvian Towns.* Ann Arbor: University of Michigan Press, 1981.

Bunster, Ximena, and Elsa M. Chaney. *Sellers and Servants: Working Women in Lima, Peru.* New York: Praeger, 1985.

Caballero Aquino, Olga. *Por order superior.* Asunción: Intercontinental Editora, 1989.

Calderón de la Barca, Fanny. *Life in Mexico.* Garden City: Doubleday, 1966.

Castillo Bueno, María de los Reyes. *Reyita: The Life of a Black Cuban Woman in the Twentieth Century.* Durham: Duke University Press, 2000.

Caulfield, Sueann. *In Defense of Honor: Sexual Morality. Modernity, and Nation in Early Twentieth Century Brazil.* Durham: Duke University Press, 2000.

Chaney, Elsa M. *Supermadre: Women in Politics in Latin America.* Austin: University of Texas Press, 1979.

Chaney, Elsa, and Mary Garcia Castro, eds. *Muchachas No More: Household Workers in Latin America and the Caribbean.* Philadelphia: Temple University Press, 1989.

Chassen-López, Francie R. "From Casa to Calle: Latin American Women Transforming Patriarchal Spaces." *Journal of Women's History* 9 (Spring 1997): 174–89.

Chuchryk, Patricia. "Subversive Mothers: The Women's Opposition to the Military Regime in Chile." In *Women, the State and Development,* edited by Sue Ellen M. Charlton, Jana Everett, and Kathleen Staudt, 130–51. New York: NYU Press, 1989.

Coordinadora de la Mujer. *Feminismo y política.* La Paz: Coordinadora de la Mujer, 1986.

Cordero, Isabel. "Women in War: Impact and Responses." In *Shining and Other Paths: War and Society in Peril, 1980–1999,* edited by Steve J. Stern, 345–74. Durham: Duke University Press, 1998.

Cortés, Rosaliá. "¿Marginación de la fuerza de trabajo femenina? Estructura de ocupaciones, 1980–1993." In *Acción pública y sociedad: Las mujeres en el cambio estructural,* edited by Haydée Birgin, 83–101. Buenos Aires: CADEL y Feminario Editora, 1995.

Cortina, Regina. "Gender and Power in the Teacher's Union in Mexico City." *Mexican Studies/Estudios Mexicanos* 6 (Summer 1990): 241–62.

Craske, Nikki. *Women and Politics in Latin America.* London: Polity Press, 1999.

Deere, Carmen. *Rural Women and State Policy: Feminist Perspectives on Latin American Agricultural Development.* Boulder: Westview Press, 1987.

de Jesus, Carolina Maria. *Child of the Dark.* New York: Penguin Mentor, 1963.

———. *I'm Going to Have a Little House: The Second Diary of Carolina Maria de Jesus.* Lincoln: University of Nebraska Press, 1997.

Díaz, Arlene J. *Female Citizen, Patriarchs, and the Law in Venezuela, 1786–1904.* Lincoln: University of Nebraska Press, 2004.

Dore, Elizabeth, ed. *Gender Politics in Latin America.* New York: Monthly Review Press, 1997

Dore, Elizabeth, and Maxine Molineux, eds. *Hidden Histories of Gender and the State in Latin America.* Durham: Duke University Press, 2000.

Dujovne, Alicia. *Eva Perón: A Biography.* New York: St. Martin's Press, 1996.

Ehrick, Christine. "Affectionate Mothers and the Colossal Machine: Feminism, Social Assistance and the State in Uruguay, 1910–1932." *The Americas* 58 (July 2001): 121–39.

Facio, Alda. "Repensarnos como mujeres para reconceptualizar los derechos humanos." *Género y Sociedad* 3 (1995): 1–54.

Farnsworth-Alvear, Ann. *Dulcinea in the Factory: Myths, Morals, Men and Women in Colombia's Experiment, 1905–60.* Durham: Duke University Press, 2000.

Feijóo, Maria del Carmen. *Alquimistas en la crisis: Experiencias de las mujeres en el Gran Buenos Aires.* Buenos Aires: UNICEF/Siglo Veintiuno, 1991.

Fernández-Kelly, Maria Patricia. *"For We Are Sold" I and My People: Women and Industry in Mexico's Frontier.* Albany: SUNY Press, 1983.

Fernández Poncela, Anna M., comp. *Las mujeres en Mexico al final del Milenio.* Mexico City: El Colegio de Mexico, 1995.

Fowler-Salamini, Heather, and May Kay Vaughn, eds. *Women of the Mexican Countryside, 1850–1990.* Tucson: University of Arizona Press, 1994.

Franco, Jean. *Plotting Women: Gender and Representation in Mexico.* New York: Columbia University Press, 1989.

Fraser, Nicholas, and Maryssa Navarro. *Eva Perón.* New York: W. W. Norton, 1981.

Frederick, Bonnie. *Wily Modesty: Argentine Women Writers, 1860–1910.* Tempe: Arizona State University Center for Latin American Studies, 1998.

French, John D., and Daniel James, eds. *The Gendered Worlds of Latin American Workers: From Household and Factory to the Union Hall and Ballot Box.* Durham: Duke University Press, 1997.

French, William. "Prostitutes and Guardian Angels: Women, Work and the Family in Porfirian Mexico." *Hispanic American Historical Review* 72 (Nov. 1992): 529–53.

García Pinto, Magdalena. *Women Writers of Latin America: Intimate Histories.* Austin: University of Texas Press, 1991.

Gaviola, Edda, Eliana Largo, and Sandra Palestro. *Una historia necesaria: Mujeres en Chile, 1973–1990.* Santiago: Aki and Aora, 1994.

Generali da Costa, Silvia. *Assédio sexual: Uma versão brasileira.* Porto Alegre: Artes e Ofícios Editora, 1995.

Gil Lozano, Fernanda et al. *Historia de las mujeres en la Argentina.* 2 vols. Buenos Aires: Taurus, 2000.

Gill, Lesley. "Painted Faces: Conflict and Ambiguity in Domestic Servant–Employer Relations in La Paz, 1930–1988." *Latin American Research Review* 25, no. 31 (1990): 119–36.

Gogna, Mónica. "Mujeres y sindicatos en la Argentina actual." In *Participación política de la mujer en el Cono Sur.* Buenos Aires: Fundación Friedrich Naumann, 1987, 1:69–89.

Gómez Gómez, Elsa, ed. *Género, mujer y salud en las Américas.* Washington: Organización Panamericana de la Salud, 1993.

González, Victoria, and Karen Kampwirth, eds. *Radical Women in Latin America, Left and Right.* University Park: Pennsylvania State University Press, 2001.

González Montes, Soledad, coord. *Mujeres y relaciones de género en la antropología latinoamericana.* Mexico City: El Colegio de Mexico, 1993.

Graziano, Rodolfo C. *Amos de la noche: Conversaciones con homosexuales tramposos, prostitutas, drogadictos, ladrones y lesbianas.* Caracas: Planeta, 1994.

Green, James. *Beyond Carnival: Male Homosexuality in Twentieth-Century Brazil.* Chicago: University of Chicago Press, 1999.

Guttman, Mathew C. *The Meaning of Macho: Being a Man in Mexico City.* Berkeley: University of California Press, 1996.

Guy, Donna. *Sex and Danger in Buenos Aires.* Lincoln: University of Nebraska Press, 1991.

Guzmán Bouvard, Margarite. *Revolutionizing Motherhood: The Mothers of the Plaza de Mayo.* Boulder: Westview Press, 1995.

Hahner, June. *Emancipating the Female Sex: The Struggle for Women's Rights in Brazil, 1850–1940.* Durham: Duke University Press, 1990.

———, ed. *Women through Women's Eyes: Latin American Women in Nineteenth-Century Travel Accounts.* Wilmington: Scholarly Resources, 1998.

Herrera, Hayden. *Frida Kahlo.* New York: Rizzoli, 1992.

Herzog, Kristin. *Finding Their Voice: Peruvian Women Testimonies of War.* Valley Forge: Trinity Press International, 1997.

Hispanic American Historical Review 81 (Aug.–Nov. 2001). Special issue on "Gender and Sexuality in Latin America."

Homines (Universidad Interamericana de Puerto Rico) 4 (1987). Special issue on "Mujeres Puertorriqueñas, Protagonistas en el Caribe."

Hunefeldt, Christine. *Liberalism in the Bedroom: Quarreling Spouses in Nineteenth-Century Lima.* University Park: Pennsylvania State University Press, 2000.

———. *Paying the Price of Freedom: Family and Labor among Lima's Slaves, 1800–1854.* Berkeley: University of California Press, 1994.

Hutchison, Elizabeth Quay. *Labors Appropriate to Their Sex: Gender, Labor, and Politics in Urban Chile, 1900–1930.* Durham: Duke University Press, 2001.

Iglesias Prieto, Norma. *Beautiful Flowers of the Maquiladora: Life Histories of Women Workers in Tijuana.* Trans. Michael Stone. Austin: University of Texas Press, Institute of Latin American Studies, 1997.

Jaiven, Ana Lau. *La nueva ola del feminismo en Mexico.* Mexico City: Grupo Editorial Planeta, 1987.

James, Daniel. *Doña Maria's Story: Life History, Memory, and Political Identity.* Durham: Duke University Press, 2000.

Jaquette, Jane S., ed. *The Women's Movement in Latin America: Participation and Democracy.* 2d ed. Boulder: Westview Press, 1994.

Jelin, Elizabeth. "Engendering Human Rights." In *Gender Politics in Latin America,* edited by Elizabeth Doré, 65–83. New York: Monthly Review Press, 1997.

———, ed. *Women and Social Change in Latin America.* London: Zed Books, 1990.

Karasch, Mary. *Slave Life in Rio de Janeiro.* Princeton: Princeton University Press, 1987.

———. "Slave Women in the Brazilian Frontier in the Nineteenth Century." In *More Than Chattel: Black Women and Slavery in the Americas,* edited by David B. Gaspar and Darlene Clark, 79–96. Bloomington: Indiana University Press, 1996.

Kettenham, Andrea. *Frida Kalho: Pain and Passion.* New York: Taschen, 1995.

Kirkendall, Andrew J. *Class Mates: Male Student Culture and the Making of a Political Class in Neneteenth-Century Brazil.* Lincoln: University of Nebraska Press, 2002.

Kirkwood, Julieta. *Ser política en Chile: Las feministas y los partidos.* Santiago: Facultad Latinoamericana de Ciencias Sociales, 1986.

Klubock, Thomas Miller. *Contested Communities: Class, Gender, and Politics in Chile's El Teniente Copper Mine, 1904–1951.* Durham: Duke University Press, 1998.

Knaster, Mary. *Women in Spanish America: An Annotated Bibliography from Pre-Conquest to Contemporary Times.* Boston: G. K. Hall, 1977.

Kuppers, Gaby, ed. *Compañeras: Voices from the Latin American Women's Movement.* London: Latin American Bureau, 1994.

Lagarde, Marcela. *Los cautiverios de las mujeres: Madresposas, monjas, putas, presas y locas.* Mexico City: Universidad Nacional Autónoma de Mexico, 1997.

Lau, Ana, and Carmen Ramos. *Mujeres y revolución, 1900–1917*. Mexico City: INEHRM/ CONACULTA/INAH/SG, 1993.

Lauderdale Graham, Sandra. *House and Street: The Domestic World of Servants and Masters in Nineteenth-Century Rio de Janeiro*. New York: Cambridge University Press, 1988.

———. "Slavery's Impasse: Slave Prostitutes, Small-Time Mistresses, and the Brazilian Law of 1871." *Comparative Studies in Society and History* 33 (Oct. 1991): 669–94.

Lavrin, Asunción. "International Feminisms: Latin American Alternatives." *Gender and History* 10 (Nov. 1998): 519–34.

———. "Unfolding Feminism: Spanish American Women's Writing, 1970–1980." In *Feminisms in the Academy*, edited by Donna Stanton and Abigail J. Stewart, 248–73. Ann Arbor: University of Michigan Press, 1995.

———. "Women, the Family and Social Change in Latin America." *World Affairs* 150 (Fall 1987): 109–28.

———. *Women, Feminism and Social Change: Argentina, Chile, and Uruguay, 1890–1940*. Lincoln: University of Nebraska Press, 1995.

———. "Women in Twentieth-Century Latin American Society." In *The Cambridge History of Latin America*, edited by Leslie Bethell, vol. 6, pt. 2, 483–544. New York: Cambridge University Press, 1994.

León, Magdalena, ed. *Las trabajadoras del agro*. Bogota: ACEP, 1982.

———, and Carmen Diana Deere, eds. *La mujer y la política agraria en América Latina*. Mexico City: Siglo Veintiuno Editores, 1986.

León de Leal, Magdalena. *La mujer y el desarrollo en Colombia*. Bogota: ACEP, 1977.

Levine, Robert M., ed. *Bitita's Diary: The Childhood Memoires of Carolina Maria de Jesus*. New York: M. E. Sharpe, 1998.

Levine, Robert M., and José Carlos Sebe Born Meihy. *The Life and Death of Carolina Maria de Jesus*. Albuquerque: University of New Mexico Press, 1995.

———, eds. *The Unedited Diaries of Carolina Maria de Jesus*. New Brunswick: Rutgers University Press, 1999.

LeVine, Sarah, and Clara Sunderland Correa. *Dolor y Alegría: Women and Social Change in Urban Mexico*. Madison: University of Wisconsin Press, 1993.

Logan, Kathleen. "Personal Testimony: Latin American Women Telling Their Lives." *Latin American Research Review* 32, no. 1 (1997): 199–211.

Lumsden, Ian. *Machos Maricones and Gays: Cuba and Homosexuality*. Philadelphia: Temple University Press, 1996.

MacCreary, David. "'This Life of Misery and Shame': Female Prostitution in Guatemala City, 1880–1920." *Journal of Latin American Studies* 18, no. 2 (1986): 333–53.

Macías, Anna. *Against All Odds: The Feminist Movement in Mexico to 1940*. Westport: Greenwood Press, 1982.

Mallon, Florencia E., ed. *When a Flower Is Reborn: The Life and Times of a Mapuche Feminist, Rosa Isolde Reuque Paillalef*. Durham: Duke University Press, 2002.

Masiello, Francine. *Between Civilization and Barbarism: Women, Nation and Literary Culture in Modern Argentina*. Lincoln: University of Nebraska Press, 1992.

Matos Rodríguez, Felix V., ed. *Puerto Rican Women's History: New Perspectives*. New York: Sharpe, 1990.

McGee Deutsch, Sandra. "The Catholic Church, Work and Womanhood." *Gender and History* 3 (Autumn 1991): 304–25.

———. *The Extreme Right in Argentina, Brazil and Chile, 1890–1939*. Stanford: Stanford University Press, 1999.

————. "The Visible and Invisible Liga Patriótica Argentina, 1919–1928: Gender Roles and the Right Wing." *Hispanic American Historical Review* 64 (May 1984): 233–58.

Mead, Karen. "Gender, Welfare and the Catholic Church in Argentina: Conferencias de Señoras de San Vicente de Paul, 1890–1916." *The Americas* 58 (July 2001): 91–119.

Melhuus, Marit, and Kristin Ann Solen, eds. *Machos, Mistresses, Madonnas: Contesting the Power of Latin American Gender Imagery.* London: Verso Press, 1996.

Menchú, Rigoberta, with Elisabeth Burgos. *I, Rigoberta Menchu: An Indian Woman in Guatemala.* London: Verso Press, 1984.

Miller, Francesca. *Latin American Women and the Search for Social Justice.* Hanover: University Press of New England, 1991.

Millobovsky, Matilde. *Circle of Love over Death: Testimonies of the Mothers of the Plaza de Mayo.* Willimantic: Curbstone Press, 1997.

Molineux, Maxine. "Mobilization without Emancipation? Women's Interests, the State and Revolution in Nicaragua." *Latin American Perspectives* 13 (Winter 1985): 227–54.

Morley, Helena. *The Diary of Helena Morley.* Trans. Elizabeth Bishop. New York: Farrar, Straus and Giroux, 1995.

"Mujeres Puertorriqueñas, Protagonistas en el Caribe." *Homines: Revista de Ciencias Sociales.* Special issue no. 4 (1987).

Murguialday, Clara. *Nicaragua, revolución y feminismo (1977–1989).* Madrid: Editorial Revolución, 1990.

Nash, June, and Helen I. Safa, eds. *Women and Change in Latin America.* New York: Bergin and Harvey, 1986.

Navarro, Maryssa, and Virginia Sánchez-Korrol, eds. *Women in Latin America and the Caribbean.* Bloomington: Indiana University Press, 1999.

Nazzari, Muriel. *Disappearance of the Dowry: Women, Families, and Social Change in São Paulo, Brazil, 1600–1900.* Stanford: Stanford University Press, 1991.

New American Press, ed. *A Dream Compels Us: Voices of Salvadoran Women.* Boston: South End Press, 1989.

Ortiz, Altagracia. *Puerto Rican Women and Work: Bridges in Transnational Labor.* Philadelphia: Temple University Pres, 1996.

Page, Joseph A. Introduction to *In My Own Words: Evita.* New York: New Press, 1995.

Palmer, Steven, and Gladys Roas Chaves. "Educating Señoritas: Teacher Training, Social Mobility, and the Birth of Costa Rican Feminism, 1885–1925." *Hispanic American Historical Review* 78 (Nov. 1978): 45–82.

Participación política de la mujer en el Cono Sur. 2 vols. Buenos Aires: Fundación Friedrich Naumann, 1987.

Partnoy, Alicia. *The Little School: Tales of Disappearance and Survival.* San Francisco: Cleiss Press, 1998.

Patai, Daphne. *Brazilian Women Speak: Contemporary Life Stories.* New Brunswick: Rutgers University Press, 1988.

Perón, Eva. *My Mission in Life.* New York: Vantage Press, 1953.

Potthast-Jutkeit, Barbara. *Paraíso de mahoma o país de las mujeres?* Asunción: Instituto Cultural Paraguayo-Alemán, 1996.

Power, Margaret. *Right-Wing Women of Chile: Feminine Power and the Struggle against Allende, 1964–1973.* University Park: Pennsylvania State University Press, 2002.

Rago, Margareth. *Os prazeres da noite: Prostituução e códiglos da sexualidad feminina em São Paulo, 1890–1930.* Rio de Janeiro: Paz e Terra, 1991.

Ramírez, Rafael L. *What It Means to Be a Man.* New Brunswick: Rutgers University Press, 1999.

Randall, Margaret. *Gathering Rage: The Failure of Twentieth-Century Revolutions to Develop a Feminist Agenda.* New York: Monthly Review Press, 1992.

———. *Sandino's Daughters: Testimonies of Nicaraguan Women in Struggle.* New Brunswick: Rutgers University Press, 1995.

Rodríguez, Eugenia. *Hijas, novias v esposas: Familia, matrimonio y violencia doméstica en el Valle Central de Costa Rica (1750–1850).* Heredia, Costa Rica: EUNA/Plumsock Mesoamerican Studies, 2000.

Rodríguez, Ileana. *Registradas en la historia: 10 años de quehacer feminista en Nicaragua.* Managua: CIAM, 1990.

Rodríguez, Victoria, ed. *Women's Participation in Mexican Political Life.* Boulder: Westview Press, 1998.

Rosenblatt, Karin A. *Gendered Compromises: Political Cultures and the State in Chile, 1920–1950.* Chapel Hill: University of North Carolina Press, 2000.

Ruggiero, Kristin. "Honor, Maternity, and the Disciplining of Women: Infanticide in Late Nineteenth-Century Buenos Aires." *Hispanic American Historical Review* 72 (Aug. 1992): 353–73.

———. "Wives on 'Deposit': Internment and the Preservation of Husband's Honor in Late Nineteenth-Century Buenos Aires." *Journal of Family History* 17, no. 3 (1992): 253–70.

Saffioti, Heleith I. B., and Mónica Muñoz-Vargas, org. *Mulher Brasileira é Assim.* Rio de Janeiro: Rosa des Tempos, NIPAS, Brasilia and UNICEF, 1994.

Saporta, Nancy, et al. "Feminisms in Latin America: From Bogotá to San Bernardo." *Signs* 17 (Winter 1993): 393–434.

Seminar on Feminism and Culture in Latin America. *Women, Culture, and Politics in Latin America.* Berkeley: University of California Press, 1990.

Sepúlveda, Emma, ed. *We, Chile: Personal Testimonies of the Chilean Arpilleristas.* Falls Church: Azul Editions, 1996.

Silva Diaz, Maria Odila. *Power in Everyday Life: The Lives of Working Women in Nineteenth-Century Brazil.* New Brunswick: Rutgers University Press, 1995.

Smith, Lois M., and Alfred Padula. *Sex and Revolution: Women in Socialist Cuba.* New York: Oxford University Press, 1996.

Stephen, Lynn. *Hear My Testimony: María Teresa Tula, Human Rights Activist of El Salvador.* Boston: South End Press, 1994.

———. *Women and Socialist Movements in Latin America: Power from Below.* Austin: University of Texas Press, 1997.

———. *Zapotec Women.* Austin: University of Texas Press, 1991.

Stevens, Evelyn P. "'Marianismo': The Other Face of Machismo in Latin America." In *Female and Male in Latin America,* edited by Ann Pescatello, 89–101. Pittsburgh: University of Pittsburgh Press, 1973.

Stevenson, Marcia. *Gender and Modernity in Andean Bolivia.* Austin: University of Texas Press, 1999.

Stoll, David. *Rigoberta Menchu and the Story of All Poor Guatemalans.* Boulder: Westview Press, 1999.

Stoner, K. Lynn. *From the House to the Streets: The Cuban Women's Movement for Legal Reform, 1898–1940.* Durham: Duke University Press, 1991.

———. *Latinas of the Americas: A Source Book.* New York: Garland Publishing, 1989.

————, and Luis Hipólito Serrano Pérez. *Cuban and Cuban-American Women: An Annotated Bibliography.* Wilmington: Scholarly Resources, 2000.

Suárez Findlay, Eileen J. *Imposing Decency: The Politics of Sexuality and Race in Puerto Rico, 1870–1920.* Durham: Duke University Press, 1999.

Sullivan, Edward J. *Latin American Women Artists of the Twentieth Century.* New York: MOMA, 1992.

Tinsman, Heidi. *Partners in Conflict: The Politics of Gender, Sexuality, and Labor in the Chilean Agrarian Reform, 1950–1973.* Durham: Duke University Press, 2002.

Tirado, Thomas C. *Celsa's World: Conversations with a Mexican Peasant Woman.* Tempe: Tempe Center for Latin American Studies, 1991.

Tuñon, Enriqueta. *¡Porfin . . . ya podemas elegir y ser electas!* Mexico: Plaza y Valdés, CONACULTA INAH, 2002.

Valdés, Teresa, and Enrique Gomariz, coord. *Latin American Women: Compared Figures.* Madrid: FLASCO, 1995. Volumes for each of the nineteen Latin American nations are available.

Valenzuela, María Elena. *Todas íbamos a ser reinas: La mujer en el Chile militar.* Santiago de Chile: Ediciones Chile y America, CESOC, 1987.

Vaughan, Mary Kay. "Women School Teachers in the Mexican Revolution: The Story of Reyna's Braids." In *Expanding the Boundaries of Women's History: Essays on Women in the Third World,* edited by Cheryl Johnson-Odim and Margaret Strobel, 278–302. Bloomington: Indiana University Press, 1992.

Wainerman, Catalina, with Elisabeth Jelin and María del Carmen Feijóo. *Del deber ser y el hacer de las mujeres: Dos estudios de caso en Argentina.* Mexico City: El Colegio de Mexico, 1983.

Zabala, María Lourdes. *Nos/Otras en democracia: Mineras, cholas y feministas (1976–1994).* La Paz: Instituto Latinoamericano de Investigaciones Sociales, 1995.

6

Women's and Gender History in Global Perspective: North America after 1865

ELLEN DUBOIS

The history of women in the United States since 1865 reveals several important unifying themes. Three are particularly notable: women's increasing participation in paid labor outside the home and the changes this shift brought about in family life; women's expanding desires and struggles to take control over their reproductive and sexual lives; and the steady aspiration of women to gain entry into and influence over electoral politics. Taken together, these three processes represent the gradual collapse of the antebellum regime of "separate spheres" that confined women to domestic and private affairs while allowing men full reign over public life. What emerged instead was a more modern structure of male/female relations, one we might call "integration-with-discrimination."

But in order to present a sufficiently nuanced and situated history of women in the United States through this period, these unifying processes must be considered together with other forces that shaped women's lives. Throughout American history, the differences among women, who represent the full racial, religious, socioeconomic, and ethnic spectrum of American life, have been as significant as the similarities—never more so than in this period of great population expansion and diversification. Furthermore, women were affected by political, demographic, economic, and cultural developments shaping American society as a whole, especially the abolition of slavery, industrialization, urbanization, mass immigration, the rise of consumer culture, and the social upheavals of the last thirty-five years of the twentieth century. Making these connections links what we learn about women's past to what we know about U.S. history more broadly conceived.

1865–1900

With these concerns in mind, the place to start to explore the history of women in the United States between 1865 and 1900 is the Civil War and the abolition of slavery, which had a transformative impact on the social, economic, and political life of all Americans. The United States went into its Civil War with three geographically distinct socioeconomic systems: northeastern industrial capitalism, western subsistence agriculture, and southern chattel slavery. The destruction of slavery reverberated through all aspects of national life. Slavery had been simultaneously a system for organizing production and disciplining labor, a source of tremendous wealth for a privileged few, the means for dividing society into two antagonistic "races," and a way of conceiving and running domestic life. Although the Civil War did not begin, at least according to the majority of Northerners, as a crusade to end slavery, that was precisely its result, and thus abolition brought with it the need for sweeping social and economic changes. To take just one example, inasmuch as emancipation destroyed one of the fundamental "domestic" bonds of southern life—the one between master and slave—it also unsettled southern marriage and gender relations as well, as poor white women began to insist, as ex-slaves did, that they had rights too.

As the seemingly most masculine of historic events, war presents great challenges to the women's historian. Because the Civil War was a domestic war, however, the difference in experience between men on the battlefield and women at the home front was never absolute and often disappeared entirely. Soldiers frequently left their ranks to go home and get the crops in, and wives and daughters left home to be near military camps, to cook, clean, and care for their men. Because both armies were hastily organized and not very professional, neither was systematically provisioned, and women South and North organized to take up the slack. Not only were women active behind the front lines, but they were also on the battlefield, many as nurses and a few, disguised as men, as soldiers. African American women escaped slavery and fled to Union lines for protection, where their help as cooks and laundresses was accepted, albeit under the ambiguous category of "contraband of war."

"Reconstruction," the massive postwar effort to remake both southern society and the constitutional basis of the Union itself after the Confederacy's defeat in 1865, reshaped the lives of southern women and men. Freedmen and freedwomen fought for political, social, and economic rights, while their former masters and mistresses battled to maintain a white supremacist order. Whites founded the Ku Klux Klan to try to terrorize freed people back into near-servitude and keep them from claiming their rights as citizens. The ex-slaves' greatest victories were winning the right to marry and form families and to farm on family plots; their most serious disappointment was being denied their claim to the land they had worked as slaves. Without land, they emerged from slavery, although free, impoverished and economically dependent on white society.

With freedom came new sex and family roles. The much-prized ballot went to men alone. Freedwomen refused to work for white people whenever possible and protested the sexual access to black women that white men had simply taken for granted under slavery. Together, men and women began the hard work of constructing their own communities by building churches, establishing schools, and acquiring education. While the majority remained exceedingly poor, a few acquired property and became the core of an African American middle class. The center of African American life remained the agricultural South.

At the constitutional level, Reconstruction also brought women mixed results. The three postwar amendments radically broadened the scope of individual rights for all. In 1865, the Thirteenth Amendment abolished chattel slavery, making freedwomen and men of people who had once been slaves and depriving their masters of a major form of wealth and property. The Fourteenth Amendment, ratified in 1868, was the constitutional answer to the Supreme Court's 1857 *Dred Scott* decision declaring slaves property, not persons. It established the supremacy of national citizenship for "all persons"— not just all men—"born or naturalized in the United States." The Fifteenth Amendment, ratified in 1870, put the power of the federal government behind the right to vote, without respect to "race, color or previous condition of servitude."

But despite the insistent claims of woman suffragists, "sex" was not included in this list. When it came to the question of political rights for women, which women's rights activists had been demanding for twenty years, the outcome of constitutional Reconstruction was thus deeply disappointing. Indeed, it was not only the Fifteenth Amendment that codified women's inferior status in the Constitution. The second section of the Fourteenth Amendment defined the basis of representation as "male citizens over the age of twenty-one." This was the first direct reference to the distinction of gender in the Constitution. "If that word 'male' be inserted, . . . it will take us a century at least to get it out again," Elizabeth Cady Stanton ominously predicted in 1866.[1] Thus, the passage of these three amendments, precisely because they did not recognize women's claims to participate in a citizen's right to suffrage, inaugurated a fifty-year-long battle to win constitutional recognition for female enfranchisement. The National and the American Woman Suffrage Associations, later to combine as the National American Woman Suffrage Association, were formed in 1869 to this end.

The Civil War also was a major spur to industrialization. Women were drawn along with men into the growing wage-labor force; they represented about one-quarter of industrial workers nationwide. But the profile of the average female worker was radically different from that of her male counterpart. First and foremost, she was young. Most female workers were under twenty; they were literally working girls. The great majority were unmarried and lived in their parents' households, where their wages provided a crucial supplement to the family income. The minority who lived elsewhere, such as in commercial or charity boardinghouses, risked sexual disreputability because the combination of personal independence and straitened economic circumstances was thought to lead young women "into temptation."

The 10 to 15 percent of women wage-earners who were adult, married, and mothers were regarded as tragic deviations from the norm of economically dependent wives and breadwinning husbands. African American women could be found disproportionately in this category of working wives. In retrospect, we can now see that what appeared then as an aberration, concentrated among black women, from the normal arrangement of family and working roles was actually the beginning of a more modern pattern in which most women who work are, like most working men, adults, parents, and lifetime wage-earners.

Nineteenth-century men and women worked in such different industries, and for such different wage rates, that it makes sense to speak of separate male and female wage-labor forces. On average, women earned less than half of what men were paid. They were concentrated in a few sectors of the economy where most of the other workers were female as well. The most common female occupation—employing perhaps three-fourths of the whole female labor force at the beginning of the postwar era—was paid domestic labor. It would only be a small exaggeration to say that in these years a woman was either a domestic servant or the employer of one. Although domestic service was as well or better paid than other jobs women could get, most women disliked the work, especially the total lack of personal independence involved in live-in service, and left it whenever they had alternatives. Thus domestic servants were usually the women with the fewest economic options: Asian immigrants in the West, recent European immigrants in the East, and African Americans in the South.

The next-largest category of women wage-earners worked in industrial manufacturing, the expansion of which was almost directly proportional to the contraction of the domestic sector. Women were concentrated in what were called the "needle trades": textiles, shoemaking, and the relatively new industry of ready-made garments. A much smaller but fast-growing category of women workers found employment in clerical and retail occupations, both of which had previously been men's work. Despite long hours and a pronounced tendency to pay women less than men, these "white-collar" jobs were the most preferred form of wage-work for women inasmuch as they were considered more respectable and involved less physical labor than other jobs open to them.

At the other end of the class ladder, the postwar surge in industrialization helped make the "Gilded Age," as Mark Twain dubbed the period, an era characterized by new levels of wealth and the sudden emergence of a conspicuously lavish American upper class. For those women who rose from middle- to upper-class status, wealth meant many things. Women were deeply involved in translating this affluence into unheard-of levels of "conspicuous consumption." Increasingly, wealthy women devoted less time to productive labor— which is why they had domestic servants—and more time to the work and pleasure of consumption. This was the era of the first great urban department stores, to which leisured women were welcomed by all manner of inviting devices. Dazzling displays, lavish lounges, and elegant tea rooms were all designed to attract female shoppers. As the late-nineteenth-century social critic Thorstein Veblen observed, the elegantly attired upper-class woman herself became one of the great commodities of the age, a means to display her husband's wealth and status.[2]

And yet the very idleness accompanying the reduction of women's productive labor in middle- and upper-class families also fostered female aspirations to assume a more active, public place in community life. One of the most dramatic and portentous changes in women's history in the post–Civil War era was the development of higher education for women. In 1848 Lucy Stone became the first American woman to receive a B.A. (at Oberlin College), but it was not until later, with the passage in 1862 of federal legislation providing for public universities in the West and the founding of Vassar College in 1865, that college education became a genuine possibility for large numbers of women. By 1900, 40 percent of college graduates were women. The two institutions granting the largest numbers of B.A.s to women were Smith, an all-female private college in the East, and the University of California, a coeducational public institution in the West. But college education alone was not enough to quench the thirst of this new generation of bourgeois women for a more expansive sphere for their sex. Indeed, female college graduates often found themselves suffering from a "crisis of vocation," unable to find public or professional outlets for their newly cultivated energies and capacities.

For a slightly older generation of women, born too early to take advantage of these new educational opportunities, the women's clubs that proliferated in the late nineteenth century served a parallel function. All over the country, in large cities and small towns, middle-aged, middle-class women formed societies to pursue both learning and community influence. They read great books together, set up libraries and playgrounds for local children, and established large charitable institutions such as hospitals and orphanages. Gradually, they were leaving behind the exclusively domestic sphere that women like them had once enthusiastically occupied. Black and white middle-class women organized similar but separate clubs, both because each group had significantly different interests and because white women did not welcome black women into their organizations. Both groups gathered their clubs into racially exclusive national federations during the 1890s. White women formed the General Federation of Women's Clubs, and black women the National Association of Colored Women.

Middle-class women also tried to venture outside their "sphere" without quite shattering its boundaries in less public, more intimate ways, as evidenced by the era's sharply declining birthrate. By 1900 American women were having on the average half as many children as women a hundred years before had. How this was accomplished remains a bit of a mystery. The exact details of sex and reproduction must always evade historians, but in the last quarter of the nineteenth century silence on such matters became official legal and medical policy. State and then federal laws made it a crime to advocate or even describe contraceptive techniques. The newly formed American Medical Association began a campaign against abortions, which had been commonly available earlier in the mid-nineteenth century. In part, the crackdown on contraception was a reaction to widespread fears that white, middle-class women, by not bearing as many children, were neglecting their duty to their families, nation, and race. These repressive efforts were not completely successful. Some women were still able to learn, from each other and from their private physicians, the basic principles of contraception: when not to have intercourse, what concoctions seemed to interfere with conception, and how to keep sperm and egg apart. The fact that the birthrate continued to decline is a measure of stubborn aspirations among women to gain some degree of control over their reproductive lives.

Invidious racial distinctions continued to thrive in post–Civil War America despite emancipation of the slaves. In the former Confederacy, the battle between black aspirations for full citizenship and white efforts to maintain political and economic supremacy took on new forms and greater intensity. New laws made interracial marriage, especially between black men and white women, a serious crime; meanwhile, white men continued to lay claim to black women's bodies. African American men who insisted on their "manhood rights"—to vote, to earn, to support and protect wives and children—were the special objects of white assault, literally and figuratively. To help, to educate themselves, and ultimately to provide leadership where and when men could or would not, African American women in the South began to step forward. Many found their own public voices in these years. A particularly notable example was Ida B. Wells, a courageous Memphis journalist and daughter of former slaves, who began a nationwide campaign against lynching in 1892. Whites often justified the lynching of black men by alleging that they had committed sexual offenses against white women. Wells's willingness to contest these charges meant risking the fragile claim to sexual respectability that she and other African American women had struggled to achieve since emancipation.

The dynamics of race and racism deeply affected social struggles outside of the South as well. As white settlers moved westward across the American continent, they brought their racist habits and laws along with their Bibles and copies of the Constitution. In the decades after the abolition of slavery, the ever-growing need for low-paid wage-workers subjected new groups of nonwhite laborers to discrimination and prejudice. Although nonwhites now had to be compensated for their work, most were paid at the lowest possible levels, which made their labor attractive to employers and anathema to white workers. To many white Americans, the Fourteenth Amendment's broad-based guarantee of the rights of citizenship did not ensure racial equality so much as make it all the more imperative to keep the nation's population racially homogeneous.

The Chinese were particularly victimized by racism during the years after the Civil War. Many Chinese initially came to the United States expecting to stay temporarily, make money, and then return home. Like other such "sojourners," the great majority were men. Unlike other immigrant groups, however, those Chinese who ended up staying found their way to integration into American society blocked by racially discriminatory laws. Ever since 1790, federal law had limited naturalization to "free white" immigrants.[3] At the state level, "antimiscegenation" laws banning interracial marriages, which had been originally directed against African Americans, were expanded to include Asians. These economic forces and legal constraints condemned the Chinese immigrant men who remained in the country to the permanent status of unmarried noncitizens.

The growing population of bachelor workers in the West generated a highly profitable prostitution industry there. This is where many of the first Chinese women to come to the United States could be found. As of 1870 there were approximately sixty thousand Chinese men in the United States, most of them working on the transcontinental railways, and only two thousand Chinese women, of whom more than half were prostitutes. For other groups of women, western prostitution offered good money that could be quickly if disreputably earned, but not for Chinese women. The sale of their sexual services primarily profited American speculators and Chinese merchants, who could sell a woman in the United States for ten times what they paid for her in China. The conditions under which these Chinese women were brought to this country and lived, worked, and died call into question the claim that American slavery ended in 1865.

As the numbers of Chinese immigrants grew so did white westerners' hostility, fueled by economic competition and moral concerns. Among white women, those who were dependent on their own or their husbands' wages aligned themselves with working-class anti-Chinese forces. In 1876 a group of white women workers petitioned the California legislature to stop Chinese immigration, arguing that Chinese labor undermined their own status as a "class of respectable and working women."[4] Middle-class white women, in a position to respond more benevolently, reacted differently. They began to organize moral crusades to "rescue" Chinese women from prostitution and convert them to Christianity. They established nineteenth-century versions of domestic shelters to which Chinese women could flee, provided that they were willing to live a respectable Christian life under the rescuers' guidance.

In 1875 the anti-immigration faction took the lead. The U.S. Congress passed the Page Law banning the immigration of women "for criminal or demoralizing purposes." The law was used to bar virtually all Chinese women from entering the country, on the assumption that they were prostitutes. It was the first piece of federal anti-immigrant legislation and was followed seven years later by the Chinese Exclusion Act of 1882, which curtailed Chinese immigration in general.

Mexican Americans faced different racial and class pressures. Those who were residents of the Southwest when it was transferred to American control in 1848 retained their rights as citizens but lost much of their land to Americans. At first there was a great deal of intermarriage, usually between Anglo men and Mexican women. (Because courts tended to classify Mexicans as "white," these marriages did not violate the antimiscegenation ordinances.) After the Southwest was absorbed into the United States and laws determining wives' property rights there were made more consistent with Anglo American practices, ownership of land was transferred from Mexican wives to Anglo husbands. More and more Mexican American women could be found in the wage-labor force, primarily serving as domestics for the growing Anglo population. Toward the end of the century this shrinking and impoverished Mexican American population began to be supplemented by immigration from the South, especially into California, where Mexicans replaced the "excluded" Chinese as the lowest-paid workers.

Finally, native people, despite their best efforts to keep away from encroaching American "civilization," were drawn nonetheless into the racial conflicts of the postbellum period. Men, native warriors and American aggressors both, fought the "Indian wars" that raged across the western plains, ending with the brutal massacre and defeat of the Sioux at Wounded Knee in 1890. White women were associated with a more benevolent approach to resolving America's "native problem." They prescribed Yankee ways—family farms, male breadwinning, female domesticity, and Protestantism—as the best means to save Indians from destruction.

In 1886 New Englander-turned-Californian Helen Hunt Jackson published *Ramona: A Romance of the Old Southwest,* a novel deliberately patterned after *Uncle Tom's Cabin,* to protest the genocide of western Indians.[5] The Paiute author and speaker Sarah Winnemuka was particularly notable among a handful of individual Indians sufficiently at home in white society to act as advocates for native people. The efforts of women like these helped gain passage for the Dawes Act in 1887. This piece of federal legislation was designed to advance Indian family life, foster an ethos of individual proprietorship, and lead eventually to Indian citizenship, although at the cost of traditional tribal cultures, which were considered doomed in modern American society.

1900–1920

By the end of the nineteenth century new historical dynamics were thus becoming apparent: a growth in industrial power, national wealth and class inequality, reassertion of white supremacy, and expansion and diversification of the American population. In all parts of American society the first decades of the twentieth century were marked by massive changes in women's lives and prospects, perhaps greater than in any other twenty-year period in the nation's history. Most fundamental was what was happening in the female labor force. As it continued to grow larger and more visible, working women took on new roles in American society and saw themselves in new ways. The political realm was also important for women in the early twentieth century as female activists and professionals demanded and designed new government initiatives to modernize work and family life. In 1920 these political achievements were capped by the long-overdue enactment of nationwide woman suffrage.

By 1900 more than 20 percent of the labor force was female. Domestic service was rapidly losing primacy to manufacturing, and women's white-collar labor was expanding faster than any other sector. College-educated women were starting to break into male-dominated professions. Wage labor had long been regarded as an unfortunate necessity for women at the bottom of the socioeconomic scale whose husbands and fathers could not adequately support them. But the emergence of middle-class "career women," who expected personal independence and upward mobility from their jobs and worked as much out of desire as need, signaled a new attitude about work for pay among American women.

Despite the formation of this new class of female professionals, women industrial workers were nonetheless considered the representative working women of the era. They achieved this visibility collectively through a series of spectacular strikes in the industries in which they were concentrated. The first and most famous of these was the massive strike in the New York City women's garment industry in 1909 and 1910, known as the "Shirtwaist Strike" or the "Uprising of the Thirty Thousand." Over the next few years, women workers participated in other dramatic industrial conflicts: in the men's garment industry in Chicago, in the silk factories of Paterson, New Jersey, and among the wool spinners and weavers of Lawrence, Massachusetts. Contemporary commentators expressed surprise that women were capable of the level of political determination, labor militancy, and group solidarity that these strikers displayed. Their actions created or strengthened important unions such as the Ladies Garment Workers Union and the Amalgamated Clothing Workers Union, which laid the foundation for a more broadly based industrial labor movement. Middle-class women activists, feeling a new "sisterhood" with the young, heroic, working-class women, became sympathizers and supporters of the women's trade union movement. In 1903 they joined with women labor organizers to found the Women's Trade Union League, which nourished the collaboration between wage-earning women and their middle-class female "allies."

Immigrant women were prominent in the labor upsurge of the early twentieth century. Starting in the 1880s, immigration to the United States increased dramatically, a response to the burgeoning industrial economy with its insatiable need for labor power. Most newcomers came from Southern and Eastern Europe, but a few came from Japan, the Philippines, and Mexico. Toward the end of this period a growing number of African Americans left the rural South to come to the urban North. These were truly momentous population movements. One-third of East European Jews came to the United States between 1880 and 1915, and 10 percent of the population of Mexico moved north between 1910 and 1930.

On the one hand, immigrant gender and family patterns differed along ethnic lines. The Japanese came as families; Italians and Catholic Slavs sent men to the United States to make money and return home; and East European Jews and African Americans allowed young women to migrate alone before the rest of their families. On the other hand, some kinds of family experiences, particularly generational conflicts, cut across ethnic lines. Young girls from a wide range of backgrounds came together in the female labor force, eager to earn their own wages and live their own lives. By contrast, their mothers lived and labored largely within immigrant ghettos, often unable to

read or write English. They were responsible for preserving whatever traditions of family life, food, worship, and language survived the American melt-
ing pot. Immigrant mothers and daughters thus experienced the upheavals
of Americanization differently. They clashed over maintaining Old World ways
versus embracing new ones, battling over everything from how daughters
should dress to whom they should marry. In their own way, immigrant wom-
en thus experienced the conflict between dependent motherhood and individual wage-earning that was coming to affect all American women.

In their battle to maintain control over their daughters, immigrant mothers found unanticipated support from middle-class, socially concerned, Amer-
ican-born women who elected to live and labor in urban working-class districts.
Predecessors of today's social workers, these reformers took it as their task to
help immigrant families adjust to America and vice versa. Jane Addams, the
reformers' most famous spokeswoman, explained that their goal was to extend
democracy from the political world into the realm of social relations. The institution of the settlement house, which Addams brought to the United States
from England in 1889, became a major venue for the work of these urban social reformers. A cross between a charity institution and a community center,
the settlement house provided a place for recent immigrants to meet, learn,
organize, and confront the values and expectations of their new homeland.

Middle-class women established settlement houses not only out of a desire to help others but also, again in the words of Jane Addams, out of their
own "subjective necessity." For many, including Addams, the settlement house
became a permanent home, and work among the immigrant poor a life-long
vocation. In her autobiography *Twenty Years at Hull-House*, Addams described
the longing of college-educated women for purpose beyond the care of their
own families and for a way of living that placed them at the exciting if chaotic
core of modern urban life. In search of a personal alternative to the dependent and increasingly ornamental role of the bourgeois wife, these female
reformers had a tendency to romanticize what they regarded as the more
socially productive lives of immigrant women.

The spread of settlement houses was part of the larger political movement
in this period that was known as Progressivism. Progressives called for expanded government programs and policies to address what they saw as the devastating social consequences of rapid economic expansion. In particular, they
battled for new labor laws and social welfare policies, arguing that the fate of
society's most impoverished sector was linked to the general national welfare.
After decades of retreat from social reform and strong government, a "lais-
sez-faire" backlash against the activist state of the Reconstruction period, many
Americans, particularly in the middle and professional classes, embraced this
new spirit of public stewardship.

Women played an extremely important role in the development of a new social welfare ethic during the Progressive period. The leader of these pioneering female policy makers was Florence Kelley, executive secretary of the National Consumers' League, which advocated better conditions for working women. Among the Progressives' more successful welfare initiatives was passage of state laws that limited the number of hours women could work and provided public "pensions" for widows and mothers who were without male support. Progressive women activists' most notable failure was their attempt to make child labor illegal; the courts ruled that prohibiting child labor was an unconstitutional restraint on freedom of contract. Ironically, despite Progressive women's willingness to challenge the unfettered workings of the free market, and despite their pathbreaking activism in the political arena, they supported policies that rested on traditional notions of the male-breadwinning, female-dependent family pattern, a system that women's wage labor was already beginning to undermine.

The labor militancy of women workers and the political involvement of Progressive women activists together fueled a great and final drive for women's enfranchisement. Ever since the constitutional revisions of the Reconstruction years, the woman suffrage movement had been accumulating advocates and reformulating its demands in terms of new political realities. In the 1880s radical suffragists had negotiated a surprising alliance with the women's temperance movement, which helped link the demand for political rights to mainstream domestic and religious values and thus draw many more conventional women into the suffrage movement.

Then, in the 1890s, woman suffrage was taken up by the Populist movement as one of several reforms that promised a more democratic political system. Male citizens in many western states in which Populists held power voted to amend state constitutions to enfranchise women. (Fundamental constitutional ambiguities over control of the electorate made it possible to pursue woman suffrage simultaneously at the state and national levels.) In the 1890s woman suffrage was passed in Colorado and Idaho and only narrowly lost in Kansas and California. Two other western states—Utah and Wyoming—came into the Union with woman suffrage in their original constitutions. Thus, at the beginning of the twentieth century women in four states already enjoyed full (federal as well as state) voting rights.

In order to continue to gain ground, suffragists had to make their movement, originally fueled by a particularly nineteenth-century passion for equal political rights, seem modern and compelling to the American public. In the twentieth century, a new generation of suffragists thus changed their rallying cry from the antiquated "woman suffrage" to the more modern-sounding slogan "votes for women." They called themselves "suffragettes" in imitation of

British suffrage advocates who had turned that term of trivializing opprobri-
um into a label of pride. The movement rapidly generated enthusiasm in the
nation's largest cities and most industrialized states.

In 1911 California club women, college women, and working women
joined together to win a second voters' referendum on votes for women (the
first had been lost in 1896). They were successful in part because they ran a
sophisticated publicity campaign that used the latest advertising techniques,
including billboards, mass-produced posters, and even little political commodities like playing cards and postage stamps. In Chicago, well-organized African American women joined with white women to get the support of the Progressive wing of the Republican Party for an innovative legislative strategy that
granted the women of Illinois partial suffrage, allowing them to vote but only
in municipal campaigns and for presidential electors. These victories inspired
a uniquely ambitious campaign from 1913 through 1915 in New York state,
an intensive effort that featured giant suffrage parades and brought a whole
new level of public visibility to the votes for women movement. Wealthy wom-
en were recruited to fund this costly campaign and joined the large number
of wage-earners who filled the movement's ranks.

This state-by-state strategy for enfranchising women had limitations. Victory in one state campaign often spurred opposition in the next. The narrow
win in California in 1911 was followed in 1915 by solid defeats on similar
measures in four eastern states, most significantly New York. Nor could votes
for women ever be won by popular referenda in the single-party South. In 1913
a group of younger suffragists, styling themselves militants, moved to reinvig-
orate suffrage activism at the federal level and formed the first new national
organization to be established since the movement had begun in 1869. Initially called the Congressional Union and then renamed the Woman's Party
in 1916, its goal was to reignite the stalled campaign to achieve woman suffrage through an amendment to the U.S. Constitution. The group's leader
was a young charismatic Pennsylvanian named Alice Paul. On the day in 1913
before Woodrow Wilson was inaugurated as president she led five thousand
suffragettes in a parade down Constitution Avenue in Washington, D.C.

The goal of militant suffragettes was not to implore but rather to force
Congress to pass a constitutional amendment and send it to the states for
ratification. To do this they intended to mobilize women voters in the steadi-
ly growing roster of "suffrage states" to put pressure on the national Democratic Party, which controlled both Congress and the presidency. But the militants' plans for the 1916 election were confounded by the growing clamor
for the United States to enter the war raging in Europe. Campaigning for his
second term, Woodrow Wilson ran as the antiwar candidate, which made it
difficult for suffragettes to convince women to vote against him. On the con-

trary, it was said that it was women's antiwar votes that secured for Wilson the all-important state of California and victory in 1916. Then, six months after his reelection and despite his campaign promises, Wilson took the United States into war. Women, like men, divided over this action. The majority supported the war effort. A much-maligned minority, including the first woman elected to the House of Representatives, Montana congresswoman Jeanette Rankin, opposed U.S. entry into the war.

This division between pro- and antiwar women, along with strategic differences between militants and moderates in the votes-for-women movement, shaped the final stages of the struggle for a constitutional amendment. Militant suffragettes refused to suspend their campaign against President Wilson, despite wartime prohibitions against criticizing the administration, and took up civil disobedience tactics, for which they were arrested and imprisoned. Meanwhile, mainstream suffragists, led by Carrie Chapman Catt of the National American Association for Woman Suffrage, tried to influence the president and the nation through pro-war activities and displays of extravagant patriotism. By 1918 pressure and persuasion together convinced President Wilson to support the amendment, and the House to pass it by the required two-thirds vote. Opposition in the Senate, however, held up the amendment for another seventeen months. Leaders of the southern wing of the Democratic Party were especially opposed to federal action on votes for women, which they feared would interfere with their ability to disfranchise African American male voters. They recognized that the charges of immorality that they habitually flung against black men who wanted to vote would not work so well against black women. But the combined pressure of suffragist determination and of larger events was too great, and in May 1919 the Senate finally gave way, passing the Nineteenth Amendment and sending it to the states for ratification. The thirty-sixth and final legislature to ratify the amendment was that of the border (and hence two-party) state of Tennessee. There a young Republican named Harry Burn cast the deciding vote because, as he reported, his mother had told him "to be a good boy" and vote to ratify.[6]

Ironically, the passage of the Nineteenth Amendment seems to have contributed to a decline in the political activism of American women after 1920. There are many reasons for this surprising development. First, protesting their common disfranchisement had given women of all ranks and classes a sense of solidarity and collective purpose. Once they could participate in mainstream politics women, like men, acted out of different interests and conflicting perspectives. Second, the political atmosphere of the 1920s was more conservative than that of the 1910s, and the ebbing of support for the kinds of social policies championed by the Progressive generation marginalized many women activists. Third, women's entry into regular, party-oriented politics was only beginning in 1920. It took almost as long for women's influence and concerns to move to the center of the political stage as it had taken for women to win formal voting rights.

Finally, the winning of votes for women coincided with and contributed to a deeper shift in the aspirations and inclinations of American women. "Emancipation" remained an inspiring call for the generation who came of age during World War I, but these women had a different idea of emancipation than their mothers and grandmothers, less public and more personal, less collective and more individual, less political and more sexual. Indeed, the term *feminism*, which we now use to characterize the long tradition of women struggling for freedom and equality, was coined in just these years to refer not to the convictions of the many who supported votes for women but to the ideas of those few who longed instead for liberation from their womanly timidity, what Emma Goldman called "inner tyranny." This modern turn in the women's rights tradition could be detected in the emergence, just before World War I, of a small, underground feminist campaign on behalf of "birth control," a neologism invented in these years by Margaret Sanger, this movement's greatest leader.

1920–45

Underlying the reorientation in women's values and interests was a deeper shift in American culture, away from "Victorian" values of restraint, industriousness, and public decorum and toward a more modern mode of pleasure, display, and recreation. Although economics and culture are never linked in a simple one-to-one equation, this subtle but fundamental change was inextricably linked to developments in capitalism. The nineteenth-century emphasis on capital accumulation, industrialization, and massive mobilization of a whole population's labor power became the twentieth-century emphasis on the creation of markets for new goods and commodities, the expansion of industrial methods into new areas of human activity, and the cultivation of a consumerist ethic that valued immediate enjoyment over deferred gratification. Put most simply, American society was undergoing a reorientation from production to consumption. While the roots of this change lay in the prewar years, the rapid economic expansion of the 1920s greatly accelerated the process.

From the beginning of this grand elaboration of the American consumer market, women were the most active purchasers. Younger women concentrated on purchasing clothes and cosmetics, while married women bought household appliances. Each of these commodities linked new industries to new markets. Cosmetics, for instance, were no longer the sign of a disreputable woman with a "made-up" face, but the product of a multi-million-dollar industry marketed to respectable women of all classes. Widespread urban elec-

236

trification, undertaken at public expense, made possible an aggressive advertising campaign to get automatic washing machines and iceboxes in every middle-class home. Women learned how they should look and what they should buy by reading magazines that had elaborate pictorial advertisements and by watching movies starring highly publicized actresses. Popular marketers targeted women not only for the "rational" economic reason, that they made the many small purchasing decisions of daily life, but also for the "irrational," psychological reason that women's growing desires for personal fulfillment provided perfect fuel for the new ethic of mass consumerism.

In particular, a marked generational shift in sexual styles and standards contributed significantly to intensified efforts to market to women consumers. A new, more openly sexual style of femininity had first made its appearance in the 1910s among "advanced" women in larger cities. By the 1920s, bold young flappers—so named because of their highly revealing clothing styles—could be found among all groups. Sociological studies done in the 1920s showed that women born after 1900 had a markedly different attitude to premarital heterosexuality, which they were twice as likely to have experienced than women born in the late nineteenth century. In immigrant communities, rebellious daughters participated in the new culture of teenaged dating against their parents' wishes. Although the small beginnings of an open lesbian culture could be detected in these years, the era's new sexual permissiveness was mostly directed at male-female relations. Indeed, "homosociality," the intense attachments to other women that were common in the nineteenth century, gave way to a more exclusive heterosocial emphasis on dating and marriage with men.

These cultural changes among women were uneven. On the one hand, the repudiation of Victorian notions of femininity and the acceptance of a more openly sexual female style were often strongest outside the middle class. Working women, especially urban white-collar women workers, tended strongly to the flapper lifestyle. African American urban communities, which were being transformed by thousands of migrants from the rural South, were relatively accepting of alternative sexual styles. Many newcomers were working women who were impatient with the pursuit of respectability that had long motivated the tiny black middle class. Blues songs and cabaret dances enjoyed crossover popularity with white audiences, who regarded them as exotic and exciting. New York's Harlem, the national center of urban black culture, was the home of inventive African American artists and writers, women as well as men.

On the other hand, the postwar prosperity that underwrote expanding consumerism did not reach to the bottom levels of the society. The trend toward unionization, which had continued throughout the 1910s, was dramatically reversed as businesses incorporated and industrial employers consoli-

dated power. The textile industry, long the most important employer of female labor, "escaped" from the well-organized Northeast to the low-wage, unorganized South. Other sectors of women's labor, especially domestic and agricultural work, were also depressed in the 1920s. Downward pressure on
wages may have contributed to the intensifying racial antagonisms of the
postwar years. The Ku Klux Klan and Marcus Garvey's United Negro Improvement Association thrived equally in the 1920s; although both movements encouraged men's patriarchal ambitions, they also counted on the participation
of newly enfranchised and politicized women. When the stock market crashed
in October 1929, rural areas, mining districts, textile towns, and urban ghettos and barrios were already in an advanced state of economic collapse.

By 1932 the dramatic and sustained contraction of the American economy had put one-quarter of the labor force out of work. Although women made
up more than 20 percent of the nation's workers, most were employed in different industries than men, making garments, shoes, clothing, and small elec-
trical appliances and canning and packing fruit and vegetables. This deep and
structural division of labor by gender meant that women and men experienced
the unemployment crisis of the Great Depression differently. Men, who
worked in the most highly capitalized and critically struck industries, bore the
brunt of industrywide layoffs, for instance those in steel and rubber. Women's
wages were already so low that employers had less to gain by firing them.

Working women, then, tended to experience the Great Depression as a
time of relentless downward pressure on wages and of reverse job mobility.
White-collar workers went to work in factories, factory operatives became
domestic workers, domestic workers slipped into day labor, and everyone's
wages declined. At the top end of the female labor force, women were being
pushed out of the professions. There were fewer female doctors in 1930 than
in 1920, and women who had advanced degrees and had expected to become
professors worked instead as lecturers and research assistants. At the lower
end, the domestic service sector, after nearly a half-century of steady decline,
began to grow again among the daughters and granddaughters of European
immigrants. In big cities, African American women desperate for any sort of
work gathered on street-corners, forming what were chillingly nicknamed
"slave markets" and hoping for the opportunity to work for a day here and
there in white women's kitchens. In southern California, public funds were
used to "repatriate" not only Mexican immigrants but also their American-
born children.

Although women workers suffered terribly from the employment crisis of
the Great Depression, they neither left the labor force nor moved into the jobs
that men had vacated. Patterns that had existed before the economic collapse—
steady growth in the female work force coupled with the maintenance and re-

inforcement of the occupational and wage differential between men's and women's labor—were intensified rather than reversed in these years. So, too, was a fundamental change in the character of the female labor force itself as the adult woman, staying in or returning to paid labor after marriage and motherhood, replaced the young unmarried girl as the typical female worker. Indeed, this process accelerated during the 1930s as families in which male breadwinners were laid off depended increasingly on adult women to survive the depression. The proportion of married women in the female labor force grew from 29 to 35 percent during this decade. Wives replaced teen-aged children as the second earners in families that needed more than one income.

During the depression, hostility once directed at women workers in general focused on the growing new population of adult, married women workers. High rates of male unemployment were made all the more intolerable by the subtle alteration in family dynamics that wives' wage labor signified. Politicians seeking popular yet superficial ways to address the employment crisis advocated bans on the employment of married women in public-sector jobs, and by 1940 more than three-quarters of all school systems in the country refused to hire married women as teachers. The trend reached its pinnacle in 1932 when the federal government announced a prohibition on federal employment of spouses of federal employees, a theoretically gender-neutral policy that in practice worked overwhelmingly against wives. In 1936 one of the first "scientific" polls of public opinion ever taken found that 80 percent of men and 75 percent of women believed that a woman should not take on paid labor if her husband was working. This conviction, which ran in the face of long-term demographic trends favoring adult women workers, was only temporarily reversed during World War II and returned with a vengeance in the 1950s.

The economic suffering of the 1930s had a varied impact on American family and sexual patterns. The divorce rate, which had been rising, declined, in part because separation was more costly than maintaining a single household. The marriage rate went down even more precipitously. Birth rates also declined. Indeed, the government began to reverse its policies on birth control. Instead of prosecuting birth control advocates for violating obscenity laws, the government publicly funded health programs that encouraged contraceptive practices. These policies definitely had a troubling aspect because certain groups were targeted for population reduction for reasons similar to the racist policies taking hold in Nazi German. Among Puerto Ricans and Native Americans, for instance, aggressive federal campaigns resulted in as many as one-third of women of childbearing age being permanently sterilized. Similarly, many states mandated sterilization of women labeled as "feeble-minded," a large, vague category that included uneducated and emotionally troubled as well as physically handicapped persons.

The United States entered the depression without a government strategy for meeting the pressing needs of an entire population in structural economic crisis. Many of the social welfare efforts initiated by the Progressive-era generation had been small in scope and voluntary and extra-governmental in nature. The Republican Party regarded the use of government funds to offset mass unemployment as a morally dangerous reliance on "the dole" that would only encourage indolence and dependency. The few state and local programs that did exist were thoroughly inadequate and, moreover, available only to men. Women turned instead to private charity institutions like the YWCA and suffered out their poverty in ladylike privacy. The urgency of widespread need inspired a new generation of northern Democrats; led by New York state's former governor, Franklin D. Roosevelt, they assumed responsibility in 1932 with an expansive vision of federal involvement in economic stabilization, industrial growth, public employment, and social welfare.

To win the 1932 presidential election Roosevelt assembled an electoral coalition that brought organized labor and descendants of European immigrants together for the first time with black voters. Black women voters, less attached to "the party of Lincoln" than their husbands and brothers and more influenced by the suffragist ethic of nonpartisanship, may have played an important role in African Americans' willingness to change parties a half-century after Reconstruction. The most influential black New Deal Democrat was, in fact, Mary McLeod Bethune. Bethune, an educator and the founding president of the National Council of Negro Women, was appointed director of the Negro Division of the National Youth Administration, the highest post any African American held in the Roosevelt administration.

Because the 1932 election occurred in an era before exit polls, however, conclusions about the contribution of women to this epochal party realignment must necessarily remain hypothetical. Nonetheless, it is worth considering the part enfranchised women's maturing electoral behavior played in creating the winning Roosevelt Democratic coalition. Several processes were at work. The Republican Party, to which many leading women Progressives had been inclined, squandered its goodwill among female voters and alienated a generation of aspiring women politicians. Ruth Hanna McCormick, daughter and widow of GOP leaders, was elected twice to the House of Representatives, but in 1930 party leaders prevented her from winning what would have been the first female seat in the U.S. Senate. Meanwhile, first- and second-generation immigrant women, whose family associations were to the Democratic Party, were becoming citizens and voters. At the same time, the ratification of two constitutional amendments, the first prohibiting the sale of alcohol and the second repealing this prohibition, worked to depoliticize the temperance issue, which had long kept many women away from the "wet" Democrats.

An influential group of women, many of them with roots in the social welfare movements of the 1910s, were prominent among New Deal policymakers. Eleanor Roosevelt herself had been drawn into social settlement work in the 1920s when personal crises, beginning with her husband's polio in 1921 and culminating in the discovery of his adulterous affair with her own secretary, pushed her into a more independent and politically oriented life of her own. By 1932 she was at the center of a network of Democratic women activists and had become a major influence on her husband's domestic social welfare policy. Veterans of the Women's Trade Union League held positions in the Women's and Children's divisions of the Labor Department, which itself was headed by the nation's first woman cabinet officer, Frances Perkins. As secretary of labor in a pro-labor administration, "Madame Secretary" oversaw policies that shaped working people's lives at home as well as at work.

Were these women the missing generation between the first and second waves of feminism? Many of them (although not Eleanor Roosevelt) had been suffrage activists in the 1910s. Moreover, the needs of women and families were high on their list of policy concerns. Yet they did not consider themselves "feminists," a term reserved for a small, rival group of ex-suffragists who were already working for another constitutional amendment, this time to prohibit legal discrimination on the basis of sex. The Roosevelt Democratic women were committed instead to a strategy of legal "protection" for women's needs. Ironically, the Fair Labor Standards Act, passed by the administration in 1938 to establish nationwide standards for minimum wages and maximum hours, contained no reference to gender, thus departing from the long tradition of lower rates and shorter hours for women workers. Still, New Deal women held to the conviction that working women were more vulnerable than their male counterparts, and thus in need of special legislative protection not applicable to male workers. True to their Progressive-era roots, they designed federal welfare legislation to underwrite and reinforce the male-breadwinner, female-dependent family form.

Nowhere was this tendency clearer than in the mammoth Social Security Act, one of the New Deal's greatest legislative achievements. The bill designed an old-age insurance system that assumed the normality of nonworking wives and granted benefits to the surviving wives of working men that it did not extend to the surviving husbands of working women. These assumptions also shaped a small subsection of the Social Security bill, Aid to Dependent Families (ADF), which later expanded into the much larger federal program that we now commonly call "welfare." ADF (later Aid to Families with Dependent Children, or AFDC) was meant to provide for those mothers, mistakenly presumed to be declining in number, who were deprived of the normal ability to rely on a male breadwinner. The very things that this program would be criticized for a half-century later—that its recipients didn't work for wages and didn't have functioning marriages—were initial requirements for aid and reflections of New Deal notions of normative family life.

It is commonly observed that the employment and production crises of the Great Depression were only ended by the intense economic mobilization of World War II. For women workers the economic upswing was reinforced by a pronounced wartime reversal of the prejudice against working wives and mothers that had flourished in the previous decade. The sudden mobilization of men into the armed forces, combined with the intense demand for production from those "heavy" industries (steel, rubber, and airplanes) in which male workers predominated, created tremendous new opportunities for women where they had never had them.

Convincing the public, however, that women should take on traditionally male jobs proved to be an ideologically delicate task. A year after the bombing of Pearl Harbor, the newly created Office of War Information undertook a concerted campaign to recruit women into war work. The commercial advertising industry, just coming into its own, developed propaganda campaigns, using the magazine and movie industry to encourage women to do work for which they had long been told they were unsuited. The campaign became identified with a generic woman war worker, nicknamed "Rosie the Riveter" after a character in a Hollywood movie made early in the war and later identified with the sweet-faced, big-bicepted cartoon figure created by illustrator Norman Rockwell for the August 1943 issue of the *Saturday Evening Post*.

The increase in the female labor force consisted mainly of women who had left jobs to get married and have children and were recruited back into war work. Within a year, pollsters found that the majority of Americans, male and female, thought that the presence of women, even wives, in the labor force was not only appropriate but also patriotic. But this new tolerance pertained only to "the duration," that is, the extraordinary conditions of world war and societywide mobilization. The propaganda message was clear: Women war workers were working to support their sons and husbands and to serve their country. When peacetime conditions returned they were expected to be happy to give men back "their" jobs and return to primarily domestic lives.

The downward pressure on the female labor force that had been so pronounced during the depression was temporarily reversed in these years. As a significant portion of women workers crossed over into the well-paying, unionized industries traditionally reserved for men, others moved up from manufacturing to clerical work and from domestic and service work to manufacturing. Women of color particularly benefited from these shifts because they were admitted for the first time in significant numbers to factory shop floors in America's fundamental industries. Fannie Hill, an African American "Rosie" from California interviewed many decades later about her wartime work, acidly observed that Lincoln hadn't freed the slaves. Hitler had.[7]

The war helped create new opportunities for other groups as well. The Chinese, for instance, were suddenly regarded as "good" Asians, as distinct from the Japanese, who were—citizens or not—considered enemy aliens. As a result, Chinese American women were able to find clerical and retail work outside the confines of their "Chinatowns," and in 1943 the federal ban on Chinese immigration, dating from the 1880s, was finally repealed. To some degree, therefore, we can speak about the war years as the beginning of the desegregation of the American labor force. African Americans and Latin Americans pushed for these changes, organizing to pressure the federal government to give interracial substance to its claims to be fighting a war for democracy.

There is, of course, one colossal exception to this generalization about an upturn in racial relations. A month after Pearl Harbor, President Roosevelt signed Executive Order 9066, which mandated rounding up Japanese and Japanese Americans living on the West Coast and imprisoning them in federally administered internment camps. No equivalent measures were taken against Germans and German Americans. The driving force seems not to have been wartime concerns for national security but rather a hostility to Asians that had flourished ever since the first Chinese immigrants arrived in the United States. Living and working conditions in the camps undermined traditional family relations. Women were paid the same (paltry) wages as men, and tight family networks gave way to homogeneous age groups, ironically accelerating Americanizing tendencies among the younger generation. The racialized government bias was also evidenced by U.S. refusal to waive immigration barriers against European Jews despite growing evidence of the monstrous German genocide being conducted against them.

1945–90

From one perspective, the immediate postwar years signaled a conservative turn in women's lives: return to a primary commitment to family life, repudiation of workplace ambitions, and reassertion of traditional femininity. In part, all of these grew out of a desperate desire for a "return to normalcy" after decades of depression and war. But new forces were at work as well, and what appeared conventional and traditional was actually fractured and contentious, providing hints of the dramatic changes in women's lives and perspectives that were to become unmistakable by the late 1960s. Despite postwar economic demobilization and cultural images that emphasized women's essential domesticity, the female labor force continued to grow and mature. And while the dominant political message emphasized a vision of men in charge and women at home, numerous women continued to provide political vision and leadership, especially in the all-important civil rights movement of the period. Perhaps most fundamental, under the calm surface of family life in the 1950s, sexual politics began a shift that would erupt in the cultural revolution of the 1960s.

The Feminine Mystique, the term by which we characterize the domestic revival of the postwar years, was the title of a book published in 1963 by Betty Friedan. Friedan described how psychologists, educators, and publishers of popular magazines led a campaign to convince women to focus their hopes and ambitions on home and family and reject any other lifestyle as abnormal and perverse. Writing of her own postwar decision to give up a journalism career to live in a New York suburb, Friedan observed, "Domestic bliss had suddenly become chic."[8] This feminine revival was declared from many quarters. In 1949 Benjamin Spock published *Baby and Child Care,* directed at full-time, stay-at-home mothers; all other child-rearing arrangements, he declared, were damaging to children. Fashion styles—long, full skirts and narrow waists—celebrated a return to femininity. And magazine articles praised fulfilled young wives who dedicated themselves to family welfare and relegated their own talents and interests to side pursuits. Television, the new medium of the postwar years, featured domestic comedies designed to be watched at home by the entire family, sitting at their television tables and enjoying their television dinners in blissful "family togetherness."

Yet the actual story was more complicated. Friedan's book was less a dispassionate sociological portrait than a carefully designed polemic intended as her contribution to the vigorous public debate about women's appropriate roles that had thrived earlier in the century. This debate, of course, had never been entirely quelled, although it served Friedan's purposes in the book to argue that it had. In 1947, for instance, psychologists Marynia Farnham and Ferdinand Lundberg had written their own manifesto, *Modern Woman: The Lost Sex,* in which they characterized feminism as the result of "disturbed libidinal organization."[9] Friedan had come out of a background in the labor movement and throughout the 1950s remained a dedicated community activist. Other women political activists worked behind the scenes in this era, especially a largely unsung generation of southern black women who led many local desegregation campaigns that followed the Supreme Court's landmark *Brown v. Board of Education* decision (1954).

Friedan did not, however, overstate the forceful impact of the era's pro-domestic propaganda. Much of it had a repressive edge as if its creators believed women had to be disciplined into adhering to the family-first regime. Writers and educators condemned high school girls for rock-and-roll frenzies and backseat petting. Participants in a small bohemian culture, which repudiated mainstream materialism and family complacency, were simultaneously lampooned and promoted under the distorted rubric of "beatniks." Lesbians who challenged men's dearest prerogative, that of exclusive sexual access to women, were regularly beaten. Special criticism was reserved for African American women, who, by participating in the paid labor force at substantially higher rates than white women, failed to meet dominant standards of proper femininity. The high point of this condemnation was the publication, two years after Friedan's *Feminine Mystique*, of a federally funded study of "the negro family" by the urban sociologist Daniel Patrick Moynihan. "The Moynihan Report," as it came to be known, combined a sympathetic description of the plight of the black urban poor with a diagnosis of black family pathology, which Moynihan blamed on overstrong, underfeminine "black matriarchs."

Unacknowledged in all this domestic rhetoric was the fundamental fact that more women than ever were spending more years working for wages outside the family. The female labor force, which had declined briefly after the war, began to grow again. In contrast to wartime, however, women were back in their "women's jobs," the majority earning less than two-thirds of the average male wage. Nonetheless, a momentous change had taken place: The average working woman was no longer a young, unmarried girl but rather an adult married woman, often with children. By 1960 the majority of working women were married, and 40 percent were mothers as well. Still, many women worked only seasonally or part time, and their earnings were regarded as secondary to the main (male) family wage. Nevertheless, under the surface, the growth of the female labor force was generating important changes in family life and social structure.

Behind the anxious complacency of the "feminine mystique" lay the larger political environment of cold war America and nuclear threat. "Domestic security" meant more than a well-paid male breadwinner supporting mom and the kids in the suburbs; it meant a national government strong and vigilant enough to keep the communist menace at bay behind the Iron Curtain. As Vice-President Richard Nixon announced to USSR Premier Nikita Khrushchev when they met in Moscow in 1960 during a brief thaw in the cold war, Western capitalism's best defense against the class warfare predictions of communism was the American middle-class family, complete with a happy mom in her well-equipped kitchen. What Nixon didn't say was that extensive federal funding was required to provide the suburban infrastructure of low-cost mortgages and a modern highway network.

Back at home, the family romance of the period was barely able to contain unruly sexual forces that threatened to disrupt, even destroy, the traditional family. Not for nothing were sexy women referred to as "bombshells," while the new, revealing, two-piece women's bathing suits were nicknamed "bikinis" after the Pacific atoll where the first atomic bombs were exploded. Behind the era's dramatically declining age of first marriage and high birth rates among women in their twenties lay trends that would become more pronounced in the future—boys and girls becoming sexually active ever earlier but without the blessings of teenage conjugality, and young women's widespread use of birth control, no longer simply to concentrate their childbearing in a few years but to escape it altogether. In 1960 "the pill," funded through the efforts of aging birth control pioneer Margaret Sanger, became available.

The civil rights movement was the wellspring of the political conflict and cultural upheaval of the 1960s. To be sure, the bus boycott in Montgomery, Alabama, and the integration of Little Rock High School in Arkansas happened in the 1950s. But it was in the 1960s that a new generation of bold black southerners, college-age women and men, first began to alter the tone of civil rights protest. Theirs was a youth rebellion directed not only against the segregationist structures of the white South but also against what they saw as the timidity and "internalized racism" of their parents' generation. Young black women in particular rejected the regime of female respectability to which their mothers' generation still clung. (In Montgomery, a young, unmarried, pregnant woman had been the first to challenge the "back of the bus" rule, but she was judged by the community as unsuitable to be the campaign's central symbol. Instead, the more mature Rosa Parks, a local civil rights activist, got the role.)

In 1960 young African Americans formed their own civil rights organization, the Student Non-Violent Coordinating Committee (SNCC). Ella Baker, a remarkable activist of the prior generation and acting coordinator for the Southern Christian Leadership Conference, encouraged the young organizers' independent efforts. Perhaps her own experiences as a woman in a male-dominated organization made Baker sympathetic to the students' generational frustrations. SNCC, although led by African Americans, was a racially integrated organization. It was also a group in which young women and men confronted the terrors of white supremacy together. Refusing to be cowed by the threat of imprisonment, they flooded into southern jails in great numbers. Diane Nash, one of the leaders of SNCC, chose to go to jail although she was four months pregnant because, she explained, her baby would be born a prisoner of southern racism in any case. The judge, however, refused to incarcerate her.

Building on their dramatic campaigns to desegregate public accommodations and interstate transportation, SNCC workers organized to challenge the widespread de facto disfranchisement of black southern citizens. They brought their bold voter registration campaign to the small towns and back country of the Mississippi Delta region. There, college-educated activists discovered the political dedication and abilities of rural African Americans. Fannie Lou Hamer, a tenant farmer from Sunflower County, Mississippi, became the symbol of southern blacks' determination to force their way back into the American political system. In 1964 Hamer led a delegation of Mississippi citizens into the Democratic National Convention in Atlantic City. The group demanded that they, rather than the white segregationists who controlled the state party, be officially seated as convention delegates. Their failure to win the support of national party leaders, including longtime liberal and vice-presidential candidate Hubert Humphrey, was a devastating and demoralizing defeat.

The growing national visibility of the civil rights drive put women's rights back on the political map. In late 1963, in the wake of the great March on Washington and the assassination of John F. Kennedy, President Lyndon Johnson made the passage of an omnibus Civil Rights Bill one of the first goals of his presidency. Title VII of the bill prohibited employers from discriminating on the basis of race. In an effort to both ridicule and derail the bill, a southern white congressman added an amendment to Title VII prohibiting discrimination by sex. Martha Griffiths of Michigan, one of the few female members of Congress, took advantage of this cynical act to rally support for the bill, which passed in 1964.

Two years later, when the federal agency established to carry out the bill's provisions, the Equal Employment Opportunity Commission, refused to pursue complaints of sex discrimination, a group of women's rights activists led by Betty Friedan organized the National Organization for Women (NOW), a legislative and lobbying group. Although some later critics claim that early second-wave feminism was limited to middle-class white women, NOW's membership included women of color and union activists. Civil rights activists won another victory in 1965 with the passage of the Voting Rights Act, which gave federal authorities the ability to challenge state-based disfranchisements. A half-century before, black suffragists could not persuade white suffragists to protest the obstacles they faced in securing their new right to vote. From one perspective, then, the legislation marked the final stage in an effort begun in 1848.

Meanwhile, the youth wing of the civil rights movement was moving beyond legislative and political demands to a more militant approach known as black power. New organizations began to stress group determination and defense. The most influential of these was the Black Panthers, founded in 1966, the same year as NOW. Although the Panthers emphasized community self-help and initiated educational and health programs in their hometown of Oakland, California, they were most widely known for confronting the police, brandishing guns, and employing violent rhetoric. In contrast to the previous decade of civil rights activism, virtually all the leaders of the Panthers were men, although they frequently invoked women as symbols of black nationhood. Black feminist Michele Wallace memorably characterized this ideological turn as the rise of "Black Macho."

White student activists, finding no place for themselves in black power organizations, threw their energies into protesting U.S. military involvement in Vietnam, which had escalated significantly in the mid-1960s. Students protested the collusion of universities with military programs, corporate profit-making off the war, and above all the army draft system, which was drawing more and more young men into the war. Thus the antiwar movement, while mobilizing enormous numbers of young women, developed a militant style and masculinist emphasis similar to those of the black power movement. Folk singer Joan Baez, one of the few women nationally known for antiwar activism, inadvertently revealed the subordinate and sexualized roles available to movement women in her famous draft-resistance slogan "girls say yes to boys who say no."[10]

The black power and antiwar movements together inspired the rise of youth revolts among Chicano/as, Native Americans, and Asian Americans, especially on the West Coast. Starting in 1968, students on California campuses organized a series of "third world strikes" in which they demanded more professors of color and the creation of "ethnic studies" programs. The campaigns were models for the subsequent movement to push universities to create women's studies programs and affirmative action hiring of more women professors.

In each of these political environments women activists began to notice the subordinate roles into which they were placed and protest what they called "sexual racism" or just "sexism." Toni Cade, editor of the 1970 anthology *The Black Woman*, described how "every organization you can name has had to struggle with seemingly mutinous cadres of women getting salty about having to man the telephones or fix the coffee while the men wrote the position paper and decided on policy."[11] More often than not, the initial male response to women's protests was hostile. A white woman speaker at a 1969 antiwar demonstration who dared to talk about "women's liberation" was harassed with catcalls to "take her off the stage and fuck her."[12] Chicanas who voiced feminist opinions were labeled as *vendidas* or *agringadas*.

Yet because of the racially conscious atmosphere of the period, a common feminist consciousness did not produce a unified feminist movement. Most black women and Chicanas protested repressive sexual standards and family forms, established consciousness-raising groups, and challenged oppressive norms of femininity from within their racially based movements. (The

National Welfare Rights Organization, a largely minority protest organization of the female poor, was an exception.) "Women's liberation," when it surfaced as an independent exclusively female movement, was thus primarily white, although, ironically, the black power movement served as its model. Just as black power activists insisted that "black was beautiful," feminists said that "sisterhood was powerful."

The surfacing of feminist awareness in the youth movements of the period provided a mass base of support that, combined with the organizational sophistication and policy leadership of the National Organization for Women, gave form, momentum, and strength to a new feminist movement. By the early 1970s the movement focused on two issues: an Equal Rights Amendment and abortion rights. (A wing of NOW that had sought to focus on economic and employment issues was defeated in intraorganizational battles.) At first both campaigns seemed to be coasting to quick victories. The ERA, languishing in Congress since the 1920s, passed smoothly through both houses in 1972, and in 1973 the Supreme Court ruled in *Roe v. Wade* that state antiabortion laws unconstitutionally violated women's rights to privacy.

But in both cases a well-organized antifeminist opposition developed to challenge these gains. The leader of the STOP-ERA campaign was Phyllis Schlafly, a right-wing Republican activist who had gotten her start in the anticommunist politics of the 1950s. She built opposition to the ERA by insisting that the heretofore uncontroversial amendment had sufficient power to break down sexual barriers everywhere from the armed forces to public toilets. By 1979 the ratification process ground to a halt, and even the three-year extension granted by Congress could not produce the magic number of thirty-eight ratifying states.

The antiabortion rights movement drew strength from the defeat of the ERA as well as from the considerable financial support of the Catholic Church. In 1976 Rep. Henry Hyde of Illinois gave his name to the first federal antiabortion law, which prohibited using Medicaid funds to pay for abortions, thus depriving many poor women of access. The ultimate goal of the antiabortion camp was to reverse *Roe v. Wade*. Since the Supreme Court decision, virtually every candidate for appointment to the Supreme Court has been evaluated, by both pro- and antiabortion forces, on his or her stand on the issue.[13] The forces defending abortion rights were strengthened and extended by joining up with poor women and women of color who were protesting welfare system practices that submitted them to sterilization procedures without their full consent. Eventually, the opposing movements renamed themselves "pro-life" (antiabortion) and "pro-choice" (for reproductive rights).

The antifeminist backlash had various sources. American politics was moving to the right through the 1970s and 1980s. Despite the revelations of malfeasance in the Nixon White House, the GOP controlled the White House for three of the next four administrations. The growing influence of the Republican Party's ultraconservative, antifeminist "New Right" wing was marked by the party's dramatic reversal of its thirty-year-long support of the ERA; starting in 1976, the Democratic Party adopted the issue. At the same time, the postwar boom years came to an end in the depression of 1973. As inflation and unemployment rose, women's demands for workplace equality became a harder sell; it seemed there was no longer enough economic prosperity to go around.

Above all, the strength of the antifeminist backlash was a reaction against (as well as a measure of) epochal transformations in women's lives. These were as momentous as simultaneous changes in the country's racial relations and reflected widespread sympathy for gender equality that extended far beyond the ranks of the feminist movement proper. Women now constitute almost 50 percent of the labor force, and 60 percent of mothers of small children are working outside their homes. Women in major professions such as law and medicine are reaching numeric parity with men. Even the income gap is narrowing. The average female wage went from 59 percent of the male wage in 1960 to 73 percent in 1998.[14] The great majority of women have experimented with sex before or outside of marriage. Female fertility is declining, and the average age at the birth of a woman's first child is rising. Heterosexual couples living together before marrying are now the norm. Even more dramatic deviations from the status quo ante are increasingly visible. Lesbianism has gone public in a big way as significant numbers of women openly choose to organize their lives around sexual intimacy with each other. The availability of abortion has not only increased the number of childless women but also, ironically, has led to greater willingness among women without male partners to keep and raise their children.

But if we can speak of a feminist revolution in the last quarter of the twentieth century, its greatest failure has been the unequal distribution of its benefits among American women. Historical change in women's lives and expectations are running in two very different tracks, with one class enjoying greater personal independence and financial rewards for its labor and the other becoming increasingly underpaid, overworked, and underserved by public policy. While women at the top are moving into high-paying, previously "male" jobs, women at the bottom remain confined to the underpaid sector of women's work, especially the fast-growing service sector of the economy. This development closely parallels the bifurcation of African Americans into an increasingly stable middle class and a publicly maligned "underclass." In a quite extraordinary development, domestic service, which seemed to be decreasing to the point where it was headed for oblivion, has revived as women at the lower end of the class scale, many of them recent immigrants, are called on to care for the children and the homes of women at the top. Upper-tier women's growing incomes combine with those of their husbands to fuel an extraordinarily high level of consumer spending as the two-income, upper-middle-class marriage becomes the modern standard for affluent family life.

Meanwhile, poverty in America is not disappearing; instead, it is becoming "feminized." While women at the top enjoy new levels of autonomy and liberation, women at the bottom are increasingly forced to support their children without a male wage. As of 1990 one out of three female-headed families is officially impoverished. The shiny new promises of the postfeminist era, ironically, are working to deny these poor women political sympathy. Aren't there good-paying jobs for women? Hasn't equal opportunity been made as available to women as to men? On the contrary, sexist undercurrents have run through the campaign, begun under Republicans and completed under Democrats, to "reform welfare" (that is, to end the Social Security Act's Aid to Families with Dependent Children), a program that by 1980 served eleven million families. The organized feminist movement, which has increasingly made "choice" its sole criterion for political endorsement, has had little to say about this campaign directed against poor women and their children.

By the 1990s the profound and complex changes in women's lives and attitudes over the previous thirty years made their way to the very center of American politics. The nomination of Geraldine Ferraro as the Democratic Party's vice-presidential candidate in 1984 marked a historic first, as did the 1996 appointment of Madeline Albright as secretary of state, the first woman ever to reach such a high level in the order of presidential succession. The most impressive breakthrough for women in public office occurred in 1992 when an unprecedented number of women were elected to Congress, including the first black woman ever to sit in the U.S. Senate.[15] During the 1996 presidential campaign there was a sense that the wives of the nominees might have made more credible candidates than their husbands.

The "gender gap" that first appeared in the late 1980s, when women more often voted Democratic while men voted Republican, reflects differences of opinion about issues as well as candidates. Pollsters report that women are more supportive of domestic spending than men and less supportive of military expenditures. Although critical issues directly affecting women—such as the lack of a comprehensive health-care policy, failures in the educational system, and a generation of American families facing new stresses without adequate public resources—remain unresolved, political conflicts over abortion and sexual relations in the workplace have taken center stage. These issues may be more symbolic battles over the upheavals in sex and gender relations with which Americans are currently grappling than strategic attempts to address them directly.

At century's end, women were unquestionably a presence in politics and in the workplace; they were insistent about taking charge of their own sexual and reproductive lives. These momentous historical developments are best seen as processes rather than events, with their ultimate consequences impossible to predict. One thing is sure, however: American women will continue to make history, and history will continue to (re)make them—and at a very fast pace indeed.

Notes

1. Stanton to Gerrit Smith, Jan. 1, 1866, in *The Selected Papers of Elizabeth Cady Stanton and Susan B. Anthony*, vol. 1 in *The School of Anti-Slavery, 1840–1866*, ed. Ann D. Gordon (New Brunswick: Rutgers University Press, 1997), 569.

2. Thorstein Veblen, *The Theory of the Leisure Class* (1899, repr. New York: Penguin, 1979).

3. This law was not declared unconstitutional until after World War II.

4. U.S. Congress, *Report of the Joint Special Committee to Investigate Chinese Immigration*, 44th Cong., 2d sess., 1877, S. Doc. 689, 897–901, as cited in Rebecca Mead, "Working Class Women and the Anti-Asian Movement in San Francisco, 1870–1920," unpublished paper.

5. Helen Hunt Jackson, *Ramona: A Romance of the Old Southwest* (1884, repr. New York: New American Library, 1988).

6. Quoted in Anastasia Sims, "Armageddon in Tennessee: The Final Battle over the Nineteenth Amendment," in *One Woman, One Vote*, ed. Marjorie Spruill Wheeler (Troutdale, Ore.: New Sage Press, 1995), 347.

7. Sherna Gluck, *Rosie the Riveter Revisited: Women, the War and Social Change* (New York: New American Library, 1987), 42.

8. Betty Friedan, *It Changed My Life* (New York: W. W. Norton, 1976), 10.

9. Marynia Farnham and Ferdinand Lundberg, *Modern Woman: The Lost Sex* (New York: Harper, 1947), 173.

10. Joan Baez, *And a Voice to Sing With: A Memoir* (New York: New American Library, 1987), photo after 253.

11. Toni Cade, *The Black Woman: An Anthology* (New York: New American Library, 1970), 107.

12. Alice Echols, *Daring to Be Bad: Radical Feminism in America, 1967–1975* (Minneapolis: University of Minnesota Press, 1975), 117.

13. In 1981 Sandra Day O'Connor became the first female Supreme Court justice.

14. William H. Chafe, "The Road to Equality, 1962–Today," in *No Small Courage: A History of Women in the United States*, ed. Nancy F. Cott (New York: Oxford University Press, 2000), 577.

15. Carol Moseley-Brown was defeated for reelection in 1998; on the eve of the millennium there were no African Americans seated in the U.S. Senate.

Contributors

BONNIE S. ANDERSON is the Broeklundian Professor of History at Brooklyn College and the Graduate Center, City University of New York, where she has developed courses on the history of feminism and of sexuality. With Judith P. Zinsser, she coauthored *A History of Their Own: Women in Europe from Prehistory to the Present*. Her most recent book is *Joyous Greetings: The First International Women's Movement, 1830–1860*.

ELLEN CAROL DUBOIS is a professor of history at the University of California, Los Angeles, where she is also affiliated with the Women's Studies Program. She is the author of numerous books on the history of the woman suffrage movement, most recently *Harriot Stanton Blatch and the Winning of Woman Suffrage;* coeditor (with Vicki Ruiz) of *Unequal Sisters: A Multicultural Reader in U.S. Women's History;* and coauthor of *Through Women's Eyes: A Gendered History of the U.S.*

BARBARA A. ENGEL is a professor of history at the University of Colorado, Boulder. She is the author of *Mothers and Daughters: Women of the Intelligentsia in Nineteenth-Century Russia; Between the Fields and the City: Women, Work, and Family in Russia, 1861–1914;* and *Women in Russia, 1700–2000*. She is also coeditor of *Five Sisters: Women against the Tsar; Russia's Women: Accommodation, Resistance, Transformation;* and *A Revolution of Their Own: Russian Women Remember Their Lives in the Twentieth Century*. Her articles have appeared in *Slavic Review*, *Signs*, and the *Journal of Modern History*.

CHERYL JOHNSON-ODIM holds a doctorate in history from Northwestern University and is dean of the School of Liberal Arts and Sciences and a professor of history at Columbia College Chicago. A past member of the board of directors of the African Studies Association and the American Council of Learned Societies, she is also on the board of directors of the Illinois Humanities Council and the editorial board of the *Journal of Women's History*. Johnson-Odim was a Fulbright Scholar in Nigeria and has published frequently in learned journals and written chapters in edited collections, among them *For Women and the Nation: Funmilayo Ransome-Kuti of Nigeria* (with Nina Mba). Along with Marjorie Strobel, she is coeditor of the four-volume collection *Restoring Women to History: Women in Africa; Women in Asia; Women in Latin America and the Caribbean; Women in the Middle East.*

NIKKI R. KEDDIE, professor emerita of history, University of California, Los Angeles, has written numerous books and articles. Among her seven single-authored books are *Modern Iran: Roots and Results of Revolution, Iran and the Muslim World: Resistance and Revolution,* and *An Islamic Response to Imperialism.* Among her edited or coedited books are *Women in Middle Eastern History* and *Women in the Muslim World.* She was founding editor of the journal *Contention,* and a selection of her work on women was published in 2004. Keddie was graduated from Radcliffe College and received a Ph.D. from the University of California, Berkeley. She has had numerous national fellowships and is a Fellow of the American Academy of Arts and Sciences. Her lifetime awards include the Distinguished Scholar Award of the American Historical Association, the Mentoring Award of the Middle East Studies Association, and the Persian History Award of the Encyclopedia Iranica Foundation. Her other interests include politics, photography, and art.

ASUNCIÓN LAVRIN, a professor of history at Arizona State University, holds a Ph.D. from Harvard University. She has received several NEH fellowships and a John S. Guggenheim Fellowship. The author of thirty-eight articles in journals and thirty-six chapters in books, she has published *Monjas y beatas: La escritura femenina en la espiritualided barroca novohispana, siglos XVII y XVIII* (coedited with Rosalva Loreto); *Women, Feminism, and Social Change in the Southern Cone, 1890–1940; Sexuality and Marriage in Colonial Latin America;* and *Latin American Women: Historical Perspectives.* Lavrin's books and articles have received three academic prizes. She is the past president of the Conference on Latin American History and director of two National Endowment for the Humanities summer institutes.

BONNIE G. SMITH is Board of Governors Professor of History at Rutgers University. She is the author of *Changing Lives: Women in European History since 1700, The Gender of History: Men, Women, and Historical Practice,* and other books and articles. She has edited *Global Feminisms since 1945* and coedited *Gender Meets Disability Studies.* She is also general editor of the *Oxford Encyclopedia of Women in World History.*

JUDITH P. ZINSSER is a professor of history at Miami University in Ohio. She is coauthor of *A History of Their Own: Women in Europe from Prehistory to the Present* and author of *History and Feminism: A Glass Half Full.* Her articles on the United Nations Decade for Women have appeared in *Women's Studies International Forum* and the *Journal of World History.* She served as president of the World History Association from 1996 to 1998 and is on the editorial board for the Berkshire Encyclopedia of World History. Her current project is a biography of an eighteenth-century *philosophe,* the Marquise Du Châtelet. Her articles on the Marquise Du Châtelet have appeared in collections here and in Europe and in such journals as *French Historical Studies, Notes and Records of the Royal Society,* and *Rethinking History: The Journal of Theory and Practice.*

Index

University of Illinois Press

1325 South Oak Street

Champaign, IL 61820-6903

www.press.uillinois.edu